The Garden Manual

You are holding a reproduction of an original work that is in the public domain in the United States of America, and possibly other countries. You may freely copy and distribute this work as no entity (individual or corporate) has a copyright on the body of the work. This book may contain prior copyright references, and library stamps (as most of these works were scanned from library copies). These have been scanned and retained as part of the historical artifact.

This book may have occasional imperfections such as missing or blurred pages, poor pictures, errant marks, etc. that were either part of the original artifact, or were introduced by the scanning process. We believe this work is culturally important, and despite the imperfections, have elected to bring it back into print as part of our continuing commitment to the preservation of printed works worldwide. We appreciate your understanding of the imperfections in the preservation process, and hope you enjoy this valuable book.

THE GARDEN MANUAL;

FOR THE

CULTIVATION AND OPERATIONS REQUIRED FOR THE

KITCHEN GARDEN, | **FLOWER GARDEN,**
FRUIT GARDEN, | **FLORISTS' FLOWERS,**

ILLUSTRATED WITH ENGRAVINGS AND PLANS.

By the Editors and Contributors of "The Journal of Horticulture."

SEVENTH EDITION.

REVISED AND CORRECTED.

LONDON:
JOURNAL OF HORTICULTURE AND COTTAGE GARDENER OFFICE,
162, FLEET STREET.

MDCCCLXIII.

LONDON:
Printed at the Horticultural Press,
17, Johnson's Court, Fleet Street, E.C.

KITCHEN GARDEN.

FORMATION OF THE KITCHEN GARDEN.

SITUATION.—A gentle slope towards the south, with a point to the east, is the most favourable aspect; to the north-east the least so: in short, any point to the south is to be preferred to one verging towards the north. It is a great desideratum to have a hill on the south-west, as a shelter from the high winds proceeding from that quarter.

The garden is best situated at a moderate elevation; the summit of a hill, or the bottom of a valley, is equally to be avoided.

SIZE.—Making allowance for all circumstances, as near as can be estimated, we should say, twelve square perches to each head in a family (exclusive of servants), but rather more than less, is sufficient.

FORM.—We prefer a parallelogram, with its sides placed as near as may be to the cardinal points, and having the two lines of walling running north and south one-third longer than those running east and west.

SOIL.—A lightish loam, three feet deep, resting upon a subsoil of gravel, or of chalk, is the best for all gardening purposes. If the soil be too heavy, that is, if it contains too much clay, it must be rendered lighter and more open by the addition of sand, bricklayers' rubbish, and coal-ashes. If the subsoil be clay, it must be thoroughly drained.

WALLS.—Walls are usually built in panels, from fifteen to thirty feet in length, one brick thick, with pillars at these specified distances, for the sake of adding to their strength, and the foundation a brick and a half thick.

In every instance a wall should never be lower than eight feet. The thickness usually varies with the height of the wall—being

feet. For perpendicular and *table trellises*, the trees may be about twelve feet.

Vines, Figs, Peaches, Nectarines, and Apricots must, in the main, be on the *south* aspects; nevertheless, we have known Apricots, especially *Shipley's*, and sometimes Figs, succeed to admiration on east or west. Where early desserts are required, there should always be one *May Duke* Cherry, and an early Plum—say *Rivers' Early Prolific*—on the south wall; and one *Morello Cherry* highly deserves a place there also.

The very best Pears, and especially those which look tempting while growing, should be on the *east* and *west* in the interior, and, of course, all luscious Plums, Cherries, &c., and the slip must receive all the harder-featured later and hardier kinds, and some bush fruit.

Morello Cherries succeed well on a *north* aspect.

WALKS.—Their place and width being fixed—the width should not be less than three feet—and the edges, if of Box, being planted, some little excavation will be necessary. Six inches deep will do, unless there are other reasons for making it deeper —such as obtaining soil from the foundation, or in order to bury rough stones and other materials otherwise difficult to dispose of. In that case you may go to any depth you like, taking care, as you advance to the top, that smaller and closer-fitting materials be used; and what is equally important, those to which worms have an antipathy may then be more freely employed, and brickbats or small stones, with mortar adhering, or mortar in some shape, may be thrown amongst the stones. Clinkers, or rough cinder-ashes, are equally obnoxious to this class of underground enemies; but whatever is used, be sure that a fair share is added, as nothing disfigures a walk more than unsightly worm casts, and nothing is more likely to prevent this disfigurement than the abundance of such offensive substances as noted above. Rough gravel will follow next, and then that which is firm. Now, though gravel may be said to be requisite, yet we have made very good walks without it; two or three inches of rough stones, like road metal, being covered with coarse black (or any other coloured) sand, so as amply to hide all the stones, and the surface being rolled and made smooth, about an inch or so of white shells was laid on. This makes, perhaps, the most pliant walk of any, the shells soon getting broken, and every shower washing them to the top, making the best appearance of any for walks, and after rain, or even when it is raining, they are in better order than at any other time; and weeds are more easily removed than when on a hard firm-setting gravel. We strongly advocate the use of shells to all who are within reach of them.

Such is the course to be pursued if the usual system of gravel walks is adopted; but we prefer and recommend the adoption of either *concrete* or *asphalte* walks, accordingly as chalk or gas-tar may be most easily obtained.

Late in March, and all through April and May, is the best time to make *concrete walks*; four inches, or, at most, five inches is deep enough for any walk whatever. The bottom should be formed into the same shape as the walk is to be finished, or say two inches higher in the middle than at the sides, before any of the materials are laid on. The old way of draining the centre of a walk, by drawing in the water from right and left, is radically bad in principle, and will not answer for the concrete system at all, as the drier the bottom the firmer the walk, and the longer it will endure. On very heavy clay land, where chalk and gravel are dear, burnt clay will make an excellent and enduring bottom to a walk; three inches of the burnt clay should first of all be put in the bottom, and be well rolled in dry weather, then two inches of the concrete on the top, this to be well rolled also, and to be heavily watered the last thing in the evening; then, the following morning, *a very thin* layer of fine-sifted gravel, of good colour, should be laid on the top of the damp concrete, and the roller passed over it several times until the good gravel is thoroughly embedded in the concrete, and forms part of it, as it were. When the concrete is very wet, and the good gravel over it too thinly put on, the weight of the roller will cause the white juice of the concrete to come up through the gravel, and that is the best sign. To hide that, put on a little more gravel, and roll again, and when the whole is dry, in two or three days, a pick could hardly break the surface.

On light dry lands four inches is deep enough for walks, and the first two inches at the bottom may be laid with any of the rough materials, without chalk or lime, and the next two inches in concrete. The roller will press this sufficiently to allow a slight coat of clean good gravel on the top, without the walk being more than four inches deep in the whole.

The concrete is made with any coarse gravel, with the largest stones taken out or broken, five parts or loads, and one part or load of fine chalk, all mixed well together, and put on the walk, then well watered. In dry weather this is soon dry enough for the roller. The usual way is to begin this in the morning, and water every three or four yards in length as soon as the mixture is got in, and so on till towards four o'clock in the afternoon, when the whole is ready for the roller; or if it is not dry enough that day, to keep on till six o'clock, and roll it the first thing next morning, and then put the fine gravel on and roll again immediately. If the concrete is too wet it will stick to the roller; and after rolling, if it is allowed to get dry before the colouring gravel is put on, the fine gravel will not stick to the concrete, so that the state of the weather has much to do with the perfect success of the operation, and wet weather is much against it.

Gas-tar or *asphalte* walks are very common at Derby, and still more so at Nottingham, where they not only use it for footpaths, but for horse-roads, and where they have arrived at the greatest perfection in laying them down. Their method of doing so is this:—

The materials are gravel and gas-tar. The gravel for footpaths must be the common fine gravel used in gardens, with as little dust amongst it as possible. This must be procured some time before it is wanted, and laid under cover, and turned occasionally, to get it *as dry as possible,* which is the great secret in making a good road. Fine weather must be chosen for mixing, when the gas-tar is to be mixed with the gravel in just sufficient quantity to give every pebble a little, and no more; and this can only be accomplished by well mixing and turning about, and doing only a small quantity at once. This is the second great point. The third is, heavy pressure when laid down, the road having been previously well rolled or rammed, so as to have a solid foundation. The gas-tar may be laid on from two to three inches thick, according to the traffic, and a little fine gravel sprinkled over it, to give a fresh and pleasant appearance. It should be rolled occasionally until set, which, if the first two points are carefully attended to, will be very soon, say, in favourable weather, in about a fortnight. It should not be attempted in frosty weather, as it is certain to fail in making a good and level road.

For horse-roads larger gravel may be used; and that would be improved by being broken as for a common macadamised road. Ashes are to be avoided, as they and the fine dust of gravel absorb the tar, and during a hot day the road is swimming with tar, in consequence of the ashes giving out the tar again. This, also, is the case when there is too much tar used in mixing.

EDGINGS.—Box and other live edgings being a harbour for snails, slugs, and other vermin, are best excluded, and the limits of the beds and walks marked by a single course of bricks, as these are not only durable, but save much labour in keeping them up. On the edges of the cross-paths Parsley, Thyme, or other potherbs may be employed for this purpose.

CROPS ON BORDERS.

We recommend the *south* border to be devoted to early vegetables, and such things as *Lettuce, Endive,* and *Cauliflowers,* which stand the winter; the *east* and *west* borders form suitable places for small crops, seldom cultivated to such an extent as to come into the general square. *Sweet Herbs,* especially of the annual kind, seed-beds for *Lettuce*, and the whole *Cabbage* tribe, *Pricked-out Celery*, prior to its final planting, may occupy these borders; and many other things which are not deep-rooted, or severe exhausters of the soil, may be sown or planted there, observing that, as such borders are generally bounded by an important walk, it would be advisable not to plant anything likely to look rubbishy at any period of its growth. Besides, we would always have a small plot or so in such borders unoccupied, in order to receive anything new that might arrive, or to serve for successional crops that might require putting in from time to time.

The *north* border we shall suppose eight feet wide, running along the north side of a wall somewhat less than that in height. This slip of ground we expect will have been partly planted with a late kind of Strawberry, as the Elton, in order to prolong the season of that much-esteemed fruit, by having some as late as possible. This fruit, we will suppose, occupies something like one-third of the whole, and, on the remainder, we propose to plant such things as the dry weather, and other circumstances, render an uncertain product in other parts of the garden. In many gardens such a border is of great value, for though, in the coldest or moistest parts of the kingdom, it may be less necessary, still there is often some crop which wants retarding, or a space more than ordinarily cool—as *Radishes* in summer, or a shady spot may be required for striking *hardy cuttings*, and other purposes; yet it is more especially fitted to meet the wants of a garden where a hot gravelly, or sandy soil, and a dry season, render the production of many vegetables a matter of much difficulty in the full exposure which the central part insures. We advise the major part of the border not appropriated to *Strawberries* to be reserved for such things as *Lettuce, Radishes, Kidney Beans*, during the hot, dry weather, and such other crops as there may be room for, which demand particular attention.

ROTATION OF CROPS.

Cabbages we suppose to require nutriment of the same kind as *Broccoli, Cauliflowers*, and the other members of this family; they ought not, therefore, to be followed by any of these, and the crop that first points itself out to our use is *Potatoes*. *Carrots* we strongly object to; the slugs that usually harbour in the ground where *Cabbages* have been grown are generally too numerous and difficult to destroy to leave much chance of obtaining a crop of that delicate-topped young vegetable; besides, the wire-worm and other casualties have induced us to prefer a piece of ground for *Carrots* that has lain all winter exposed to the action of the elements, one or two turnings in frosty weather being also given, and the previous crop may have been *Scarlet Runners*, or one of a similar character.

There are many things which mar that arrangement of rotation, which, in theory, we think the most beautiful; nevertheless, there are some rules which ought not to be departed from. *Celery* is usually favoured with the best ground or situation; and in planting the crop the previous season, it should be done sufficiently early that a portion of it may be got off the ground intended for *Onions* some little time before this crop is to be sown. In fact, all *Celery* but the very latest may be grown in ground intended for Onions the following year, observing, as the *Celery* is removed, to dig or trench the ground, and add what dung you do apply in as rotten a state as possible; that green or fresh condition, which enhances its value for some crops, is not suitable for this.

Peas, which occupy a considerable section of the garden, might follow some of the *Cabbage* tribe, were it not that we strongly advise *Broccoli* of the late kinds to be planted amongst them, which, for that reason, we sow in drills wide apart. Where the *Peas* may have followed such a crop as *Winter Spinach*, then *Broccoli*, *Brussels Sprouts*, &c., may be advantageously planted between.

The early period at which the *Onion* crop is gathered off allows of that space being occupied by *Winter Spinach*, or, it may be, the first crop of *Spring Cabbages*, planted in September; while *Parsnips*, *Leeks*, and sometimes *Beet*, remaining in the ground all winter, afford a fair place for *Peas* and *Broccoli*, or it may be *Broad Beans*.

The last crop of *Broccoli*, which ought to carry on the supply up to the time the first *Cauliflowers* are fit for use, will be off in time to sow the second and after crops of *Kidney Beans*. *Lettuce*, and other small crops, we suppose to be grown on borders, where the rotation may be varied by *Early Potatoes*. Beds of seedlings, as sweet herbs, the Cabbage tribe, &c., and other minor crops, may also be placed in such situations.

AMERICAN CRESS (*Barbarea præcox*).

This, sometimes called Winter and Belleisle Cress, is considered a good autumn and winter salad, and where the Watercress, for which it is an excellent substitute, cannot be conveniently procured, may be cultivated in any corner of the garden. The seed should be sown thinly in drills, and the plants pricked out at the final thinning to eight or ten inches apart, or it may be sown in a drill, to form an edging similar to a Parsley edging. It is fit for use as soon as the leaf is three inches long, and should be pulled or picked in the same manner as Parsley. A single sowing about Midsummer is usually enough, so that it may become luxuriant and well established by the autumn. If the crop is found to be pretty strong by the middle of August, a portion of it should then be cut back to insure a good supply of new and tender leaves for autumn and winter use. We make it a rule to cut a portion of it back at three different times, by which means an excellent succession is secured.

ARTICHOKE (*Cynara scolymus*).

Varieties.—There are two; the *Conical* or *French*, which is of a milky-green colour, with the scales spreading; and the *Globe*, which has its scales tinged with purple, curved inwards, and closely folding over each other. This is the best.

Soil and Situation.—They should have a rich, deep loam allotted to them. Manure must be applied every spring; and the best compost for them is a mixture of three parts well-putrefied dung, and one part of fine coal-ashes. They should always have an open exposure.

Propagation.—Plant suckers from the old roots in the spring. When the suckers are eight or ten inches high, in open weather, about the end of March, or early in April, select such as have much of their fibrous roots, and are sound, and not woody. The brown, hard part, by which they are attached to the parent stem, must be removed, and, if that cuts crisp and tender, the suckers are good, but if tough and stringy, they are worthless. They should be set in rows, four feet and a half by three feet apart, and about half their length beneath the surface. Turn a large flower-pot, or a Sea-kale pot, over each, and water them abundantly every evening until they are established, as well as during the droughts of summer. It is an excellent plan to have some mulch kept about their roots during dry weather, immediately after planting, and during the whole summer, and to remove all small, weak suckers about June. The plants will produce a succession of heads from July to October in the year they are planted. At the end of five years a fresh bed should be made.

Winter Dressing.—As soon as a stem is cleared of all its heads in the summer, it should be broken down close to the root, and early in November the beds dressed for the winter. Cut away the old leaves close to the ground, but without injuring the centre or side-shoots. Fork over the bed, throwing the earth in a ridge, about eight inches high, over each row, putting it close round each plant, but being careful to keep the heart free from the crumbs of soil. After this has been done, pile round every plant some long litter, or pea-haulm, three or four inches thick; and, to keep this from blowing away, as well as to help in preserving the roots from severe frosts, cover over the litter, or haulm, two inches deep with coal-ashes. The ashes may be turned into the soil in the spring, being a manure much liked by the Artichoke.

ASPARAGUS (*Asparagus officinalis*).

There are five conditions essential for obtaining an abundance of fine Asparagus. 1. Beds well drained. 2. Abundance of rich dung in the autumn. 3. Weekly sprinklings of salt and strong liquid-manure during the whole period of growth. 4. Leaving off cutting by the middle of June. 5. Not cutting down the seed-stems until they are quite yellow.

Making the Bed.—This is best done at the end of March, or early in April, this being the best time, also, for planting. If the ground is common loam, and well drained, or having a subsoil of gravel or chalk, nothing more is needed than to trench the space intended for the bed, and to mix with the soil as much rich, thoroughly decayed dung as can be worked in.

Planting.—Have only two rows of plants in each bed, as this enables them to be cultivated and cut from easily. Set the rows out two feet apart, stretching the line, and drawing with a hoe a drill on each side of it, sufficiently deep for the roots to be extended on each side of the little ridge which is thus left between the two drills, and on which ridge the plants are placed. Their roots being equally divided on each side, nothing more is required than filling up the drills with a hoe or rake. The plants should be chosen when they have started into growth two or three inches; they should be forked out carefully, and their roots not allowed to get dry after being taken up. No heads should be cut the first year after planting, and very few the second.

Summer Dressing the Beds.—When the beds have come into production, do not continue cutting after the end of June. Keep a thoroughly open surface. Apply slight dredgings of salt, and if a little guano and charred dust can be given alternately, the vigorous growth of the Asparagus will be increased. No one would think of applying salt, guano, or liquid-manure, in hot, parching weather. Advantage should, at all times, be taken of applying them at the commencement of rain, that they may be immediately washed in. If the manures are sprinkled on the surface of the soil when dry, this should at once be well scarified, and then thoroughly soaked with water.

Winter Dressing.—In November, or as soon as the stalks are yellow, they may be cut down close to the ground. Should there be any weeds to be seen when the stems are all cut off, let them all be hoed up lightly on a dry day, and raked off. Then let the beds be carefully forked up, and give them a good coat of very rotten manure, or pigeons' dung, regularly all over the surface. In giving the winter dressing we draw off with a hoe about an inch in depth of the surface soil of each bed; put on about the same depth of thoroughly decayed dung; sprinkle over the dung some common salt, a quarter of a pound to every square yard; return the earth, and then leave undisturbed until the spring.

Spring Dressing.—In March the beds are again forked over carefully, the manure and soil well broken up and mixed together, and some of the rougher parts of manure, with all the rakings, are forked into the alleys after the beds are raked over nicely.

Cutting Asparagus.—Two or three inches' depth of soil above the crowns of the Asparagus plants is quite enough. Never cut Asparagus shoots until they are six inches above ground, and cut them only half an inch below the surface. Nearly the whole shoot is then eatable, and the flavour beyond all comparison superior to that which has scarcely seen daylight. There will be no injury either to the roots or rising shoots if you cut only just below the soil's surface.

BEAN (*Faba vulgaris*).

Varieties.—Small early varieties to be sown from the last week in November until the end of January, the Beans to be gathered from the middle of May to the middle of June following.

1. *Early Mazagan.*—Not more than eighteen inches or two feet high; sown in November beneath a south wall or paling, they will usually afford a gathering in the second week of May.

2. *Dwarf Fan, or Cluster.*—Stems ten or twelve inches high, spreading like a fan from the root. Sown in November; we have gathered them in May.

3. *Long-pod.*—About four feet high. Sown in November; first gathered from beginning of June.

Large late varieties for sowing from January to July, and which will usually be gathered from in twelve weeks from the time of sowing.

1. *Windsor.* 2. *Green Windsor.* 3. *Green Long-pod.* All about four feet high. There are several other varieties of Garden Beans, such as the White-blossomed Long-pod, Red-blossomed, Violet seeded, and others, all of which possess no intrinsic merit, and are more curious than useful.

Soil and Situation.—For the winter-standing and early crops, a moderately rich and dry soil; whilst a cool-bottomed, more tenacious soil is best for the spring and summer sowings. The situation cannot be too free from shade.

Times and Modes of Sowing.—For the first production, in the following year, a large sowing may be made at the end of November, and plantations may be continued to be made, from the beginning of January to the end of June, once every three weeks. Not later than the 1st of July a last sowing may be made.

Winter Sowing.—As the rows should run north and south, they need not be more than two feet and a half from each other. Dig enough ground for one row, and then insert the Beans two inches deep and four inches apart: by thus putting in one row at a time, the ground need not be trampled on.

Spring and Summer Culture.—The sowings at these seasons may be done as directed above, and for all the crops. Earth-stirring, &c., may be practised so long as it can be done without injury to the plants, by working amongst them; and, when the blooms are fully expanded at the bottom, nip off the extreme tops: this prevents their running away in a long, useless stalk, and they become more fruitful in consequence, and the bottom pods come sooner into use.

BEET (*Beta*).

Two kinds of Beet are grown as garden vegetables; the one for its leaves, and the other for its roots. The varieties cultivated for their leaves are sometimes called *Sea Kale Beet*, and are distinguished by their long, thick, broad, and succulent foot-stalks, which have a strong resemblance to the blanched stalks of Sea Kale, and are used in the same way as that vegetable. The variety most worthy of cultivation is the *White*, or *Silver-leaved*.

Of the varieties cultivated for their roots the only ones worth growing are those of the Red Beet (*Beta vulgaris*). The best are Nutting's Dark Red, Short's Pine Apple, and Castelnaudary, which is an excellent kind for the main crop, if obtained genuine.

The Red Beet is used sliced in salads, or alone with an acid dressing. It is much better baked than boiled.

Soil and Situation.—Beet requires a rich, deep, open soil. Its richness should rather rise from previous application than the addition of manure at the time of sowing. We have always found it beneficial to dig the ground two spades deep for these deep-rooting vegetables, and to turn in the whole of the manure intended to be applied with the bottom spit, so as to bury it ten or twelve inches within the ground. Salt is a beneficial application to this crop, the Beet being a native of the sea-shore.

Time and Mode of Sowing.—The best time for inserting the main crop of Red Beet-root for winter supply is early in May. Leaf-Beet may be sown at the same time for supply in summer; and at the beginning of July or August a successional crop may be sown for use in the winter and following spring.

Sow in drills a foot asunder, and half an inch deep; or dibble in at the same distance each way, and at a similar depth, two or three seeds being put in each hole. The White Beet requires eighteen inches space between the rows.

The beds, for the convenience of cultivation, should not be more than four feet wide. At the close of May, according to the advanced state of growth, the plants must be cleared thoroughly of weeds, both by hand and small hoeing; the Red Beet thinned to ten or twelve inches apart, and the White to eight or ten. The plants of this last variety which are removed may be transplanted into rows at a similar distance, or to fill up vacancies. Moist weather is to be preferred for performing this; otherwise the plants must be watered occasionally until they have taken root. They must be frequently hoed and kept clear of weeds throughout the summer.

It is a great improvement to earth up the stalks of the *White Beet* in the same manner as Celery when they are intended to be peeled and eaten as Asparagus. No vegetable is more benefited by the application of liquid manure than the White and Brazil Beets.

Taking up the Red Beet.—In October the Beet-root may be taken up for use as wanted, but not the entire crop, for preservation during the winter, until November or the beginning of December, if the weather continues open; then bury the roots in sand, in alternate layers, under shelter. Before storing, the leaves and fibrous roots must be trimmed off, but the main root not wounded.

Gathering from the White Beet.—The largest outside leaves should be first taken, and the inner left to increase in size, when the same selection may be continued whilst they remain perfectly green and vigorous.

BORECOLE OR KALE (*Brassica oleracea fimbriata*).

The varieties of this Cabbagewort yield the most unfailing supply of sprouts for table during winter and early spring.

There are many prolific hardy varieties, the best being the *Dwarf* and *Tall Curled Kale*, only differing in height; *Egyptian* and *Jerusalem Kale*, both very hardy and productive, and throwing out shoots in spring which form an excellent substitute for Asparagus; *Heading Kale*, which forms a close head, and is a valuable winter green; *Red Kale*, of first-rate quality, and very productive; and *Cottager's Kale*, which also produces abundantly. *Melville's Variegated Kale*, of various colours, is valuable for garnishing, and may also be used at table. *Brussels Sprouts*, though scarcely so hardy as the Kales, are vastly superior in quality, and, being equally productive, should be principally planted, but not to the exclusion of the other kinds, which come in very useful in severe winters.

Sowing.—The first crop sow the beginning of March, the seedlings of which are fit for pricking out towards the end of April, and for final planting at the close of May, for production late in autumn and commencement of winter. Sow again about the middle of May; for final planting, early in July and early in August, for use during winter and spring.

Prick out the Seedlings when their leaves are about two inches in breadth; set them about six inches apart each way, and water frequently until established. In four or five weeks they will be of sufficient growth for final removal.

Planting.—Set them in rows two feet and a half apart each way; the last plantation may be six inches closer. They must be watered and weeded. If, during stormy weather, any of those which acquire a tall growth are blown down, they should be supported by stakes, when they will soon firmly re-establish themselves.

Cutting.—With the exception of the Brussels Sprouts, all the varieties must have their centre shoot, or heart, cut first, as this causes them to produce side-shoots, or sprouts; but of Brussels Sprouts the side-shoots must be cut first, whilst firm, and about the size of a walnut. Cut the largest first, and the smaller will continue to increase, and must be cut as fast as they attain the size named.

BROCCOLI (*Brassica oleracea botrytis*).

Varieties.—These are in a very confused state, and many of the old sorts seem to have entirely disappeared, or to have become totally changed in character. The best are the *Walcheren*, which is more properly a Cauliflower, *Snow's Superb, Chappell's Cream, Wilcove, Knight's Protecting, Purple Cape,* and *Dancer's Late Pink.*

Sowing.—For a successional supply of the *Walcheren*, sow in the end of March, the middle and end of May, the middle and end of June, and the middle and end of July, which will give a regular supply till the end of the year. Sow, for succession, *Snow's Superb* early in March and in the middle of May; *Chappell's Cream* in end of March and middle of April; for late use, till Cauliflowers come in, sow *Wilcove,* or *Knight's Protecting* middle of April and middle of May. The *Purple Cape,* sown in the middle of March, middle of May, and middle of June, will come in successionally from August or September till the end of the year. Each variety should be sown separately, and marked with a tally, and the sowing performed thin; the beds not more than three or four feet wide for the convenience of weeding. The seed must not be buried more than a quarter of an inch, and the beds netted to keep away the birds. The seed should be of the previous year's growth.

The March sowings may be planted out in the end of May or early in June, and the others in succession as they become fit, the late crops being put out in July and August.

Soil.—A loamy, well-manured soil, rather light than heavy, suits it best. It should not follow next to a crop of any other kind of Cabbagewort.

Pricking out.—The plants are fit for pricking out when having five or six leaves rather more than an inch in breadth; set them

CABBAGE.

...inches apart each way, and water every night until ...inches in breadth. They must not again be moved until they ...ted out, they must be set on an average ... way. Water to be given at the time of ...afterwards, until they are established; ...ever it may be given plentifully with ...must be hoed between frequently, ...their stems. Liquid-manure ...three cases which have to with-... is beneficially applied, as ...in the neck. The salt ... in summer, at the rate ...destruction by ...first week of ...the adjoining ...the back than the ...surface of the ...immediately ...Then every ...is scarcely...

to the 12th of August, and the seedlings may remain in the seed-bed all the winter, if not too thick; or any number may be finally planted out into the open quarters from October to November, or pricked out into nursery-beds, banks, &c., so as to have a good stock of plants for final planting out whenever favourable opportunities offer.

Should the winter be so severe as to have destroyed many of the autumn-sown plants, then early spring sowing becomes of importance. Sow towards the middle or end of January, so as to have good plants for final planting out, if the weather be mild and open, about the end of February. To effect this, a pinch of seed may be sown in pans or boxes, and placed in some steady-heated structure, and when the seedlings are large enough to prick out, have a warm border, or very gentle hotbed, ready to prick them out upon, to be protected either by glass or hoop and mat. Also, any kind may be sown in the open warm border in February and March, should the August sowing have been destroyed.

Mode of Sowing.—The soil should be soaked with water twelve hours before the seed is sown, for, after raking and forking, it is thus rendered less liable to become hard and surface-bound. The seed should also be soaked twelve hours previously to sowing in dry weather. In hot, dry weather, the evening is always the best time to sow, not covering the seed more than a quarter of an inch, and the seed-beds should be slightly shaded with boughs, straw, or any other article of a similar description, until the young plants are just appearing above the surface, when the covering must be removed. A slight sprinkling of water must then be applied, and a top-dressing of charcoal-dust, so that it may adhere to the young plants whilst moist, which will not only prevent the attacks of the fly, but promote growth.

Pricking out.—When about three inches high, thin the seedlings to four inches apart, and prick out those removed into beds prepared as for the seed-bed, planting them four inches apart.

Planting.—We never make but two plantings in the year; one from the 21st of July sowing, which planting is made during the first fortnight of September; and the second planting is made in the spring, towards the end of February or beginning of March. This last planting is either made from plants raised in August, or, if the winter destroyed that sowing, it is made from early spring sowings, our soil being made so rich for these two plantings that we never want for Coleworts, or even young Cabbage, which are produced after the principal heads have been cut away.

Plant in rows from one foot and a half to two feet and a half asunder each way, the smaller, earlier kinds being planted the closest. The *Red Cabbage*, the principal plantation of which should be made in March for pickling in September, is benefited by having the distances enlarged to three feet. They must be well watered at the time of removal, and until fully established. The best mode of applying the water is to make the hole with the dibble, and pour in about a quart *before* inserting the plant; frequently hoe to keep the weeds under, and as soon as their growth permits, the earth should be drawn round the stems.

Frame Seedlings.—The heat must never exceed 60°, nor sink more than two or three degrees below 50°, which is the most favourable minimum. Air should be admitted freely in the day, and the glasses covered, as necessity requires, at night with matting.

Cutting Cabbages.—If young sprouts are required, the side-leaves should be left on for about five days after the principal head is cut. The side-sprouts will be found to put forth very much the stronger and quicker for the leaves being thus left.

CAPSICUM.

The kinds generally cultivated are almost endless varieties of *Capsicum annuum*, consisting of various forms and colours of fruit.—*C. cerasiforme*, Cherry Pepper; *C. baccatum*, the Bird Pepper; *C. grossum*, the Bell Pepper; and *C. frutescens*, the Chillies, or Cayenne Pepper. The last-named kind, if kept in a plant-stove, pruned back, and fresh potted, or well top-dressed every year, will yield large crops for a number of years, and, from its habit, will be neat and compact to look at.

The fruit is used for pickling when green; for mixing with other pickles; for placing in vinegar, so as to form Chili vinegar; and for grinding, when ripe, for Pepper. Unless in favourable situations, it does not often ripen sufficiently in the open air, though forwarded under glass till the end of May.

The seeds (which may be kept in their ripe cases until wanted) should be sown under glass, towards the end of March, in a very rich soil, and if in a hotbed all the better. As soon as the plants are four inches high they should be pricked off, either singly in small pots, or four in a five-inch pot, and well watered, syringed, and smoked, to destroy the green fly, and shifted again, if necessary, until the first or second week in June, when the plants may be turned out into nice mellow soil, in front of a south wall, in front of forcing houses, or on a south border, when a good quantity of green fruit will be obtained in September and October. If, by the middle of September, they should not have produced ripe fruit enough, take them up with a ball of earth, repot them, shade them in a frame, pit, or hothouse of any kind for a few days, and keep them under glass. They will hardly feel the moving, and will produce abundance of either green or ripe fruit, whichever may be most required for use, all winter and next spring.

CARROT (*Daucus carota*).

Varieties.—*Dutch Horn*, very short, for forcing. *Long Horn*, for summer crop, and for all crops on shallow soils. *Long Red* and *Altrincham*, largest, for main crop on deep soils.

Young Spring Carrots.—Sow some Dutch Horn in the last week of August, or first week in September, in a dry, sheltered situation; those who have lights to spare need not sow so soon by a month. Cast out a shallow pit in a sheltered spot, forming the outsides with the earth, and finishing it level on the top with turf, upon which place any old rough boards or slabs. Into this pit put any kind of refuse, sweepings, and rakings, leaves, &c., or, indeed, anything that will secure drainage and a little bottom warmth; upon this place from ten to twelve inches of open, sandy soil, raising it quite to the top of the pit; drills are to be pressed into the soil, eight or nine inches apart, with a straight-edge, and every alternate drill sown with Carrots, and the other drill with Radishes, which, being up early, nurse and shelter the young Carrots by the time they appear. These Radishes being thus early and well thinned, are quickly ready for use, and when drawn out of the way, leave the Carrots in rows eight or nine inches apart. Take care to make such beds the same width as the frame or pit lights, in case you have any of them to spare for a short time when needed, but otherwise cover with slight protectors the size of a light, covered with straight straw, fixed on closely and neatly; or light protectors made in the same way, covered with asphalte felt.

For the out-door crops without any bottom-heat or protection the *soil* should be warm, light, and rich, dug full two spades deep. With the bottom spit turn in a little well-decayed manure; but no general application of it to the surface should be allowed.

Time and Mode of Sowing.—The first sowing, for the production of plants to draw whilst young, should take place in a warm border in the end of February, or early in March. At the close of the last month, or preferably in the first half of April, the main crop must be sown, though, to avoid the maggot, it is even recommended not to do so until its close. In May and July sow for production in autumn.

For *sowing*, a calm day should be selected; and the seeds should be separated by rubbing them between the hands, with the admixture of a little sand or dry coal-ashes, otherwise they cannot be sown regularly. Sow thinly in drills eight inches apart for the Horn, and twelve inches for the Long, and the beds not more than four feet wide, for the convenience of after cultivation. The larger weeds must be continually removed by hand, and when the plants are seven or eight weeks old, or when they have got four leaves two or three inches long, they should be thinned,—those intended for drawing young to four or five inches apart, and those to attain their full growth to ten; at the same time the ground must be small-hoed. At the close of October, or early in November, as soon as the leaves change colour, the main crop may be dug up, and laid in alternate layers with sand in a dry outhouse, previously to doing which the tops and any adhering earth must be removed. A dry day should always be chosen for taking them up. If, in cutting off the tops, a slice of the Carrot itself is cut off also, entirely removing the ring, whence the leaves again spring forth, and the Carrots are buried in sand, they will never sprout at all, and remain serviceable to a much later time in the year following.

CAULIFLOWER (*Brassica oleracea cauliflora*).

Varieties.—There are many names, but they are only different names for the following:—*Early Cauliflower; Large Asiatic*; and *Walcheren*. The last named is included also among the Broccolis, for it unites these to the Cauliflowers.

Soil.—A well-drained, rich loam suits it best. We like to grow it upon the ground upon which Celery was the previous crop. So soon as the head begins to form, no plant is more benefited by a weekly application of very strong liquid-manure.

First Sowing.—For the first main crop, sow in the third week, or about the 24th of August, to raise plants for winter protection, so as to form the first, principal, and main crops of the following year. Should the weather be very dry at the time of sowing, the soil should be thoroughly well watered before the seed be sown, and the watering continued to encourage the growth of the seedlings; as soon as these are up large enough to handle, prick them out; if in dry weather, late in the afternoon or in the evening. By this attention, strong, healthy plants will be ready for either finally planting out under hand-glasses about the middle of October, or for protection in frames, or at the foot of walls. These protected plants are to form a second crop to those which were planted out under the hand-glasses, and may be finally planted out towards the end of February, if the weather is favourable, two feet and a half asunder each way; and should severe weather set in again, flower-pots just large enough to cover the plant may be turned over each, but taken off in all favourable weather. Care should always be taken to lift up the plants out of the nursery-beds, so as to insure uninjured roots.

Should the weather be very severe in the winter, the hand-glass crop must have a little protection more than that of the hand-light itself. But particular attention should be paid to airing at all times when the weather will permit, by either taking the lights entirely off or tilting them.

Plants raised from this August sowing may be so treated as to give a successional produce during June and July following.

Take up some of the plants in October, trim their roots, pot them, and plunge the pots under a cold frame, close to the glass, until the end of February; then turn them out under hand-glasses. Their heads will be ready for use in June. Other plants prick out at the beginning of October in a south border, and leave unmoved until March is ended; then finally plant them out. These will produce heads for use at the close of June. A third portion of plants prick out at the end of October, and do not plant them out finally until the middle of April. They will be fit for use early in July.

If, through some mismanagement or misfortune, the winter stock should become short, a sowing towards the end of January becomes of importance. A very little seed must then be sown in a pan or box, placed in some moderately-heated structure, or in a gentle hotbed made for the purpose; and when the seedlings are up, and large enough to handle, they should be pricked out on other very gentle hotbeds, care being taken to keep the plants up close to the glass, and inured to the open air. Plants raised in this way will be nearly as forward as those sown in August, and protected in cold frames through the winter.

Planting under Hand-glasses.—Do this about the third week in October. Choose an open quarter, and let the ground be well manured and trenched; let the rows be four feet apart from row to row, and the plants three feet apart in the row. Two-feet wide paths and two-feet wide beds will give four feet in the clear between the rows. Insert your plants four or five together under each glass, choosing some of the best and strongest from your nursery-beds; lift them up with a little care, so as not to hurt their roots. Put on the glasses, and let them remain on for three or four days, after which give a little air by tilting the glasses up on the south side for six or eight hours every day; and after this, any very fine warm days the lights may be taken quite off about nine o'clock in the morning, and put on again at three in the afternoon.

Having Cauliflowers in April.—Mr. Barnes says that they have these in Devonshire by pursuing the following course:—We sow quite at the end of September and beginning of October. We merely place one frame for sowing on the bare ground, or fill up either the Cucumber or the Melon-bed with some of the old, half-decayed linings, leaves, or refuse of any kind that may be then at hand, to secure a gentle bottom-heat. A few inches of soil are placed over this refuse, and allowed to remain a day or two, so that the warmth may rise and the materials settle; a little more soil will then be required to fill up level with the top of the frame. The seed is then sown, and beaten down with the back of the spade; a little good earth intermixed with charred dust is then covered over the seed, and the lights placed on until the young plants begin to make their appearance, when air is immediately given by propping the lights slightly at first, but increasing gradually both at the back and front, and as soon as the plants are fully up the lights are taken off entirely. The earth is surface-stirred as soon as possible, and a little dry, charred material often sifted amongst the plants to prevent mildew or shanking. As soon as the plants can be handled they are pricked out on another well-prepared bed close to the glass, or into thumb or small-sized pots, and plunged, keeping them well aired both night and day, and watering them with tepid water when necessary. As soon as required, we shift them into larger pots, never allowing them to get pot-bound, or to be still, and become stunted, as they would in that case form flower-heads so small as to be useless. The beds, where the early Celery has been taken up, are prepared by the application of a good dressing of manure, and the ground is well trenched, ready to receive the plants early in the year, when, in open weather, we turn out our Cauliflower plants under a hand-glass, where, if well attended to afterwards, they will grow freely, and become strong enough to produce good and handsome heads of flower in the month of April.

The second Sowing should be at the end of February or beginning of March, and then either in a cold frame or on a warm, open border; or, if the weather be very unfavourable, a sowing may be made on a very gentle hotbed even at this time, attention to pricking out, &c., given as before directed. From this sowing a third planting is made.

The third Sowing should be made about the last week in April or first week in May, and the seedlings attended to as before, as to pricking out, &c. From this sowing a fourth planting is made.

Fitness for Use.—When a Cauliflower has arrived at its full size, which is shown by the border opening as if it were about to run, pull up the plant, as it never produces any useful sprouts, and if hung up thus entire in a cool place, it may be preserved for several days. The best time to cut a Cauliflower is early of a morning before the dew is evaporated.

To preserve from Frost.—Bury them in sand, laying them in alternate layers with the sand in a dry situation. By this means they may be preserved to the close of January; or they may be put in a trench dug at the bottom of a wall, eighteen inches wide and deep, the plants being laid with their roots uppermost in an inclining position, so that the roots of the second cover the top of the one preceding. The earth to be laid over them thickly, a considerable slope given to it, and beaten smooth with the spade to throw off rain.

CELERY (*Apium graveolens*).

Varieties.—*Cole's Superb*, red and white; and *Nutt's Champion*.

The facts to be kept constantly in remembrance in Celery culture are, that the plants must not be checked in their growth either by injuring their roots in moving them, or by neglecting to water them, or by a deficiency in the supply of manure.

The following is the mode pursued by those who have grown Celery weighing 15 lbs. per head :—

Sowing.—Sow in pans from the 12th to the 18th of February, covering the seed as lightly as possible with rich soil, and plunging the pans under a frame in a gentle hotbed. Temperature from 70° to 75°.

Seedling Plants.—When these have been up about a week, give them a little air in the daytime, not allowing them to get drawn. After they have been in their second leaf nine or ten days, prepare frames, filling them with new stable-litter, and covering this with three inches of rich soil; and when it is nearly the same heat as the hot frames in which the seedlings have been raised, begin transplanting. Plant them in rows six inches apart each way. After the seedlings have been planted nearly a week, give a little air in the frames in the daytime, watering the plants very lightly.

Planting out.—For planting, dig the trench eighteen inches deep, and thirty-six inches wide. Manure with pig and horse-dung, with horn or bone dust, well mixed together. Put about fifteen inches of this mixture in the trench, and cover it with three inches of rich, light soil. Plant out near the middle of May, putting the plants twelve inches apart from each other. They should be four or five inches high at the time of this their final planting, and very sturdy. The trenches should be in an open situation, for the plants never attain to a large and vigorous growth if shaded by Peas, Beans, or anything else.

After Culture.—If the weather should be very dry and hot, the plants ought to be protected in the day from the scorching sun; water should be given freely after sunset from a rose water-pan. After the plants have got "hold," or commenced growing, they will need no protection from the sun; but take care to water pretty freely with clean water if the weather is hot and dry.

After the plants have attained the height of twelve inches they will require to be tied round with a little bass matting, or anything of a softish texture, but care must be taken not to tie them too tight, taking off all the lateral shoots as the plants grow. After having been tied up for some time, it will be necessary to untie them, and tie them again a little higher, taking off all the lateral shoots and superfluous stems before tying them again. They may then be suffered to grow till they have attained the height of from twenty to twenty-two inches. Care should be taken that they do not suffer for want of water. After having attained the above height, and are well cleared of lateral shoots, they should then be earthed about three inches high, and tied a little higher with matting (the tying is only done to prevent the wind and wet from breaking the outer stems. After having earthed them about twice, three inches at a time, water them once a week with liquid-manure, but still keep watering with clear water if dry weather. As the plants grow they may be earthed up a little at a time, taking care not to earth them over the centre of the heart, or they will be very likely to rot at the core. Liquid-manure must not be used oftener than once in seven days. Earth up a little at a time once a fortnight, leaving the earthing up on a slant towards the edge of the trench, so that the water will not run in so as to touch the stems of the plants, as this would cause them to rot. Be careful to remember that sandy soil is the best for earthing up with.

CIBOUL (*Allium fistulosum*).

This, also known as the *Welsh Onion*, is a perennial, never forming any bulb, but is sown annually, to be drawn young for salads, &c. Its strong taste renders it greatly inferior to the common Onion for this purpose; but, from its extreme hardiness, it is good as a winter-standing crop for spring use.

Varieties.—Two varieties are in cultivation, the white and the red.

Culture.—Sow it in August, in drills six inches apart, and about a quarter of an inch deep. Sow thickly, as the plants are to be drawn young.

Soil.—A light, rich loam is best. The leaves usually die away completely in winter, but fresh ones are thrown out again in February or March.

Scallions.—All Onions that have refused to bulb, but form lengthened necks and strong blades in spring and summer, are called Scallions.

COUVE-TRONCHUDA (*Brassica oleracea*, var. *costata*).

Although only a variety of the Cabbage, it deserves a special notice for its great excellence when grown at the proper season.

Sow in March and April, and prick out and cultivate in soil the same as directed for the *Cabbage*. It then becomes fit for use in November, and when it has endured some night frosts it is the most tender and sweetest of all the Cabbageworts.

CRESS (*Lepidium sativum*).

Varieties.—There are three varieties: *Plain-leaved*, which is the one commonly cultivated for salads; *Curled-leaved*, equally good, and employed likewise for garnishing; *Broad-leaved*, seldom cultivated. See *Mustard*.

CUCUMBER (*Cucumis sativus*).

Varieties.—These are divided into glaucous and non-glaucous: in the former the fruit is covered with a fine bloom; in the latter this characteristic is absent, the fruit being of a bright lively green. Of glaucous varieties the best are *Dr. Livingstone*, fruit black-spined, seventeen inches long; *Hamilton's Market Favourite*, very handsome, sixteen inches long; *Butler's Empress Eugénie*, white-spined, eighteen inches long; and *Improved Manchester Prize*, white-spined, twenty inches long. Of the non-glaucous kinds the best are *Carter's Champion*, smooth, twelve inches long; and *Kenyon's Improved*, white spined, fifteen inches long. All the above are excellent bearers. For Ridge Cucumbers the *Early short prickly* is often preferred for the first crop, as being a very plentiful bearer, quick in coming into production, and the hardiest of all the varieties. The *Early long prickly* is a hardy, abundantly-bearing variety, but not quick in coming into production. It is generally grown for main crops.

The sorts above enumerated have been selected after the careful trial of every known kind, but there are some others closely approaching them in point of excellence.

Times for Sowing.—To obtain fruit at Christmas the seed must be sown in the middle of August; but as the days lengthen and the temperature of the air increases in spring, the time between sowing the seed and cutting the fruit decreases much; so that if sown in May the fruit from it can be ready for table in from six to eight weeks; if sown the first week of January the cutting can be ready early in March.

Soil.—A fresh loam, as the top spit of a pasture, is, perhaps, as fine a soil as can be employed for the Cucumber.

Culture in Dung Beds.—We will commence with the dung fresh at the stable-door: the first thing is to throw it into a close body to "sweat." Shake it over loosely, and reject a portion of the mere droppings; for these take the most purifying, and, moreover, engender an over-powerful and sometimes unmanageable heat. The main bulk of the material thus thrown together will, in a week or so, become exceedingly hot, and must then be turned completely inside out; and in so doing, every lock or patch which adheres together must be divided. Water now regularly as the work proceeds, rendering every portion equally moist. After the mass has lain for about four days longer, give a liberal amount of water on the top; this will wash out at the bottom of the heap much of its gross impurities. In a few more days it must be again turned inside out, using water if dry in any portion; and after laying nearly a week it should be almost fit for use; but it is well to give it even another turn. If any tree leaves, strawy materials, &c., are to be added to the mass, they may be so at the last turning but one. The heap ought now to be "sweet;" a handful drawn from the very interior, and applied to the nostrils, will not only be devoid of impure smell, but actually possess a somewhat agreeable scent, similar to the smell of mushrooms.

Beds.—Select a spot perfectly dry beneath, or rendered so, exposed to a whole day's sun; but the more it is sheltered sideways the better, as starving winds, by suddenly lowering the temperature, cause a great waste of material as well as of labour. Some portable screens, therefore, are useful things for early work. The ground surface should be nearly level. It is well, also, to fill most of the interior of the bed, after building it half a yard in height, with any half-decayed materials, such as half-worn linings, fresh leaves, &c. This will, in general, secure it from the danger of burning, whilst it will also add to the permanency of the bed, for the Cucumber roots will descend, and thus secure an indefinite amount of food during the hot weather of summer.

A bed should be at least four feet high at the back; if five feet, all the better; and as soon as built, let some littery manure be placed round the sides in order to prevent the wind searching it. As soon as the heat is well up, or in about four days from the building of it, the whole bed should have a thorough watering. It is now well to close it until the heat is well up again, when a second and lighter watering may be applied; and now it will be ready for the hills of soil.

In making the hills of soil for the plants, make a hollow in the centre of each light half the depth of the bed. In the bottom of this place nearly a barrowful of brickbats, on this some half-rotten dung, and finally a flat square of turf, on which place the hillock. It is almost impossible for the roots of the plants to "scorch" with this precaution. The *soil* at this early season may be one half good turfy loam, six months old at least, and the other half-rotten manure, old vegetable soil, and sandy heath-soil, well blended.

In placing the hillocks, most old practitioners keep them, at first, in a globular form in the centre of each light; this enables the cultivator to apply water occasionally, in case of burning, without wetting the soil.

Culture.—This may be said mainly to comprise a due attention to ventilation, sprinkling, and constant care over the linings. If the bed is established as it ought to be, the principal of the heat will have to be furnished by the latter; for if the body of the bed is in a slight fermentable state, there will always be *bottom-heat enough*; for such should not be permitted to rise above 90° *by any means*, nor to fall below 75°. Protection to *the linings* was named at the beginning: we proceed to explain. It is well known that a good deal of labour is involved in the culture of very early Cucumbers by the ordinary dung-frame; and not only this, but the loss of much manure. Now, by having some kind of screen to ward off the wind, linings will both last double the time, and also be much less liable to injurious fluctuations.

We recommend the use of wooden frames, covered with tarpaulin, sail cloth, or anything impervious to wet. The frame may be a mere skeleton, like an old picture-frame, and bound across, for strength, at each angle; and the cloth, mats, or other material stretched tight and nailed down all round. Made in about six-feet lengths, by about four feet in depth, they can be readily shifted according to need by even lady amateurs. Such adjuncts are greater economisers than many would imagine: beds made of properly sweetened fermenting materials, and the linings kept moist and protected by screens, will almost work themselves, ventilation being, of course, attended to. Nevertheless, the linings should be turned over about once in a fortnight during February and March, choosing mild weather for the operation, never turning the whole at once, but back and front alternately.

As to *ventilation*, a good surface heat being insured, we say, give air night and day, less or more, so long as 70° can be secured by day, and from 60° to 65° by night; suffering, however, a rise at all times in a just proportion to the amount of light. Let the maximum be attained generally from about three to five P.M., during which period the frames may be closed. After this again give a little air for the night, cautiously, and slightly sprinkle round the sides of the frame.

Beds heated by Hot Water.—The general cultural directions given above are equally applicable to these. Mr. Latter, one of the most successful of Cucumber growers, employs hot water to heat his beds. He sows in the first week of September, and the vines from this sowing will be in bearing and very strong before February. The seedlings are first shifted into sixty-sized pots, secondly into twenty-fours, and lastly into the largest size. If to be trained on a trellis, the runner must not be stopped until it has, trained to a stick, grown through the trellis. The temperature in the pit or frame is kept as nearly 65° as possible during the night, and from 75° to 85° during the day, air being admitted *night and day*, little or much, according to the state of the weather. The bottom-heat is kept as near as can be to 70°, although he finds that 85° does not hurt the plants. He waters them with salt water until February, and then employs liquid-manure, taking care that the temperature of the liquid is always from 75° to 80°. The earth over the hot-water tank or pipes ought not to be less than fifteen inches deep. During severe frosts it is an excellent plan to keep a small floating light burning within the frame every night.

Hand-glass Crops.—Sow for these towards the end of March or beginning of April. The plants to be ridged out towards the middle or end of April, under hand-glasses. If the open, warm quarters are to be occupied by this fruit, trenches should be dug out one foot or one foot and a half deep, by two feet and a half wide, and ten feet wide from row to row; these to be filled with good fermenting dung that has been well worked as for other hotbeds. The trenches should be filled with the dung to six or eight inches above the common level of the soil before the earth is put on. Put on the earth in the form of a ridge until the heat is up, which will be in the course of three or four days, when it may be levelled down, the glasses put on, and the plants turned out under them, and watered with tepid water. The pots out of which the plants were turned may remain to tilt the lights with when a little air is required; and when the plants begin to fill the lights two similar pots or half bricks will be required to stand the lights upon over the plants, after which they may be trained out by degrees, and as they begin to extend over the beds the sides or alleys must be forked and well broken up, making a neat level surface for the plants to be trained out upon. The plants will require stopping, training, and plenty of water in dry, hot weather.

Open-Ground Crops.—The sowing for these crops must be at the close of May, or early in June. A rich south-west border, beneath a reed or other fence, is peculiarly favourable, as they then enjoy a genial warmth without suffering from the meredian sun. The border being dug regularly over, and saucer-like hollows, about fifteen inches in diameter and one or two deep, formed five feet apart, the seed may be sown six or eight in each.

Seed may also be sown beneath a hedge of similar aspect, and the plants either trained to it or to bushy branches placed perpendicularly. If the weather be dry, it is requisite to water the patches moderately two or three days after sowing. In four or five days, if the season is genial, the plants will make their appearance, and until they have attained their rough leaves, should be guarded from the small birds, which will often destroy the whole crop by devouring the seed-leaves.

If the season is cold and unfavourable, plants may be raised in pots, under a frame or hand-glasses, as directed for those crops; to be thence transplanted, when of about a month's growth, or when the third rough leaf appears, into the open ground, shelter being afforded them during the night. Water must be given every two or three days, in proportion to the dryness of the season, applying it during the afternoon or early in the morning.

Only three or four plants may be allowed to grow together in a patch, and these pressed far apart. The training must be as carefully attended to as for the other crops; but stopping is seldom necessary, as the plants are rarely super-luxuriant. They will come into production in August and September.

ENDIVE (*Cichorium endivia*).

Used in salads.

Varieties.—The *Green-Curled* for the main crops, as it best endures wet and cold; the *White-Curled*, chiefly grown for summer and autumn; the *Broad-leaved*, or *Batavian*, is preferred for soups and stews, but is seldom used for salads.

Soil and Situation.—A light, dry, but rich soil, dug deep and unshaded. It is best to form an artificial bed by laying a foot in depth of earth on a bed of brickbats, stones, &c.

Sow for a first crop about the middle of April, to be repeated in May, but only in small portions, as those which are raised before June soon advance to seed. Towards the middle of June the first main crop may be sown, another in the course of July, and lastly early in August; and in this month the main plantation is made. Sow in drills twelve inches apart, and about a quarter of an inch below the surface. When an inch in height, thin the plants to three or four inches apart; those taken away are too small to be of any service if pricked out. . Water should be given freely in dry weather.

When the larger seedlings have been transplanted, the smaller ones which remain should have a gentle watering, and in twelve or fourteen days they will afford a second successional crop; and, by a repetition of this management, in general, a third. The plants are generally fit for transplanting when of a month's growth in the seed-bed, or when five or six inches high.

Planting.—Set them in rows twelve or fifteen inches apart each way; the Batavian requires the greater space. Water must be given moderately every evening until the plants are established, after which only in excessive and protracted drought. Those which are left in the seed-bed, in general, attain a finer growth than those that have been moved. In November, some plants that have attained nearly their full size may be removed to the south side of a sloping bank of dry, light earth, raised one or two feet behind; to be protected by frames, mats, or thick coverings of litter during severe and very wet weather; but to be carefully uncovered during mild, dry days. The plants, in this instance, are not required to be further apart than six or eight inches. This plan may be followed in open days during December and January, by which means a constant supply may be obtained.

Blanching.—About three months elapse between the time of sowing and the fitness of the plants for blanching. This operation will be completed in from ten to fourteen days in summer, or in three or four weeks in winter. To blanch the plants tie their leaves together, or place tiles or pieces of board upon them; or tie their leaves together, and cover them to their tips with mould, making it rise to a point, so as to throw off excessive rains. Another mode is to cover the soil between the plants with sand, and turn over each of those intended for immediate blanching a flower-pot, with its drainage-hole closely stopped by a cork, so as to entirely exclude the light. The best plan is to take the pots off daily for a quarter of an hour if the weather is dry, and then to put on a fresh dry pot, stopped similarly to the one taken off. The pot taken off may be dried ready for the next day. By this means mouldiness and decay will be prevented, to which Endive is very liable during blanching. If the simple mode of drawing the leaves together is adopted to effect this blanching, they must be tied very close, and, in a week after the first tying, a second ligature must be passed round the middle of the plant to prevent the heart-leaves bursting out. A dry afternoon, when the plants are entirely free from moisture, should be selected, whichever mode is adopted. A very excellent mode is to spread over the surface of the bed about an inch in depth of pit-sand, and cover each plant with a small pot made of earthenware, painted both within and on the outside to exclude the wet—that worst hinderance of blanching. To avoid this, the pots should be taken off daily·to allow the plants to dry, and the insides of the pots wiped. A Sea-kale pot in miniature, like the annexed figure,

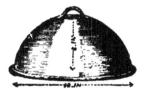

is to be preferred; and, if made of zinc or other metal, it would be better, because impervious to moisture.

Preserving in Winter.—Endive may be secured in turf or other temporary pits, and may be protected with asphalte or light-boarded shutters, thatched wood-frames, fern, furze, or other similar materials. A portion, in succession, may be placed to bleach in a dark shed or cellar, being planted thickly together in sand or earth.

ESCHALLOT OR SHALLOT (*Allium Ascalonicum*).

Varieties.—The *Common*, which puts up long, slender, dark green leaves; and the *Long-keeping*, with larger bulbs and dwarfer habit, keeping good for nearly or quite two years.

Propagation.—Each offset may be planted out either in the months of October and November, or early in the spring, from February to the beginning of April. Autumn is the best season for planting if the soil lies dry. If planted in beds, let them be three feet and a half wide, and three or four inches higher than the alleys, and the surface of the bed a little arched. Set out the rows nine inches apart from row to row; spread a mixture of soot and charred refuse along the line about to be planted, and then plant the offsets singly with the hand upon the surface of the bed, six inches apart in the row, just pressing each bulb down firm in the soil; see occasionally that they are not cast out of their places by worms or other vermin. Take them up for storing, when full grown, towards the end of June or July, as soon as the leaves begin to decay. Spread them out to dry, on boards, in some airy situation, and when dry hang them up in small bunches in a dry, cold, dark place.

FENNEL (*Anethum fœniculum*).

Used for sauce to mackarel, pickled salmon, &c. It will grow almost anywhere, but in a dry soil is longest-lived. It is propagated both by offsets and partings of the root, any time between the beginning of February and the end of April. Insert the plants a foot apart. Water must be given freely at every removal, and until established, if the weather is at all dry.

The stalks of those that are not required to produce seed must be cut down as often as they run up in summer. If this is strictly attended to, the roots will last for many years; but those which are allowed to ripen their seed seldom endure for more than five or six.

GARLIC (*Allium sativum*).

The directions given for cultivating the ESCHALLOT are entirely applicable to Garlic.

GOURD (*Cucurbita*).

PUMPKIN (*C. pepo*). SQUASH (*C. melopepo*). VEGETABLE MARROW (*C. ovifera*).

The fruit is used, when young, to boil whole as a culinary vegetable, or to pickle; and, when ripe, to boil and mash like Turnips, or to mix with soup.

Soil.—It must be a light rich loam, as for the Cucumber.

The seeds may be sown in a hotbed of moderate strength, under a frame or hand-glasses, at the end of March or early in April. In May they may be sown in the open ground beneath a south fence to remain, or in a hotbed if at its commencement, to forward the plants for transplanting at its close, or early in June.

The plants are fit for transplanting when they have got four rough leaves, or when of about a month's growth. They may be planted without any shelter on dunghills, or in holes prepared as directed for the open-ground crop of Cucumbers. Some may be inserted beneath pales, walls, or hedges, to be trained regularly over them, on account of their ornamental appearance. They may be treated in every respect like the Cucumber, only they do not want so much care. They require abundance of water in dry weather. When the runners have extended three feet, they may be pegged down and covered with earth at a joint; this will cause the production of roots and the longer continuance of the plant in vigour.

HAMBURGH PARSLEY (*Petroselinum sativum*, var. *latifolium*).

This, known also by the name *Broad-leaved* and *Turnip-rooted Parsley*, is cultivated for its root, which attains the size of a middling Parsnip, boiling exceedingly tender and palatable.

Sow at monthly intervals, from February until the middle of June, thinly in drills nine inches apart. The plants appear in about a month after sowing, and require to be thinned to nine inches asunder. Frequent hoeing is the only cultivation required. By the end of July, or during August, the earliest sowings will have acquired a sufficient size for occasional use; but the roots seldom attain their full size until Michaelmas, and the latest crops not until the following year. On the arrival of frost, some of them must be taken up, and buried in sand, in a dry situation under cover.

Soil.—A light rich loam. Dig it two spades deep, turning in a little well-decayed stable-manure with the bottom spit.

HORSE-RADISH (*Cochlearia amoracia*).

It delights in a deep rich soil, banks of a ditch, &c. It is propagated by sets, provided by cutting the main root and offsets into lengths of two inches. The tops, or crowns of the roots, form the best. Each set should have at least two eyes, in case of one refusing to vegetate. The times for planting are in October and February.

Insert the sets in rows eighteen inches apart each way. The ground being trenched between two and three feet deep, the cuttings should be placed along the bottom of the trench, and the soil turned from the next trench over them. The earth ought to lie lightly over the sets; therefore treading on the beds should be carefully avoided.

Remove the leaves as they decay in autumn, the ground being also hoed and raked over at the same season; and the hoeing may be repeated in the following spring.

In the succeeding autumn they merely require to be hoed as before, and may be taken up as wanted. By having three beds devoted to this root, one will always be lying fallow and improving, of which period advantage should be taken to apply any requisite manure.

Taking up.—To take them up, a trench is dug along the outside row down to the bottom of the roots, which, when the bed is continued in one place, may be cut off level to the original stool, and the earth from the next row then turned over them to the requisite depth; and so in rotation to the end of the plantation.

JERUSALEM ARTICHOKE (*Helianthus tuberosus*).

Used plainly boiled, or with a white sauce as a table vegetable. It deserves to be more generally cultivated, and, if attended to properly, it is very productive. It is most productive in soil that is light and moderately rich. It should never have any manure applied at the time of planting.

The best time for planting is in November; but whether planted then or in the early spring, plant with the dibble six inches deep, in rows three feet apart, and the same space between every two plants in the rows. The rows should run north and south, so as to admit as much sunshine as possible between them.

No after-culture is required but frequent hoeings, and thinning the stems produced by each set to one or two at the most. Neither earth up the stems nor cut them shorter.

In November the tubers will be fit for taking up, either as wanted, or to be stored in alternate layers with earth. The middle-sized tubers are the best for planting.

If the tubers are allowed to remain in the ground, let the stalks be cut off to within six or eight inches of the earth's surface, and a coat of mulch, leaves, or refuse of any kind put over them, so that the Artichokes may be taken up at any time, even when severe frost prevails.

KIDNEY BEAN (*Phaseolus vulgaris*).

Varieties.—There are many varieties, and so numerous are they, and so much cultivated in France, under the name of *Haricots*, that this vegetable is commonly called the "*French Bean.*" The best varieties for our climate are, of *Dwarfs*, the *Newington Wonder*, *Dun*, and the *Negro*. *Runners*, the *Scarlet* and the *Case-knife*.

Soil and Situation.—A very light, mellow, well-drained loam. For the early and late crops, a sheltered border, or in a single row about a foot from a south fence, otherwise the situation cannot be too open.

Sowing.—*Dwarfs* may be sown towards the end of January in pots, and placed upon the flue of the hothouse, or in rows in the earth of a hotbed, for production in March, to be repeated once every three weeks in similar situations during February and March, for supplying the table during April. A small sowing may be made, under a frame without heat, in the end of March or early in April, if the weather is fine, for removal into a sheltered border early in May. When planted out, it is a good plan to place them at the bottom of a trench for protection. The chief requisites for success in the hothouse are, to have them near the glass, to keep them well watered and the air moist, and ventilated as much as the season permits.

During May, and thence until the first week in August, sowings may be made of *Dwarfs* once every three weeks; but one sowing of *Runners* in May will suffice. In September forcing recommences, at first merely under frames without bottom-heat; October, and thence to the close of the year, in hotbeds, &c., as in January. Sowing, when a removal is intended, should always be made in pots. It is a good practice, likewise, to repeat each sowing in the frames without heat after the lapse of a week, as the first will often fail, when a second, although after so short a lapse of time, will perfectly succeed. In every instance bury the seed one inch deep. The rows of the main crops to be two feet apart, the seed being inserted either in drills or by the dibble, four inches apart; the plants, however, to be thinned to twice that distance. If a vacancy occurs, it may always be filled by plants which have been carefully removed by the trowel from where they stood too thick. The seed inserted during the hottest period of summer should be either soaked in water for five or six hours, laid in damp mould for a day or two, or the drills be well watered previously to sowing. Earth up the plants early, as it keeps the stems from being broken by the wind. Dwarfs may be kept in production late into November, by hooping over the rows, and covering them with mats.

The pods of both kinds are always to be gathered while young; by thus doing, and care being had not to injure the stems in detaching them, the plants are rendered prolific and long-lived.

Forcing.—The hotbed must be of moderate size, and covered with earth nine inches thick. When the heat has become regular, the seed may be inserted in drills a foot apart, and the plants allowed to stand six inches asunder in the rows. Air must be admitted as freely as to the Cucumber. The same precautions are likewise necessary as to keeping up the temperature, taking the chill off the water, &c., as for that plant. When the seed begins to sprout the mould should be kept regularly moistened; and when grown up, water may be given moderately three times a week. The temperature should never be less than 60°, nor higher than 75°.

Those sown under frames in March for transplanting into a border, when two or three inches in height, must be hardened gradually for the exposure by the plentiful admission of air, and the total removal of the glasses during fine days. If any are raised in pots in the hothouse, they must be prepared for the removal by setting them outside in fine days, and there watering them with cold water.

If the season is too ungenial to remove them even to a warm border, the plants are often inserted in patches, to have the protection of frames or hand-lights at night, or as the weather demands.

Runners.—As these are tender, and the seed is more apt to decay than those of the Dwarfs, no open-ground crop must be inserted before early in May, sowing to be continued at intervals of four weeks through June and July, which will insure a supply from the middle of this last month until October.

They are so prolific, and such permanent bearers, that five open-ground sowings of a size proportionate to the consumption will, in almost every instance, be sufficient.

They are inserted in drills, either singly three feet apart, or in pairs ten or twelve inches asunder, and each pair four feet distant from its neighbour. The seed is buried two inches deep, and four apart in the rows, the plants being thinned to twice that distance.

If grown in single rows, a row of poles is set on the south side of each, being fixed firmly in the ground, and kept together by having a light pole tied horizontally along their tops; or posts being fixed at each end of the rows, and united by a cross bar at their tops, a string may be passed from this to each of the plants. If the rows are in pairs, a row of poles may be placed on each side, so fixed in the ground that their summits cross, and can be tied together; but if the runners are nipped off as fast as they appear, the plants become bushy, are nearly as prolific as if allowed to climb, continue much longer in bearing, and the unsightliness and expense of poles are avoided.

LEEK (*Allium porrum*).

The Leek is a hardy biennial, for, although it attains perfection in size and for culinary purposes the first year, it does not run to seed, the perfecting of which it often survives, until the second. The whole plant is eaten, being employed in soups, &c., and boiled and eaten with meat.

Varieties.—The *Musselburgh* and the large *London Leek*, which are by far the best; the *Scotch* or *Flag*, which is larger and hardier; the *Rouen*, which is excellent; and the *Flanders*.

Sow first, at the end of February, a small crop for transplanting in June and July, as well as in part to remain where sown; again, for the main crop, in the course of March or early in April; and lastly, towards the close of April or beginning of May, for late transplanting. Sow, in drills, some to remain after thinning. The Leek, however, is much benefited by transplanting. Always transplant with the trowel, so as to injure the roots as little as possible.

Cultivation.—When the plants are three or four inches in height hoe and thin to two or three inches apart; water also, in dry weather, will strengthen and forward them for transplanting when six or eight inches high. They must be taken away regularly from the seed-bed, the ground being well watered previously if not soft and easily yielding. When thinned out, they may be left in the seed-bed six inches asunder, as they do not grow so large as the transplanted ones. The latter must be set by the trowel one foot apart each way in a shallow trench, thrown out similarly to that we have recommended for Celery. This is an excellent plan, as it furnishes the ready means of watering. If a dry summer and autumn occur, watering will be found essentially necessary. Also, the earth cast out will be convenient for earthing them to blanch. The rows should be planted cross-ways of the trench. The application of good liquid-manure will very much add to the size, colour, and mildness of the Leek. Water in abundance at the time of planting, and shorten the long weak leaves, but leave the roots as uninjured as possible. By this treatment, and by cutting off the tops of the leaves about once a month, as new ones are produced, the neck swells to a much larger size.

LETTUCE (*Lactuca sativa*).

Cos Varieties.—*Black-seeded Green, Spotted* or *Leopard, Early Egyptian, Green* and *Brown Silesia, White Paris Cos,* the largest and best summer kind; *Green Paris Cos,* rather hardier; and *Bath* or *Brown Cos,* the hardiest of the Cos kinds.

Cabbage Varieties.—*Drumhead, Brown Dutch* and *Common White Dutch,* both good for winter; *Tennis Ball* or *Button,* good for winter; *Hammersmith, Hardy Green* or *Capuchin,* the hardiest Lettuce known; *Imperial, Grand Admirable, Large Roman, Malta, Neapolitan,* the best for summer.

Soil.—Lettuces thrive best in a light very rich soil, with a dry substratum. For the first and last crops of the year a warm sheltered situation is required; but for the midsummer ones, a border that is shaded during mid-day.

Sowing.—The first sowing in a frame on a warm border, or slender hotbed, at the close of January, or early in February; at the close of this last month a larger one in any open situation, and a smaller sowing repeated once every three weeks until the end of July, for summer and autumn use, to be continued at similar intervals until the close of September, for winter and early spring. Mid-August is the best time for sowing the main winter crops, which should consist of *Hammersmith, Hardy Green, Brown*

Dutch, Brown Cos, and some of the *Green Paris Cos*. Sow moderately thin, each variety separate. From the middle of April until August the Lettuce does best not transplanted. During this period sow thinly in drills a foot apart. Thin the plants to nine inches apart. These are not so apt to start for seed as those transplanted. Give liquid-manure and abundance of water in dry weather.

Pricking out.—When the plants are about a month old, or two inches in height, thin them to three or four inches apart, and prick out those removed at similar distances; those from the sowings in January and February in frames, and thence until August in any open situation. Those of the August sowing must be divided into two portions, the largest being selected and planted in an open compartment for late autumn use, and the smaller on a warm border for winter and early spring.

Plant out finally in rows a foot apart each way. At the time of every removal, whether of pricking out or planting, water must be given moderately, and until the plants are rooted. Those which are planted to withstand the winter, which they easily do if sheltered with hoops and matting during severe weather, and continue in a fit state for use, are best planted on ridges, as a protection from excessive wet, from which they always suffer. In every stage of growth they must be kept well watered, and the earth around them frequently stirred, for the extirpation of slugs and snails. No vegetable is more benefited than the Lettuce by the application, occasionally, of liquid-manure. To check the Cos plants running to seed before the heart is perfectly blanched, it is a good practice, at the time of tying them up, to cut out the centre bud of each with a sharp knife.

Frame Crops.—The plants raised from the September sowing may be divided as directed for those of August; but, in addition, some of the Cos varieties may be planted on a warm border, to have the shelter of frames and hand-glasses. Some of the strongest of these may, in succession during November, December, and January, be planted in a moderate hotbed, being removed with as little injury as possible to the roots, to bring them forward for immediate use. Whilst in frames they require much attention. Being watered and shaded until established, they must afterwards have as much light and air admitted as possible, as well as a regular supply of moisture.

At night the additional shelter of matting, and in severe weather an increased covering, must be afforded. The day temperature should never exceed 80°, nor fall below 65°. The plants may be set in rows about six inches apart; but of those which are merely sheltering during the winter, on the return of mild weather at the beginning of March or April, every second one must be carefully removed, and planted in a warm border at the usual open-ground distance.

LOVE-APPLE (*Lycopersicon esculentum*).

This annual is also called the *Tomato*.

Varieties.—Of the *Red*—the Common Large, Small, Pear-shaped, Cherry-shaped. Of the *Yellow*—the Large Yellow, Small or Cherry Yellow.

Soil.—Moderately rich, light, and on a dry subsoil. Sea-weed may be applied with advantage to the border on which it is grown, as may kelp or common salt in small quantities. The situation must be sheltered. Where the natural soil is extremely stubborn in texture, a barrow-load of lime rubbish will be of great service.

Culture.—Sow in pots early in March, or even in February, if there is not a place where they can be hastened forward. Let the pots be placed in a hotbed, and the seed soon vegetates and grows freely. The seedlings will speedily require potting off, two or three plants together into a pot, and to be set into the frame again, where they may be allowed to remain until the small pots into which they were potted become full of roots, when they may be removed into larger ones; but they must then, or soon after, be placed in a cooler place, in order that they may be gradually hardened off, so as finally to be capable of enduring a sheltered situation in the garden in the open air by the 1st of May. They ought to be inured to the open air a few days before turning out of doors, and afterwards receive some shelter at night, for the slightest frost takes effect. Before planting out, the plants should have made a considerable advance of growth in the pots, and if, to a certain extent, pot-bound, it will be no worse. If the flower-blossoms are set and partially opened before the plants are turned out, all the better. The shelter of a wall seems absolutely necessary to make sure of ripening the fruit; but it will occasionally ripen very well on the open ground when the plants are three or four feet apart, with each plant tied up to a stake, and the shoots carefully thinned out. Plant on unoccupied portions of a south wall. They may also be planted on east and west walls with a tolerable certainty of success; or the south side of a close paling-fence will do very well.

If there is reason to suppose the plants are rambling too much in the latter part of summer, it is good practice to cut the roots all round each plant, at the distance of eighteen inches or so from it, about the beginning of September or before. Keep the plants to a leading shoot or two; if space will admit of it, the side-shoots should be kept thin, and stopped a joint above the show of every bunch of blossom. When the fruit is sufficiently set, each bunch should be thinned of all abortive small fruit, leaving only a few of the strongest and best-shaped ones at the base of each bunch. If any quantity of small green fruit is required for pickling, the bunches may be allowed to remain a short time longer before they are thinned, and then assistance should be given by liquid-manure.

We have seen magnificent crops grown against the back-wall in an orchard-house with a south-east aspect.

MARJORAM (*Origanum*).

There are three species. *O. majorana*, Sweet or Summer Marjoram; *O. heracleoticum*, Winter Marjoram; *O. onites*, Common or Pot Marjoram.

Soil.—Light, dry, and moderately fertile. The situation cannot be too open.

Propagation.—The Sweet Marjoram is propagated solely by seed; the others by seed, as well as by parting their roots and slips of their branches. Sow from the end of February, if open weather, to the commencement of June; but the early part of April is best. Portions of the rooted plants, slips, &c., may be planted from February until May, and during September and October.

Sow in drills, six inches apart, the seed not more than a quarter of an inch deep. When the seedlings are two or three inches high, thin to six inches, and those removed may be pricked in rows at a similar distance. Those of the annual species (*O. majorana*) are to remain; but those of the perennials to be finally removed during September, water being given at every removal, and until the plants are established.

Plant slips, &c., in rows ten or twelve inches apart, where they are to remain; they must be watered moderately every evening, and shaded during the day, until they have taken root. In October the decayed parts of the perennials are cut away, and some soil from the alleys scattered over the bed to the depth of about half an inch, the surface of the earth between the stools being previously stirred gently. The tops and leaves of all the species are gathered when green, in summer and autumn, for use in soups, &c.; and a store of the branches are cut and dried in July or August, just before the flowers open, for winter's supply.

Forcing.—When the green tops are much in request, a small quantity of seed of the Summer Marjoram is sown in January or February in a gentle hotbed.

MELON (*Cucumis melo*).

Varieties.—We cannot recommend any particular sort to be grown, as we believe the best is not known. But we have grown the following kinds, and know them to be good:—The *Bromham Hall, Beechwood, Golden Perfection, Trentham Hybrid, Egyptian Green-fleshed, Turner's Scarlet Gem*. And of the Persian varieties, we have grown the *Gezee, Ispahan, Green Hoosainee*, and *Dampsha*.

Sowing.—The seed is to be sown in pots about three weeks before the fruiting-bed is ready, and when the seed-leaves are pretty well expanded, they are potted off into five or six-inch pots, placing two plants on opposite sides into each pot, using the same kind of soil as directed for the fruiting-bed, or it may be a little more porous, but taking care to warm it to, or a little above, the temperature of the frames, previously to use. Give a very little water after potting to settle the soil, and plunge the pots in the bed, and keep the hot sun from them for a few days.

The Fruiting-bed and Soil.—We will suppose that a sufficient quantity of heating materials are at hand, and that it is fresh from the stable, and if so, it will require to be turned over several times to sweeten, or force off that foul steam so injurious to vegetation; and if a good quantity of oak leaves can be got to mix with it, or when it is finally made up into the bed, they will help materially to effect the purpose, as well as to produce a more gentle, uniform, lasting heat, which is a very important point in the culture of this plant, and one which, if disregarded, will most probably cause a failure. This point considered, the bed may be made up five feet high at the back and four at the front, mixing well the material as you proceed, and, when finished, place the frames thereon, and let them remain till the heat arises, when it will soon be known if any foulness still remain. If there does, push down the light a few inches till it has passed away, and then cover the bed a few inches thick with unsifted soil; place two or three green turves turned upside down under the centre of each light, and upon these a barrowful, or a little more, of good turfy loam that has been laid up for twelve months, and is of rather a stiffish nature than otherwise.

Planting out.—If the plants have done well from the time of potting off, they will, in about three weeks, be strong plants, and ready to transfer to their fruiting-bed. And in doing this, be careful not to let any cold winds blow upon them. Turn the plants carefully out of the pots, and insert one into each hill, covering and pressing the soil slightly round each ball of earth, and giving a gentle watering to settle the soil; shade from bright sun till they begin to grow, and afterwards, if they seem to require it. Air must be admitted as they begin to grow by propping up the lights at the back; and if the air be at all cold, a mat or piece of canvas should be hung over each opening, to prevent it entering so freely in a body; and however many lights there be, we prefer admitting a little air at each, in preference to admitting the same amount at one or two.

Cultivation.—As the plants progress, they will require watering, earthing-up, stopping, and setting the fruit. Stopping, we think, is often done too soon, the plants being thrown into fruit before they have power to nourish one.

We stop them when about a foot or eighteen inches long,

according to the strength of the plant, and allow two main shoots only to each plant, training one towards each corner of the frame, and when they have grown a considerable length we stop them again. This causes them to show abundance of fruit, which we take care to impregnate as the blossoms expand, and at the same time, or previously, we stop the lateral one or two joints above the fruit, and as soon as it can be seen which fruit are swelling-off, we select one of the best-shaped to each main shoot, and cut off all the others; thus allowing two fruits to each plant, and four to each light.

They will require rather liberal watering during their swelling period, but the amount should be regulated in accordance to the weather and the situation in which they are grown. As a general rule, give water in the morning, and not within six inches of the collar of the plants. Warm it to the temperature of the frame, and give no more at one time than will just moisten the soil through; and as the fruit is becoming ripe withhold it altogether.

Endeavour to keep a moist atmosphere at all times, excepting when the plants are in flower, and the fruit is becoming ripe, and be particularly careful to keep a uniform, gentle heat and moisture at the root, and to give a little air early, when the sun is powerful, otherwise, while the under side of the leaves is wet, they are liable to get scorched. The red spider is sometimes very troublesome; but its appearance is generally owing to a deficient amount of moisture both at the roots and in the atmosphere: therefore, particular attention should be paid to these points; for if once the red spider get a-head, it is difficult to destroy it without injuring the plants. Sulphur will effect this, but it requires a careful hand to use it, so that we would, in preference, recommend syringing with clear water, and keeping the plants shaded for a while.

MINT (*Mentha*).

SPEARMINT (*Mentha viridis*), for soups, salads, and Mint sauce; Peppermint (*Mentha piperita*), for distillation; and Pennyroyal (*Mentha pulegium*), for flavouring soups, stuffing, &c.

Propagation.—They are all increased by offsets in spring and autumn, and by cuttings of the young shoots in June. Plant them in rows a foot apart each way. Water until established, and full-grown Pennyroyal requires water during dry weather. Keep clear from weeds, and in October cut down the old stalks, and give a top-dressing an inch thick of equal parts decayed stable-manure and limy rubbish.

Soil.—A moist light loam suits them.

Gathering, for drying and distilling, is best done just when the flowers are opening.

Forcing.—To obtain young shoots of Spearmint in winter, plant some old roots either on small hotbeds made for the purpose, or in pots or large pans, according to the supply required. Use a light rich soil, and keep it moist by daily watering.

MUSHROOM (*Agaricus campestris*).

Mushroom-beds for winter supply should be formed at the end of August, and others at the end of October.

To make a bed, procure some good horse-droppings that have not been heated, and some sheep-dung that has not laid long on the ground; let these, four barrows of the first to one of the other, be well mixed. If there be any quantity of the fermenting material, let it be turned every day for a little time, then every two days, as the heat may seem to render necessary, and when it gets so far moderated as to give tokens of sweetness and steadiness, the bed may be made. If inside some building where a little fire-heat can be given, the bed need not be more than eighteen inches thick, and as long and wide as required; but if the place be open, and no means of warming it exist, a greater thickness of bed, with a more careful preparation of materials, so as to insure against their over-heating, must be resorted to. Make the bed four feet wide at the base, and sloping to the back, where it ought to be three feet high; now and then throw in pieces of half-decayed turf, and also pieces of spawn (this is on the supposition that the latter is plentiful); a good beating or treading is necessary; and, last of all, a good coating of fresh maiden loam from a pasture where Mushrooms are known to grow naturally. This coating, however, had better be delayed a few days, until there is no danger of the bed over-heating; at the same time it must heat a little. Watering should not be done to any extent, except to keep the surface moist, until the Mushrooms appear, when they may have a little; but if the bed seems to do well at first, it would be better to avoid heavy waterings until the bed begins partially to cease bearing, when a good heavy watering will sometimes revive it again.

Where there is plenty of good horse-dung to be had, a very good bed may sometimes be made against a blank wall. After the dung is sufficiently sweetened by turning, &c., as above, a bed about four feet wide should be made, the dung being well trodden down, and built up something like a steep-pitched lean-to roof; this lying against the wall presents a diagonal surface, which can easily be covered up to any extent. Spawning, covering with earth, &c., may be done the same as recommended above, and a deep coating of straw or litter will be all that is wanted, examining the bed from time to time, to see that the heat does not decrease, and that the fibrous matter of the spawn does not expend itself uselessly in running into the litter, which it will sometimes do, to the injury of the crop. In this way, the more liberal supply of dung making up, in a great measure, for the want of shelter, even the wall itself may be dispensed with; the bed, in this case, is made in the form of the roof of a house, or the letter $\wedge$ inverted, four or five feet wide at the base, narrowing to the top, which should be rather rounded, three or four feet high, and the length from ten to any number of feet. The dung must be well separated, and mixed, and beaten, but not trodden down. When completed, the bed must be covered with litter or other light covering, to keep out the wet, as well as to prevent its drying; clean dry straw will do, but sweet hay or matting is to be preferred. A good heavy covering is the principal thing; and if the dung is in a good well-tempered condition in October, when the bed is made, it is not likely to lose heat until the Mushrooms are formed and a crop secured.

Situation.—The bed should be made in a dry, sheltered situation, and on the level ground, in preference to founding it in a trench, which prevents the spawning being performed completely at the bottom, and guards against the settling of water, which may chill it. If the site is not dry it must be covered with stones, clinkers, &c., to act as a drain; for nothing destroys Mushrooms sooner than excessive moisture, except an extreme heat or cold. To obviate the occurrence of these unfavourable circumstances, it is far preferable to raise the bed under a shed. If it is constructed in a shed, it may be built against one side, sloping downwards from it. To proceed with greater certainty during the winter, a fire-flue may pass beneath the bed; but it is by no means absolutely necessary, for by the due regulation of covering it may always be kept of sufficient temperature.

Management.—The spawn must not be inserted before the temperature has become moderate.

Temperature.—The minimum is 50°, and the maximum 65°. Insert the spawn as soon as the violence of the heat has abated, which will be in two or three weeks, though sometimes it will subside in eight or ten days.

Such half-decayed, dryish, caky dung as you will frequently find in linings of hotbeds is invaluable for Mushroom-beds, especially with a casing of droppings. The spawn runs best in dryish material. When obliged to use rather moist material, wrap each piece of spawn into a handful of dry litter before inserting it. The less violently a bed heats the better. If it does so, bore holes to allow the heat to escape, and beat firmly again as it declines. When the heat is from 80° to 90° insert pieces of spawn about the size of a walnut at nine inches apart all over, and beat again. In a day or two, if the heat is declining, put half an inch of droppings all over the bed; and then, if there is no sign of over-heating, cover with an inch and a half of soil; beat that as firm as a brick, if you can; water the surface, and make it as smooth as a wall. If, in a few days, you find the heat is rather declining, cover with an inch or two of hay. When the spawn begins to work the temperature of the bed will be raised. After the first pin-head Mushroom makes its appearance regulate the covering according to the weather, so that the surface soil of the bed shall be about 55° to 60° in temperature. In very severe weather a few barrow-loads of hot dung as linings would be serviceable.

Keep the covering of litter on the Mushroom-bed all the time it is producing, regulating the thickness of the covering by the temperature of the bed. The bed ought to begin producing four or five weeks from the time of making, and should continue yielding Mushrooms for several months. All this depends upon the favourable temperature and correct spawning of the bed.

MUSTARD (*Sinapis alba*).

Soil.—Any free and open space in the garden will do.

Sow from the beginning of November to the same period of March in a gentle hotbed, or in the corner of a stove. From the close of February to the close of April it may be sown in the open ground, on a warm, sheltered border, and from thence to the middle of September in a shady one. Sow in flat-bottomed drills, about a quarter of an inch deep, and six inches apart. The seed cannot well be sown too thickly. The earth which covers the seed should be very fine. Water in dry weather, as a due supply of moisture is the chief inducement to a quick vegetation. The sowings are to be performed once or twice in a fortnight, according to the demand. Cress (*Lepidium sativum*) is the most constant accompaniment of this salad-herb, and being slower in vegetating than Mustard, it must, for the obtaining them in perfection at the same time, be sown a week earlier. Cut for use whilst young, and before the rough leaves appear. We have grown a constant succession through the winter in the border of an orchard-house without any artificial heat.

NEW ZEALAND SPINACH (*Tetragonia expansa*).

This is much liked as a substitute for summer Spinach. It continues available the whole summer.

Soil.—A rich moderately light loam.

Sow in the seed-vessel as gathered in the preceding autumn, at the latter end of March, in a pot, and place in a Melon-frame. The seedlings to be pricked while small singly into pots, to be kept under a frame without bottom-heat until the third week in May, or until the danger of frost is past. Plant in rows in a rich, light soil, at three or four feet apart each way. Twenty plants will afford an abundant supply daily for a large family.

In five or six weeks after planting the young shoots may be

gathered, these being pinched off. The plants are productive until a late period of the year, as they survive the frosts that kill Nasturtiums and Potatoes.

ONION (*Allium cepa*).

Soil, rich, open, well drained, and trenched, in a situation entirely free from trees.

Varieties.—*White Spanish* or *Reading; Silver-skinned,* for pickling; *Strasburgh; Deptford; Globe* (white or red); and *James's Keeping,* to store for winter use.

Sow for the main crop during March. Main crops may even be inserted as late as the beginning of April; at its close make a small sowing to draw young in summer, and for small bulbs to pickle; again in July and early in August, for salads in autumn; and finally in the last week of August, or early in September, to stand the winter, for spring and beginning of summer. Sow thinly in drills, twelve inches apart, and in four-feet-wide beds.

Cultivation.—In about six weeks after sowing give the first thinning and small hoeing, setting the seedlings out about two inches apart. If done in dry weather it will keep the beds free from weeds for six weeks longer, when they must be hoed a second time, and thinned to four inches apart; and now, where they have failed, the vacancies may be filled up by transplanting. The best time for doing this is in the evening, and water must be given for several successive nights. In transplanting, insert no part of the stem. No plant is more benefited by liquid-manure being given twice a week. After the lapse of another month they must be thoroughly gone over for the last time, and the plants thinned to six inches asunder. After this they require only occasionally the stirring of the surface, which the hoe effects. It is a good practice in July, before the tips change to a yellow hue, to bend the stems down flat upon the bed, which not only prevents them running to seed, but causes the bulbs to become much larger than they otherwise would. The bend should be made about two inches up the neck.

Storing.—About the close of August the Onions will have arrived at their full growth, which may be known by the withering of the leaves, by the shrinking of the necks, and by the ease with which they may be pulled up. As soon as these symptoms appear they must be taken up, the bed being frequently looked over; for, if the whole crop is waited for, the forwardest are apt again to strike root.

Spread on mats in the sun, frequently turn, and remove under shelter at night. In two or three weeks, when the roots and blades are perfectly withered, and the bulbs become firm, they are fit for storing. Previously to doing this, all soil and refuse must be removed from them. In the store-house they must be laid thin, or hung up in ropes, and looked over at least once a month.

PARSLEY (*Petroselinum sativum*).

Varieties.—The species is plain-leaved, but there is a curly-leaved or crisped variety, which is the handsomest for garnishing.

Sow annually in February, and again in the end of June, moderately thick, in narrow drills barely a quarter of an inch deep, twelve inches apart if in a bed by itself, or in a single one round the edge of a bed, the soil being raked level, and the stones immediately over the seed gathered off. The plants make their appearance in from two to six weeks. When two or three inches high they may be gathered from as required. If there are any vacancies, fill them up by transplanting into them some of the plants which are growing too thickly. Thin to nine inches apart. The closer they grow, the less curly they are. Soot is an excellent manure for Parsley, and it is much benefited by liquid-manure once a week, and frequent waterings in dry weather. In early June, when they make a show for seed, the stems should be cut down close to the bottom, and again in September, if they have acquired a straggling, rank growth. This will cause them to shoot afresh. Take up some of the strongest and best-curled plants in September, and plant them in pots, two or three plants in each, using a rich soil. If these be placed in a pit or greenhouse, and abundance of liquid-manure given, their produce will be very superior throughout the winter.

PARSNIP (*Pastinaca sativa*).

Varieties.—*Hollow-crowned* and *Guernsey*, which are nearly alike.

Soil.—A rich, dry, sandy loam, and the deeper the better. Trench the ground two spades deep, a little manure being turned in with the bottom spit. The situation cannot be too open.

Sow from the end of February to the beginning of April, but the earlier the better. Sow in drills, twelve inches apart, and half an inch deep, the compartment being laid out in beds not more than four feet wide, for the convenience of weeding, &c. When the seedlings are two or three inches high, thin to ten inches apart, and remove the weeds both by hand and small hoeing. The beds require to be frequently looked over, to remove all seedlings that may spring up afresh, as well as to be frequently hoed until the plants cover the ground.

The roots may be taken up as wanted in September, but they do not attain maturity till October, which is intimated by the decay of the leaves.

In November part of the crop may be taken up, and, the tops

being cut close off, stored in alternate layers with sand, for use in frosty weather. The remainder may be left in the ground, and taken up as required, as they are never injured by the most intense frost; but, on the contrary, are rendered sweeter. In February or March, however, any remaining must be taken up, otherwise they will vegetate. Being preserved in sand, they continue good until the end of April or May.

PEA (*Pisum sativum*).

Varieties.—These are more differing in name than in variation of merit. For open-ground culture none but these three need be cultivated,—
Sangester's No. 1, two feet and a half high, the best early; *Fairbeard's Champion of England,* four to five feet, next in succession, and much better; and *Veitch's Perfection,* three feet, which follows in production, and is a first-rate Pea. If a row of each of these varieties is sown at the same time their produce keeps up an uninterrupted supply.

Early Peas.—The best mode of obtaining these is in the last week of January to cut some turf in strips of three inches in width, the length depending on the width of the hotbed in which they are to be placed. Lay the pieces of turf in the frame, grass downwards, close together; then make in the centre of each piece of turf, by pressing it with the edge of a board, a drill, in which sow the Peas, which soon come up; and then take the lights entirely off in the daytime, unless very cold, and shut them down at night. Keep them close till the beginning of March. When the Peas are to be planted in the border lift the box entirely off, and the strips of turf, in which the Peas will be well rooted; place them on a hand-barrow, and take them to the border for planting, which do in a drill cut so deep that they shall be about an inch lower than they were in the box. It may be necessary to protect them from frost and cool winds at first, and this may be done by putting some short sticks along the rows, and laying some long litter or cuttings of evergreens over them.

Sowing.—In January they may be sown in sheltered borders, and larger supplies in an open compartment, and thence continued throughout February and until the end of May once every three weeks.

Sow in drills, or by the dibble in rows, Dwarfs at two feet, for the early and late crops, but three feet for the main ones; Marrowfats at three and a half or four and a half; Knight's Marrowfats and other gigantic varieties at six or eight. Peas not intended to be supported require the least room. At the early and late sowings the seed should be buried an inch deep, but for the main crops an inch and a half. With respect to the distances, it may be inserted in the row, of the Dwarfs, two in an inch; middle-sized varieties for the main crop three in two inches; the Tall and Knight's Marrows fully an inch apart. The best mode is to sow in single rows, and place the sticks alternately on each side of the row.

If the weather is dry when the summer sowings are made, the seed should be soaked in water for a few hours previously to sowing it, and the drills also be well watered.

When the plants are two or three inches high the rows should be hoed between during dry weather, and earth drawn up to each side of them. Earth drawn up in high ridges on each side of the winter-standing crops protects them much.

Sticking is not required until the plants show their tendrils. If, during the time of blossoming or swelling, continued drought should occur, water may very beneficially be applied, it being poured between the rows if they are in pairs, or otherwise in a shallow trench on one side of each. Watering the leaves is rather injurious. It is a good practice to nip off the top of the leading shoots of the early and late crops as soon as they are in blossom, as it greatly accelerates the setting and maturity of the fruit. Too much care cannot be taken, when the pods are gathered, not to injure the stems. In very severe weather the winter-standing crops require the shelter of litter or other light covering, supported as much as possible from the plants by means of branches; ropes or twisted straw-bands are good for this purpose, to be fixed along each side of the rows with wooden pins driven into the ground. Whichever mode of shelter is adopted, it must be always removed in mild weather.

POTATO (*Solanum tuberosum*).

Golden Rules for its Culture.—1. Grow none but those which ripen in July or August. 2. Plant whole, middle-sized Potatoes. 3. Plant on moderately light soil, manured some months previously. 4. Apply no manure at the time of planting. 5. Plant, during November, in light, dry soils, but not until February in wet soils. 6. Preserve your seed Potatoes between layers of earth until required. 7. Plant as you dig; that is, dig enough for one row, and then plant it with the dibble, so as to avoid trampling on the ground. 8. Let the top of the sets be eight inches below the surface. 9. Do not earth up the stems. 10. Do not cut down the stems. 11. Take up the crop as soon as the leaves begin to look yellow in July or early in August. 12. Store in a dry shed between layers of dry earth, sand, or coal-ashes.

Varieties.—These are too numerous for us to name even a tithe of them. The following are all good, early ripening sorts, and keep well:—*Walnut-leaved, Ash-leaved, Soden's Early Oxford, Rylott's Flour Ball, Fluke Kidney*, and *Forty-folds*.

Soil.—A dry, friable, fresh, and moderately rich soil is the best for every variety of Potato. If possible, avoid manuring. Leaf-mould, or very decayed stable-dung, is the best of all manures. Sea-weed is a very beneficial addition to the soil; and so is Epsom salts and common salt. Coal-ashes and sea-sand are applied with great benefit to retentive soils. The situation must always be open.

Planting in the open ground is best done in light dry soils during November, and may thence be continued until the end of March. This last month is the latest in which any considerable plantation should be made.

Sets.—For the main crops, whole Potatoes, weighing from two ounces to two ounces and a half, are the best. Larger sets are preferable for obtaining early crops, the tubers being required to form rapidly. In these only two eyes should be allowed to remain.

Planting.—Insert the sets with the dibble in rows; for the early crops twelve inches apart each way, and for the main ones eighteen inches; the sets, when spring-planted, six inches beneath the surface. The Potato-dibble is the best instrument that can be employed, the earth being afterwards raked or struck in with the spade, and the soil not trampled upon, but planted as sufficient is dug for receiving a row.

The compartment may be laid out level and undivided if the soil is light; but if heavy soil is necessarily employed, it is best disposed in beds six or eight feet wide, with deep alleys between.

Hoe as soon as the plants are well to be distinguished, and to the early crops draw the earth round each plant, so as to form a cup as a shelter from the cold winds, which are their chief enemy. But the main crops should not be earthed up, for earthing up diminishes the crop one-fourth.

It is very injurious to mow off the tops of the plants. The foliage ought to be kept as uninjured as possible, unless, as sometimes occurs on fresh ground, the plants are of gigantic luxuriance, and even then the stems should be only moderately shortened. It is, however, of advantage to remove the flowers as soon as they appear, unless the stems are very luxuriant. A Potato plant continues to form tubers until the flowers appear, after which it is employed in ripening those already formed.

The very earliest crops will be in production in June, or perhaps towards the end of May, and may thence be taken up as wanted until August, when they may be entirely dug up and stored. In storing, the best mode is to place them in layers, alternately with dry coal-ashes, earth, or sand, in a shed. The best instrument with which they can be dug up is a flat three-pronged fork, each row being cleared regularly away.

Potatoes should be dug up dry, and not be stored until perfectly so.

Forcing.—The season for forcing is from the close of December to the middle of February in a hotbed, and at the close of this last month on a warm border, with the temporary shelter of a frame. The hotbed is only required to produce a moderate heat. The earth should be six inches deep, and the sets planted in rows six or eight inches apart, as the tubers are not required to be large. The temperature ought never to sink below 65°, nor rise above 80°.

If the tubers are desired to be brought to maturity as speedily as possible, instead of being planted in the earth of the bed, each set should be placed in a pot about six inches in diameter, though the produce in pots is smaller.

Preparation of Sets for Forcing.—They should be of the early varieties, the Walnut-leaved being the best. To assist their forward vegetation, plant a single Potato in each of the pots intended for forcing during January. Then place in the ground, and protect with litter from the frost. This renders them very excitable by heat; and, consequently, when plunged in a hotbed, they vegetate rapidly and generate tubers. The seed Potatoes are equally assisted, and with less trouble, if placed in a cellar just in contact with each other; and as soon as the germs are four inches long they are removed to the hotbed.

Management.—More than one stem should never be allowed, otherwise the tubers are small, and not more numerous.

Water must be given whenever the soil appears dry, and in quantity proportionate to the temperature of the air. Linings must be applied as the temperature declines, and air admitted as freely as the temperature of the atmosphere will allow. Coverings must be afforded with the same regard to temperature.

From six to seven weeks usually elapse between the time of planting and the fitness of the tubers for use.

POTATO-ONION (*Allium aggregatum*).

This is also called the *Under-Ground* and the *Burns' Onion.* It produces a cluster of bulbs or offsets, in number from two to twelve, and even more, uniformly beneath the surface of the soil. Propagated by offsets of the root of moderate size.

Plant during October or November, or as early in the spring as the season will allow, but not later than April. They are either to be inserted in drills, or by a blunt dibble, eight inches apart each way, not buried entirely, but the top of the offset just level with the surface. The beds they are grown in are better not more than four feet wide, for the convenience of cultivation.

Let the earth always be cleared away down to the ring from whence the roots spring as soon as the leaves have attained their full size, and begin to be brown at the top, so that a kind of basin is formed round the bulb. They attain their full growth towards the end of July, and become completely ripe early in

September; for immediate use they may be taken up as they ripen, but for keeping, a little before they attain perfect maturity.

RADISH (*Raphanus sativus*).

Spring Varieties.—Long-rooted: *Scarlet*, or *Salmon*, or *Scarlet-transparent Radish.* Purple: the *Short-topped.*
Turnip-rooted: Early White and Red Turnip.
Autumn and Winter Varieties.—White Spanish and Black Spanish.

The *soil*, a light loam, and moderately fertile, should be dug a full spade deep, and well pulverised. Manures should not be applied at the time of sowing. The situation should always be open, but for early and late crops warm and sheltered.

Sowing.— For the earliest productions, during December, January, and February, in a hotbed; and in the open ground once a month during winter, and every fortnight during the other seasons of the year.

In the open ground sow thinly in drills, and bury a quarter of an inch deep. Drills for the long-rooted, three inches asunder; for the turnip-rooted, four or five; and for the Spanish, &c., six or eight.

When the seedlings are advanced to five or six leaves they are ready for thinning, the spindle-rooted to three inches apart, the turnip-rooted to four, and the larger varieties to six.

In dry weather they ought to be watered regularly every night. The early and late crops that have to withstand the attacks of frost, &c., should be kept constantly covered with dry straw or fern to the depth of about two inches, or with matting, supported by hooping, until the plants make their appearance, when the covering must be removed every mild day, but renewed towards evening, and constantly during frosty or tempestuous weather.

The bed should have a good watering the morning before that on which they are taken up, but none afterwards until subsequent to the drawing.

RAMPION (*Campanula rapunculus*).

The root, long, white, and spindle-shaped, is eaten raw like the Radish; it is sliced, as well as the leaves, into winter salads.

The *soil* ought to be moderately moist, but it must be light. A shady, rich border is most favourable.

Sow during March, April, and May, in very shallow drills six inches apart, formed by pressing a rod edgeways in the ground, the plants to remain where sown; though, in case of any deficiency, those which are taken away in thinning may be transplanted successfully if removed to a border similar to the seed bed, and inserted with the roots perpendicular, and without pressing the mould too close about them. The best time for the removal is of an evening.

They are fit for thinning when about two inches in height, and they must be set at a distance of six inches apart. The plants of the sowings during the two first-mentioned months will be fit for use at the close of August, or early in September, and continue through the autumn. Those of the last one will continue good throughout the winter, and until the following April. The soil throughout their growth must be kept moist by giving frequent waterings.

RHUBARB (*Rheum*).

There are three species, *Rheum rhaponticum*, *R. palmatum*, and *R. undulatum*. The best varieties are *Mitchell's Early Albert*, *Randall's Early Prolific*, *Myatt's Linnæus*, and *Myatt's Victoria*. We have named them in the order of their earliness, the Victoria being the latest.

The *soil* best suited to it is light, rich, deep, unshaded, and moderately moist.

Sowing.—Sow soon after the seed is ripe, in September or October, in drills three feet apart and half an inch deep, the plants to remain where raised. When they make their appearance in the spring, thin to six or eight inches asunder, and let the surface of the ground about them be loosened with the hoe. At the close of summer finally thin to four feet, or the Gigantic and Victoria to six. Break down all but one of the flower-stems as often as they are produced. In autumn remove the decayed leaves, and point in a little well-putrefied stable-dung, and earth-up the stools. In the spring hoe the bed, and if to be blanched dig a trench between the rows, and the earth from it place about a foot thick over the stool. This covering must be removed when the cutting ceases in June, and the plants then be allowed to grow at liberty. The more they are cut from, the less productive they are next year. As the earth in wet seasons is apt to induce decay, the covering may be advantageously formed of coal-ashes or drift sand. Chimney-pots and butter-firkins make good coverings for blanching.

Another simple and neat-looking mode is the following:—Just when the Rhubarb is about to start, drive into the ground three stakes or slips of board about three feet long round each plant, so as to be about two feet, or two feet six inches, out of ground, and slightly inclining together at the top. Round these stakes twist hay-bands, fastening off the ends by twisting them amongst the hay, so as not to get loose, and leaving the top open. By these means the rhubarb is drawn up; if it is not drawn too fast, you obtain a great length of stalk; and when you want to cut, slip away the hay-bands off the top altogether like a chimney-pot; and then, having cut what you want, put it on again like an extinguisher. Of course the hay-bands should reach close to the ground.

Forcing.—Plant a single row; the plants three feet apart in ground that has been trenched two spades deep, and dressed with well-putrefied dung at the time. The forcing may commence in December. First cover either with Sea-kale or common garden-pots (twelves), but chimney-pots are still better, the leaf-stalks becoming much longer and finer, and envelope them with fermenting dung. A frame is much less objectionable, and such may be formed by driving stakes into the ground on each side of the bed, alternating with the plants. These are to be three feet high above ground, and the space between the two rows of stakes two feet at the bottom, but approaching each other, and fastened by cross pieces, so as to be only fifteen inches apart at top. To the sides and top stout laths are fixed, as in the accompanying sketch, to prevent the dung falling upon the plants.

The dung may be either fresh, or that which has already undergone fermentation, placed all round the frame eighteen inches thick, and the top covered with long litter. The temperature in the interior should have a range from 55° to 60°. If it rises higher, two or three large holes made through the top soon correct it.

Rhubarb may be forced without either pots or frame, by merely covering the plants six inches deep with light litter, care being taken that the plants are not injured.

Mr. Knight's mode of forcing is to place in the winter as many plants as necessary in large, deep pots, each pot receiving as many as it can contain, and the interstices being entirely filled up by fine, sandy loam, washed in. The tops of the roots are placed on a level with each other, and about an inch below the surface. These being covered with inverted pots of the same size, may be placed in a Vinery or hotbed, and on the approach of spring, any time after January, any room or cellar will be sufficiently warm. If copiously supplied with water, the plants vegetate rapidly and vigorously, and each pot will produce three successional cuttings, the first two being the most plentiful. As soon as the third is gathered the roots may be changed, and those removed replanted in the ground, when they will attain sufficient strength to be forced again in a year's time. If not, it is of little consequence, for year-old roots raised from cuttings, or even seed sown in autumn, are sufficiently strong for use.

Propagation by Division.—When the Rhubarb is propagated by division of the root, care must be taken to retain a bud on the crown of each piece, together with a small portion of the root itself, with, if possible, some fibres attached to it. Rhubarb is benefited by being taken up when old, and the large stools cut in pieces, with a bud on each, and these separated where they are intended to remain, at the same distance and in the same manner as advised for seedlings.

SAGE (*Salvia officinalis*).

Varieties.—The *Common Green* and *Red*.

Soil and Situation.—A dry, moderately fertile soil in a sheltered situation.

Propagation.—Cuttings may be either of the preceding or same year's growth; if of the first, plant in April; but if of the latter, not until the close of May or middle of June. The shoots of the same year are usually employed, as they more readily emit roots, and assume a free growth. The outward and most robust shoots should be chosen, and cut from five to seven inches in length. All but the top leaves being removed, insert by the dibble almost down to these, in rows six inches apart each way, in a shady border, and during moist weather, otherwise water must be given immediately, and repeated occasionally until they have taken root.

After Culture.—The decayed flower-stalks, stunted branches, &c., remove in early winter and spring, and the soil of the beds slightly turn over. When the plants have continued two or three years, a little dry, well-putrefied dung may be turned in during early spring. Attention to the mode of gathering has an influence in keeping the plants healthy and vigorous. The tops ought never to be cropped too close, so as to render the branches naked or stumpy.

SAVORY (*Satureja*).

Used for flavouring stuffings, sausages, soups, &c.

There are two hardy species, *Satureja montana*, Winter or Perennial Savory. *S. hortensis*, Summer or Annual Savory.

They may be sown in the open ground at the latter end of March, or in April, in a light, rich soil; thin the seedlings moderately, and they may either remain where sown, or may be transplanted. Of the Winter Savory, when the seedlings are about two inches high, plant out a quantity of the strongest, in moist weather, in nursery rows, six inches asunder, to remain till September or the spring following, then to be transplanted with balls where they are finally to remain, in rows a foot asunder. When it is designed to have the Winter or Summer Savory remain where sown, the seeds may be in shallow drills, either in beds, or along the edge of any bed or border, by way of an edging.

By Slips.—In the spring, or early part of summer, the Winter Savory may be increased by slips or cuttings of the young shoots or branches, five or six inches long; plant them with a dibble, in any shady border, in rows six inches asunder, giving occasional waterings, and they will be well rooted by September, when they will be transplanted.

SAVOY CABBAGE (*Brassica oleracea bullata major*).

Varieties.—*Early Ulm*, which may be planted fifteen inches apart, and is the earliest kind known; *Dwarf Green Curled*, which comes in in succession; *Large Green German*, the best of the large kinds; and the *Yellow Curled*. All the above are very hardy; the last two are late kinds for standing the winter.

Sow at the close of February for use in early autumn: the plants will be ready for pricking out in April, and for final planting at the end of May; the sowing to be repeated about the middle of March, the plants to be pricked out in May, for planting in June, to supply the table in autumn and early winter. The main crops must be sown in April and early May, to prick out and plant, after similar intervals, for production in winter and spring.

Planting.—The plants of the small kinds should be set out fifteen or eighteen inches apart each way, but the large varieties should have two feet by eighteen inches. Water abundantly, if the weather is dry, until the plants are well established. Give liquid-manure once a week until the heart is formed.

Saving in Winter and Spring.—Bury them with the roots upwards; this not only preserves them from frost, but keeps them from sprouting. They remain perfectly good for weeks.

SEA-KALE (*Crambe maritima*).

The soil should be good, well manured, trenched, and pulverised. If intended to be raised from seed, lay the ground level in April after winter's trenching; draw drills (if the Kale is to stand on the same ground permanently to be forced, or otherwise blanched) three feet apart, and finally thin the plants to two feet apart in the rows. Liquid-manure from the piggery, cow-house, stable, sheep-shed, or brewed from the excrements of animals, or from guano, with a good portion of salt at all times dissolved in it, is what the growth of Sea-kale may be improved by very greatly.

Planting.—If the ground is to be planted with Sea-kale to stand permanently, choose one-year old plants from a poor piece of ground, no matter how small they are, so that they are clean from canker and from the distorted, crooked swellings caused in them by wounds from the grub. Plant in rows three feet apart, and the plants in the row two feet apart. Insert the plants singly. A cellar, or the bottom of a dark cupboard, or any dark corner, are excellent places for producing early shoots of it, if planted in sand, old tan, leaf, or other light vegetable soil, or even in common garden earth. The plants should be kept as much in darkness as possible if intended to be well blanched, but for our own eating we do not object to its being a little coloured. Strong plants should be taken up, and no matter how thick they are placed. Water them occasionally with tepid water, and two or three crops of excellent Sea-kale may be obtained in succession before the plants are exhausted. Those who do not choose to place the plants on the floor could put them in boxes, filled with any of the before-named kinds of materials. Those who have not a cellar or a cupboard, and have a dark corner in a stable, cow-house, wood-house, or any other fuel-house, could produce good Sea-kale from a few strong roots placed in a rough-made box as above directed.

There are several modes in which Sea-kale may be forced whilst growing in the bed where raised. Thus, after the plants have been dressed and trimmed in the autumn, the bed may be covered with a mixture of moderately-sifted light earth, and sand or coal-ashes, two or three inches deep; each stool must be covered with a pot set down close, to keep out the steam of the dung; or bricks or planks may be placed to the height of eight or ten inches on each side of the row of plants to be forced, and covered with cross spars, having a space of about an inch between each two of them. The dung employed must be well tempered, and mixed for three weeks before it is required, or for four if mingled with leaves, otherwise the heat is violent, but not lasting. When thus prepared, each pot is covered ten inches thick all round, and eight inches at the top. The heat must be constantly observed; if it sinks below 50°, more hot dung must be applied; if it rises above 60°, some of the covering should be removed. Unless the weather is very severe it is seldom necessary to renew the heat by fresh linings; when the thermometer indicates the necessity, a part only of the exhausted dung should be taken away, and the remainder mixed with that newly applied. In three or four weeks from being first covered the shoots will be fit for cutting, and they will continue to produce at intervals for two or three months, or until the natural crops come in. To have a succession, some should be covered with mulch, or litter that is little else than straw; this, by sheltering the plants from cold, will cause them to be more forward than those in the natural ground, though not so forward as those under the hot dung; and by this means it may be had in perfection from Christmas to Whitsuntide.

Another mode is, on each side of a three-foot bed to dig a trench two feet deep, the side of it next the bed being perpendicular, but the outer side sloping, so as to make it eighteen inches wide at the bottom, but two feet and a half at the top; these trenches are filled with fermenting dung, which, of course, may be renewed if ever found necessary, and frames put over the plants; the light is to be completely excluded by boards, matting, &c. The accompanying sketch represents a section of the construction:—

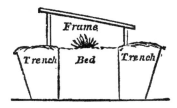

It may also be forced in a hotbed. When the heat moderates, a little light mould should be put on, and three or four-year old plants, which have been raised with as little injury as possible to the roots, are to be inserted close together, and covered with as much earth as is used for Cucumbers. The glasses must be covered close with double matting to exclude the light, and additional covering afforded during severe weather. Sea-kale thus forced will be fit for cutting in about three weeks. Instead of frames and glasses, any construction of boards and litter that will exclude the light answers as well. A common Melon-frame will contain as many as are capable of being produced in two drills of twenty yards each, and with only one-third the quantity of dung. To keep up a regular succession until the crop in the natural ground arrives, two three-light frames will be sufficient for a large family; the first prepared about the beginning of November, and the second about the last week in December.

Those who have but few plants, and have not a convenience for either forwarding them in a cellar or cupboard, or the means of forcing with fermenting materials, may produce excellent blanched Sea-kale in the spring months by covering the crowns with light, friable earth, fine cinder-ashes, old tan, or leaf-mould.

If this mode of merely *blanching* and not forcing be adopted, the most simple mode is to cover over each stool with sand or ashes to the depth of about a foot; the shoots, in their passage through it, being excluded from the light, are effectually bleached. Dry clean straw may be scattered loosely over the plants to effect the same purpose; but pots are to be preferred to any of these coverings. Butter firkins, or flower-pots of large dimensions, may be employed, care being taken to stop the hole at the bottom with a piece of tile and clay, so as to exclude every ray of light; but pots like those beneath are

generally adopted. They are of earthenware, twelve or eighteen inches in diameter, and twelve high. Frames of wicker are sometimes employed, being covered with mats, more perfectly to exclude the light. Previously to covering the stools with the pots, &c., the manure laid on in the winter must be removed; and the operation should commence at the close of February, or at least a month before the shoots usually appear, as the shelter of the pots assists materially in bringing them forward. In four or six weeks after covering, the plants should be examined, and as soon as the shoots appear three or four inches high they may be taken; for, if none are taken until they attain a fuller growth, the crop comes in too much at once. Slipping off the stalks is preferable to cutting. The plants may be gathered from until the flower begins to form, when all covering must be removed.

But one thing should never be omitted. When the Sea-kale is cut, the crown or stalk should at all times be cut down a little under the earth's surface, as any part left above the ground, after having been once forced, is almost sure to be affected by the weather, which produces canker, and the ensuing year the crowns will be weak and unfit for producing strong, healthy shoots or heads. Another thing most essential to be observed, after Sea-kale has made two or three inches of its natural summer growth, is that the shoots should be thinned, all the weak, spurious shoots being entirely removed, the strongest only being left, and those thinned according to the strength of the plants. Then, if former directions are attended to, in respect to applications of liquid-manure, fine, strong, clear, healthy buds will be established and matured in good season for the next year's produce. All blooming shoots should be removed as early as possible after they appear.

SPINACH (*Spinacia oleracea*).

Varieties.—The *Round-leaved* for spring and summer; and the *Triangular-leaved* or *Prickly-seeded* for winter, on account of its extreme hardiness; but the *Lettuce-leaved* and the *Flanders* are also hardy and generally preferred for a winter crop.

Soil.—For the Round-leaved variety, a rich, light, moist loam, in an open situation, is preferable; but for the Triangular-leaved, and other winter varieties, a light, moderately fertile, and dry border. Liquid-manure is highly beneficial to them, and when made of blood and the most fertilizing matters, the greater the benefit.

Sow of the Round-leaved variety at the close of January in a warm situation, to be repeated in larger, but still small breadths, at the commencement and end of February, and to be continued every three weeks until the middle of April, when it must be performed once a week until the close of May, and then once a fortnight till the end of July. For the summer sowings choose a somewhat shady situation; the intervals between rows of peas will answer very well. In August sow at intervals of three weeks, until the early part of September. Sow thinly in drills half an inch deep and a foot apart. The sowing should be in showery weather, otherwise an occasional watering must be given; for if there is a deficiency of moisture during the first stages of vegetation, not half of the seedlings will come up. The Triangular-leaved plants must be thinned to four or five inches apart, and the Round-leaved to eight. Thin by degrees, separating them at first only an inch or two, as the plants of the several thinnings are fit for use. The thinning ought to commence when they have attained four leaves about an inch in breadth. Regular gathering promotes the health of the plants. The outer leaves only should be gathered at a time, the centre being left uninjured to produce successional crops. This direction applies chiefly to the winter-standing crops; those of the summer may be cut off close to the root.

TANSY (*Tanacetum vulgare*).

Used for puddings, omelets, and garnishing.

Varieties.—The Curled or Double Tansy, the one chiefly grown for Culinary purposes; the Variegated; and the Common or Plain.

Soil and Situation.—A light, dry, and rather poor soil, in an open exposure, is best, as in such it is the most hardy and aromatic.

Planting.—It is propagated by rooted slips, or divisions of its fibrous, creeping root, planted from the close of February until that of May, as well as during the autumn. Established plants may be moved at any period of the year. Insert in rows twelve inches apart each way, a gentle watering being given if the season is not showery. As the roots spread rapidly, plants will soon make their appearance over a large space of ground if left undisturbed; to prevent it, a path should be left entirely round the bed, and often dug up to keep them within bounds. The plants run up to seed during summer, but the stalks must be constantly removed, to encourage the production of young leaves. Weeds should be extirpated, and the decayed stalks cleared away in autumn, at the same time a little fresh mould being scattered over the bed.

Forcing.—If required during the winter and early spring, old undivided roots must be placed in a moderate hotbed once a month, from the middle of November to the close of February. They may be planted in the earth of the bed, in pots, and plunged in a similar situation, or placed round the edges of the bark-pits in a hothouse. A frame is not absolutely necessary, as a covering of mats supported on hoops during frost at night, and in very inclement weather, will answer nearly as well.

THYME (*Thymus vulgaris*).

Varieties.—Broad-leaved Green, Narrow-leaved Green, and Lemon-scented.

Soil and Situation.—A poor, light, and dry soil is best. The situation cannot be too open.

Propagation.—*By rooted Slips.*—To obtain slips, some old stools may be divided into as many rooted portions as possible, or layers may be obtained by loosening the soil around them, and pegging the lateral shoots beneath the surface. They must be planted out from the beginning of February until the close of May, water and weeding being similarly required.

In autumn the decayed stalks should be cleared away, and a little fresh earth scattered and turned in among the stools.

Although it is perennial, yet after three or four years Thyme becomes stunted and unproductive, and consequently requires to to be raised periodically from seed.

TREE-ONION (*Allium proliferum*).

This, called also the *Canada Onion*, is without a bulbous root, but throws out numerous offsets. Its top bulbs are greatly prized for pickling, being considered of superior flavour to the common Onion.

It is *propagated* both by the root offsets, which may be planted during March and April, or in September and October, and from the top bulbs, which are best planted at the end of April. The old roots are best to plant again for a crop of bulbs, as they are most certain to run to stems. Plant in rows twelve inches asunder, in holes six inches apart and two deep, a single offset or bulb being put in each. Those planted in autumn will shoot up leaves early in the spring, and have their bulbs fit for gathering in June or the beginning of July; those inserted in the spring will make their appearance later, and will be in production at the close of July or early in August. They must not, however, be gathered for keeping or planting until the stalks decay, at which time, or in the spring also, if only of one year's growth, the roots may be taken up if required for planting; but when of two or three years' continuance, they must, at all events, be reduced in size, otherwise they grow in too large and spindling bunches; but the best plan is to make a fresh plantation annually with single offsets.

The bulbs when gathered must be gradually and carefully dried in a shady place, and, if kept perfectly free from moisture, will continue in a good state until the following May.

TURNIP (*Brassica rapa*).

Varieties.—For the first sowings: *Early White Dutch, Early Stone.* For the spring sowings: *Common Round White, Yellow Malta, Yellow Dutch, Altrincham.* For winter: *White Stone and Yellow Finland.*

Soil.—The best for Turnips is a light rich loam.

Sowing may commence at the end of February, a small portion on a warm border, of the first two varieties mentioned. These will be fit for use during April. The sowing to be repeated in the beginning of March, and these will produce throughout May.

These sowings are to be repeated in small proportions, at monthly intervals, until the beginning of July, when the main crop for the supply of the winter may be sown; and, finally, small crops at the commencement of August and September for spring.

Mode.—Sow in drills, twelve inches apart, and very thin. Each sowing should be performed in showery weather, or otherwise water given at the time of sowing, and three times a week afterwards.

Thin the plants, when they have four or five leaves about two inches in breadth, to at least twelve inches from each other.

Water must be given frequently and plentifully.

In November or December, before the setting-in of frost, some of the bulbs must be taken up, and, the tops and roots being removed, preserved under shelter in sand.

THE TURNIP-ROOTED CABBAGE, AND TURNIP-STEMMED CABBAGE, OR, KOHL RABI.

The Turnip-rooted is *Brassica campestris napo-brassica*, and is also known as *Knol-kohl*, and the Turnip-stemmed is *Brassica oleracea calo-rapa*, cultivated in Germany under the name of Kohl-Rabi; a designation by which it has now become generally known in English gardens, and which, if adhered to, would prevent the vegetable being confounded with the Turnip-rooted Cabbage. The root of the latter is swelled into a tuber near the origin of the stem, whilst in the Kohl-Rabi the stem is thick, rises about eight inches out of the ground, is there swollen into a globular form, very like a large Swedish Turnip growing above ground, and is crowned with leaves. There are several varieties of it; but by far the best are the *Early White Vienna*, and *Early Purple Vienna*, which, when young, are sweeter, more nutritious, and more solid than even the Cabbage or White Turnip, and excellent when boiled for table. Sow in April, May, or June, and plant out nine inches apart, in rows eighteen inches asunder, unless wanted of large size, when the quality of the bulbs is much deteriorated. The plants must have their stems left uncovered by the soil. When blanks occur, these may be filled up from the seed-bed with fresh plants. The bulbs may be kept sound and nutritious until very late in the spring, even much later than the Swedish Turnip.

The Turnip-rooted Cabbage is seldom grown in this country; it may be sown from March to June, and treated like Kohl-Rabi.

FRUIT GARDEN.

THE FRUIT GARDEN.

SITUATION AND SHELTER.

A SLOPING surface is an advantage, provided the slope is very moderate, and inclines to any of the points from south-east to south-west.

The walls or other boundaries being built, the matter next is, if the garden is exposed to cutting winds, to seek extra protection, if possible, by means of planting; indeed, this may be accounted the first step of the two. We do not by any means advocate planting large trees close to the garden wall. They prevent the training of some very useful fruits on the outside of the garden wall; and protection trees or shrubs thus situated do serious injury to the fruit trees in the interior of the garden, when their boughs have grown so as to overhang the wall. There is no real necessity for a continuous belt; a good group of trees at the north-western side, and another ranging from north to east, will suffice, provided the kinds are well selected. The Scotch Fir, the Holly, and the Spruce Fir, if moist soil, are particularly eligible as evergreens; and the Beech is by far the best deciduous tree to intermix with them.

ARRANGEMENT OF THE GARDEN.

We are now going to deal with trees under what is termed a dwarfing system, whether trained or not: with the ordinary orchard tree we have nothing to do at present.

BORDERS AND WALKS.—In laying out the borders next to a wall which is designed for the growth of fruit trees, all idea of cultivating them with garden vegetables should be abandoned. The roots of fruit trees require as much attention and skill in their management as the branches, and no crop should therefore be allowed to interfere with the routine which is necessary for the successful growth of the trees. A width of six feet will be found amply sufficient for the borders next the wall, provided it be devoted exclusively to the trees. Next to that border there should be a walk of at least four feet in width; and on the margin of the walk next the wall, a row of fruit trees, on *trellises*, may be planted, particularly on the south, east, and west wall borders. On the other side of the walk there should be another fruit border, of course parallel with the walk; this we would plant entirely with dwarfed or pyramidal trees, *without trellises*, confining the trellises (of whatever character, excepting high arcades) to the margin of the wall borders. Now, the border next the kitchen garden must have a walk behind it; this we would make from thirty to forty inches in width, according to the extent of ground at disposal; and next to this, at the south end of each quarter of the garden, we would have a huge slope for the cultivation of early vegetables: this to be the equivalent for the loss of the south wall borders. But if it is intended to cultivate the wall borders with light kitchen garden crops, such as Lettuce, Spinach, dwarf Kidney Beans, &c., then the border must be at least ten feet wide, and the trees on trellises must be confined to the border on the opposite side of the walk; in this case there will be no necessity for the huge slope above referred to.

As to *trellises* for the margins of the wall borders, we would not confine our readers to one shape alone. The table trellis, whether perfectly horizontal or with a slight incline to the walk, is a most excellent form for some kinds; whilst for others the saddle trellis might be adopted, or even perpendicular trellises, such as suggested for the Gooseberry or the Currant, might be put in requisition. Whatever be the form, none should exceed five feet in height; indeed, more would be unnecessary under a dwarfing system. Besides, it is of importance that the eye of the spectator or operator should see to the very bottom of the wall behind; and five feet is quite high enough for a lady gardener.

The following diagram will tolerably well represent the occupation of the border by the roots when the trees are established, on a wall border six feet wide, as we have recommended above.

Horizontal Section of a portion of the Wall Border, showing its entire occupation by the Roots of the Fruit Trees.

N.B.—The dots denote the position of trees.

Thus it will be seen, that the whole border will ultimately be a mass of fibres, freely ascending to the surface, and wholly unmolested by the spade. This is just as we wish it to be; and provided the border, or rather, the stations, are rightly prepared, that is to say, with soil of a proper texture, we will engage that, with a slight annual top-dressing in the end of April, the trees shall continue in prosperity, with the least possible amount of labour, for at least twenty years; if Pears, for double that time.

The garden being square or a parallelogram, we would carry the four-feet walk all round the exterior, and form two others crossing each other at right angles in the centre of the garden. This will, of course, throw the garden into four equal quarters or squares. We would carry our marginal borders all round every square; but along those which intersect each other at right angles in the centre we would plant the bush fruit, such as Gooseberries and Currants, dwarf Nuts, &c.

This arrangement will, of course, force all the Apples, Pears, Plums, Cherries, &c., which are not to be grown upon walls or espaliers, all round the exterior. The whole interior arrangement might then stand thus:—

PRINCIPAL CENTRAL WALK BORDER, to be planted with pyramids.

MARGINAL BORDERS, NORTH TO SOUTH, dwarf standards.

MARGINAL BORDERS, EAST TO WEST, the table trellis.

SOUTH WALL BORDERS, the inclined trellis.

EAST AND WEST WALL BORDERS, the perpendicular trellis.

SUBORDINATE WALKS, margin of bush fruit.

This form and arrangement of the garden will thus produce a variety of aspects; and for the information of those uninformed, we must give each a title, thus:—

INSIDE.—Interior Wall Borders. Interior Marginal Borders.

OUTSIDE.—Exterior Wall Borders. Exterior Marginal Borders.

Having now completed our observations upon the arrangement of the garden, we will proceed to describe the different forms of *trellises* adapted for the cultivation of fruit trees.

TRELLISES.—The principal are the perpendicular espalier rail and the horizontal or table trellis. Others may be suggested, but these are the principal.

The Perpendicular Espalier Rail.—This, being well known, needs little description. It is generally about five feet in height, and composed of parallel rods running in a horizontal form at about five or six inches apart. Such may be found in many of the old gardens of the nobility; and when established on sound principles, are well adapted for most fruits, especially for Apples. Some of the Cherries, too, such as those of the Bigarreau section, and some coarse-wooded Pears, which are rather unmanageable under a more prim mode of training, may well find a place here.

The Horizontal or Table Trellis.—This is well represented by an ordinary iron field hurdle thrown into a horizontal form, and supported a foot above the ground at each corner by some means. We have used these for some years, and find them well adapted for our more tender Pears. Almost all our more delicate-wooded fruits would succeed on them. The cross bars should, if possible, run only north and south.

Aspects.—Now, our readers, must learn not to confound a border with an aspect. An "aspect," in gardening phraseology, signifies that portion of a wall that is presented to any of the cardinal points. Thus, an east aspect is the east side of a wall which runs north and south; and so of every other point.

The south wall, or rather, southern aspects, should be reserved for the Apricot, the Peach, the Nectarine, and the Vine, anywhere south of the midland counties; but north of them the Vine must be omitted; if any attempt be made to grow it, the side of a house facing any point from south-east to south-west, provided there is a fireplace behind, will be the most eligible situation. The Apricot, however, in the northern counties, is by far the most profitable crop for a warm gable of this kind. In the northern counties some of the very superior Flemish Pears, such as the Winter Nelis, will deserve a place on a southern aspect. On the eastern aspect may be placed the principal of the trained Plums and Pears; and on the western, Pears and Cherries. On the north aspects, the Morello Cherry will be found a most valuable fruit; and by providing nets of a proper mesh to exclude the smallest of birds, this fruit may be kept with ease until the middle or end of October. Two-thirds of the north aspect may be occupied with this Cherry, whilst the remainder may receive a Green Gage Plum, an Orleans, and even the Late Duke Cherry, which makes a fine late dessert fruit in this aspect.

PREPARATION OF THE SOIL AND FORMATION OF STATIONS.

The first consideration before planting is the soil; for unless this is of a wholesome character clever selections of varieties will be of little avail. There are two extremes which should be at all times avoided in preparing the staple for fruit trees: the one when soils and subsoils are too retentive of moisture; the other when the staple of the soil is so sandy and weak, that the trees become exposed to sudden droughts. In the former case the trees become choked with mosses and lichens; the points die prematurely, and the fruit is starved and stunted. We need scarcely urge that a premature breaking up of the constitution of the tree is the sure result.

Before planting endeavour to correct the soil's texture. It is well known that clays may be made more open and fertile by means of sand; and sandy soils may be made more retentive of moisture by mixing with them clays or marl.

As correctors of sandy and hungry soils we would suggest the following, all of which, or any of them singly, will render such soils more fertile. The order in which they stand will indicate their beneficial quality: 1st. Marl; 2nd. Strong soil from headlands of fields; 3rd. Furrowings from low meadows; 4th. Clay; 5th. Ditchings from adhesive soils; 6th. Pond mud; 7th. Spare turf and weeds; 8th. Old and unctuous peat.

As correctors of adhesive or clayey soils we suggest, also, in a similar order: 1st. Sand of any kind; 2nd. Ordinary sand soil; 3rd. Old mortar, lime rubbish, &c.; 4th. Cinder ashes, fine; 5th. Ditchings from loose soils; 6th. Loose turf and weeds; 7th. Ordinary vegetable matter.

When it is desired to grow trees on the dwarfing system, it is astonishing what a very limited amount of soil, if of the proper staple, will suffice for a compact fruit tree; and the plan we are about to recommend frequently supersedes the necessity of any special drainage on behalf of the trees. After marking out the desired position for the stations, the first thing to be considered is, whether the ground is naturally too wet or too dry. If the former, the hole need only be half the prescribed depth; the other half may rise above the ordinary ground level. If too dry, there is no occasion to elevate the surface, only care must be taken not to place the collar of the tree too deep, which is a serious fault under all circumstances. The stations are made to extend three feet on each side the position for the tree, thus producing an excavation of six feet square. We consider two feet in depth amply sufficient for any fruit tree, especially for a dwarfing plan. The soil, then, should be thrown entirely out, and four or five inches more must be allowed for some impervious material, which we will presently describe. In throwing out the soil care must be taken to place it in samples, or both labour and material will be wasted. It very frequently happens that three distinct samples of soil or subsoil will come to hand during the operation. Of course all clayey, or sour, and badly-coloured subsoil must be rejected, and its amount will be supplied by the new material to be introduced; and if this is scarce, any ordinary surface-soil may be in part substituted. In filling the materials back again, the best of the orginal surface-soil must be kept downwards, mixing it thoroughly with the new soil; the inferior or second-rate soil may be kept to dress the surface with. As to the character of soil to be introduced, that depends partly upon the soil already existing in the garden, as well as on the kind of fruit tree about to be planted. If the soil is naturally sandy and dry, a very stiff or clayey loam should be selected; if naturally clayey, any fresh, mellow, sandy loam, or even the parings of road-sides, commons, or lanes, will prove excellent material; indeed, these should at all times be collected, as they prove of immense service, when mellowed down, for dressing Carrot and Onion beds, which are liable to the grub in old soils. The furrowings of old leys from what is considered good wheat soil is, however, of all other soils the best adapted for general fruit culture. Whatever materials are used, let it be remembered that the more of turfy matter that can be introduced, the longer will the compost endure. Any sort of turf, even from hungry situations, is most relished by fruit trees. If, nevertherless, no turf can be obtained, and the soil is loose and poor, it is well to introduce any refuse vegetables of a dry character, such as decayed bean or pea haulm, ordinary straw, old thatch, dry leaf-mould, or rotten spray; or, indeed, anything of a decaying vegetable character which is strong in fibre and enduring. If, any manure is thought necessary, it should be fresh from the stable or cow-shed, as such will endure longer in the soil; merely using one barrowful of mellow and rather rich soil to plant the tree in.

We come now to the hard materials for the bottom of the hole, four or five inches in depth, as before stated. It matters not what this is composed of: broken stones from quarries, brickbats, chalk, cinders, or clinkers, &c., all are eligible. These being rammed hard, our practice is to throw a coating of fine-riddled cinders over the whole, or very fine gravel: this secures drainage, and prevents the roots entering to any injurious extent.

PLANTING.

THE PLANTING SEASON.—We would in all cases advise early autumn planting of fruit trees, with the exception of the Vine and the Fig, provided the soil can be prepared in a mellow state. In the case of stubborn clayey soils, however, the business had better stand over till the spring; but the soil may be thrown out immediately, and by lying exposed the whole winter will be much improved for planting purposes; and then planting operations may safely be performed up to the middle of March, at which time they must be completed.

We have already described the preparation of the soil and the formation of stations, where such are necessary, for the reception of the fruit trees, and it now remains for us to give instructions as to the manner in which the trees are to be planted. In all cases, whether in the natural soil or on stations prepared for the purpose, never plant a tree deeper than barely to cover its roots. We have seen trees set *on the surface* of a soil, the subsoil of which was stiff, retentive clay, and the roots merely covered with some congenial compost, forming, as it were, a mound on the surface of the ground, and the roots have always found their way into the soil. In such cases it is necessary to support the tree with strong stakes, as it has no hold in the ground. Nothing can be more injurious, either to the present or future success of planting, than to bury the roots away from the influences of heat and air; and so long as the roots are sufficiently covered as not to be exposed to the direct influence of the air, they have all that is necessary for their prosperity. When the tree is placed in the soil, be careful to have the roots spread out horizontally, like the toes of a fowl when it treads on the ground; and let them be so disposed as to form the radii of a circle round the centre. Then let them be lightly covered with fine, mellow mould, such as we have already described, and when they have been completely covered, press the soil all round gently with the foot; but on no account tread and ram it, as is too frequently done. Should the tree be tall and furnished with a heavy head, the quantity of soil round the roots will not be sufficient to keep it in its place and enable it to withstand the influence of the winds; it must, therefore, be furnished with a stout stake, driven firmly into the ground, to which it is to be bound with a straw rope, or some such soft material, which in tying should be made to pass between the stake and the tree, to prevent rubbing and excoriation. After the first or second year the stakes may be removed and the tree left to itself.

TOP-DRESSINGS, MULCHING, &c.—By mulching, we mean such an amount of either half-rotten manure, or vegetable matters, or both in combination, as will at once ward off extreme drought, encourage the fibrous roots to the surface, and act by forming a weak liquid manure during every shower of rain, or application of water. There is little difference between mulching and top-dressing; the difference is more a matter of degree than of principle.

On light or sandy soils, too, mulching is of immense benefit; and as not every one can command sufficient strong loam, of a sound texture, when planting his trees, but is obliged to use soils of a lighter and inferior cast, mulching, in such cases, becomes more essential still. Mulch, if you can, the old trees, exhausted by bearing, in order to recruit their condition; mulch trees or bushes on hungry or porous soils, in order to retain a permanency of moisture during droughts; and mulch newly-planted trees, in order to control or regulate both heat and moisture.

GRAFTING AND BUDDING.

WHIP GRAFTING, called also *splice* and *tongue grafting*.—This is the most common mode of all others, and is that almost universally adopted in our nurseries; and, indeed, when the stock and scion are about equal in size, is perhaps the handiest plan of all. The head of the stock is pruned off at the desired height, and then a slip of bark and wood removed at the upper portion of the stock with a very clean cut, to fit exactly with a corresponding cut which must be made in the scion. A very small amount of wood must be cut away, and the surface made quite smooth; care must be taken that no dirt be upon the cuts in this, and, indeed, in all the other modes. The scion must now be prepared; this should have at least three or four buds, one of which should, where possible, be at the lower end, to assist in uniting it to the stock. A sloping cut must now be made in the scion; this cut must correspond with that on the stock.

CLEFT GRAFTING, as represented in this sketch, is practised on stocks one or two inches in diameter, and, therefore, too large for whip grafting. Cut or saw off the head of the stock in a sloping form; with a knife or chisel cleave the stock at the top, making the cleft about two inches deep; keep it open by leaving in the chisel; cut the lower end of the scion into the form of a wedge, one inch and a half long, and the side that is to be towards the middle of the stock sloped off to a fine edge; place the bark of the thickest side of the wedge end of the scion so as to correspond exactly with the bark of the stock; take away the chisel, and then the sides of the stock will pinch and hold fast the scion. Two scions may be inserted, one on each side of the cleft; but in this case the top of the stock must not be cut off sloping. Bast and clay must be put on as in the other modes of grafting.

GRAFTING CLAY.—To make this, take some strong and adhesive loam, approaching to a clayey character, and beat and knead it until of the consistence of soft soap. Take also some horse-droppings, and rub them through a riddle, of half-inch mesh, until thoroughly divided. Get some cow manure, the fresher the better, and mix about equal parts of the three, kneading and mixing them until perfectly and uniformly incorporated with each other; some persons add a little road scrapings to the mass.

A vessel with very finely riddled ashes must be kept by the side of the grafter, and after the clay is closed round the scion the hands should be dipped in the ashes; this enables the person who applies the clay to close the whole with a perfect finish. It must be so closed that no air can possibly enter; and it is well to go over the whole of the grafts in three or four days afterwards, when, if the claying of any has rifted or cracked, it may be closed finally.

GRAFTING WAX.—The following recipe has been recommended by a first-rate authority:—Take common sealing-wax, any colour but green, one part; mutton fat, one part; white wax, one part; and honey one-eighth part. The white wax and the fat are to be first melted, and then the sealing-wax is to be added gradually, in small pieces, the mixture being kept constantly stirred; and, lastly, the honey must be put in just before taking it off the fire. It should be poured hot into paper or tin moulds, to preserve for use till wanted, and be kept slightly stirred till it begins to harden.

BUDDING.—This is an operation which has for its object the attainment of the same end as grafting, but is performed at a different season of the year. While grafting is practised in the spring, by the union of one piece of wood upon another, budding is chiefly done in the autumn, and is the insertion of a bud of the current season into the bark of a tree which is intended to be budded. The time when budding is most successfully performed is when the young shoots, from which the buds are intended to be taken, have all but perfected their growth, and which will generally be from the beginning to the end of August, and when the buds on the lower part have become firm and set. With a sharp knife cut out a bud from the shoot, having about half an inch of bark both above and below it; this is called a *shield*. Then dexterously pick out the piece of wood which is found in the shield, leaving nothing but the bark and the axis of the bud; this is now ready for insertion. Having fixed upon the spot where the bud is to be inserted in the stock or tree, make a transverse cut about half round as deep as the wood, and then draw a perpendicular cut, beginning an inch and a half lower down than the first, up to it; these two cuts will make a figure like the letter T. Then with the bone end of your budding knife raise the bark on each side of the perpendicular cut, and slip in the shield; bind it round with a piece of soft matting, and in the course of three weeks it will have established itself, when the matting may be unbound, and again tied a little more loosely for a month longer, and afterwards entirely removed.

CAUSES OF UNFRUITFULNESS.—ROOT PRUNING.

The constitutional causes of unfruitfulness in fruit trees are either a too luxuriant growth, sometimes called "grossness," or premature old age, induced by abuse of culture. When we say "abuse of culture," we mean that to continue for years to dig a spade's depth and to crop over the surface roots of fruit trees, is sure in the long run to produce evil effects, more especially if the subsoil is of an ungenial character. Trees, in their earlier stages, may and will stand this foul play with impunity, because, the vital power being strong and in vigorous play, they can continue to reproduce fresh fibres, as a sort of equivalent to the mutilation they are made to endure. By degrees, however, this strong vital action becomes tamed; and at last, if the poor old tree were skeletonised at the root, it would be seen standing on a few deep props, something after the manner of a three-legged stool. This is no strained account, as would be ascertained on a close examination as above suggested.

The following sketch will illustrate the matter.

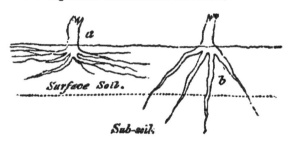

Now, when the conditions under which the roots are situated are taken into consideration, who can expect fig. *b* to continue for years in as healthful a condition as fig. *a*? Indeed, if such were the case, the ample directions given by all men of first-rate practice to take every precaution in avoiding deleterious subsoils would at once be overruled; and trees might be stuck in anywhere and anyhow, without the slightest pains. The unfortunate subject, fig. *b*, may, indeed, continue to grow for many years, but the consequences will be that the tree will be altogether thrown into a false position—the elaborations will be altogether defective.

It may here be observed, that in the case of fig. *b*, the deep roots extending into the subsoil must be cut away or extracted from the bad position they are in. Such cutting away, nevertheless, must not be done without some previous preparation. As one preliminary step, we would say, lay a compost, half manure and half turfy soil, which has been well blended for a twelvemonth, if possible, over the surface of the roots, extending from the hole nearly as far as the branches extend. This compost may be six inches deep, and a good watering with liquid manure occasionally will be a boon; the object being to do away with spade culture, if any, and to induce fresh fibrous surface roots to be produced before cutting away the tap roots in the subsoil.

When over-luxuriance is the cause of unfruitfulness a system of root pruning must also be practised, with the view of reducing the too great action of the roots. This great action is induced either by a superabundance of manure being applied to the roots at the time of planting, or from the naturally deep and rich state of the soil. Whenever it is found that trees grow too much to wood and do not produce blossom buds, dig a trench round the roots about the end of August, and cut off all those which appear to penetrate deeply into the soil, or which show a disposition to extend themselves beyond the range of their fellows. Make a layer of brickbats, stones, lime rubbish, or other rough material, under the roots, to prevent them from again shooting downwards, and then fill in the soil as before.

PROTECTING THE BLOSSOMS OF FRUIT TREES.

There are many contrivances which have been made use of for protecting the blossoms of fruit trees, which are so liable to be injured by the late frosts of spring; and of these the most effectual are canvas, woollen netting, bunting, fronds of fern, and boughs of the spruce fir.

When canvas, bunting, or netting are used, they are generally stretched upon two poles, which are inclined at an angle of 45° against the wall, the upper edge of the covering being fastened to the top of the wall by means of rings or loops hung on hooks fastened into the wall. These coverings should be fixed about the the end of February, or as soon as the buds begin to open. When the trees are in full bloom the coverings should be entirely removed during the early part of the day, and again returned about three or four o'clock in the afternoon; and about the middle of May the whole may be entirely dispensed with.

Fronds of fern and boughs of trees are applied by sticking them between the branches and the wall, and allowing them to hang down over the blossoms; but care must be taken that they are so disposed that the action of the winds will not cause them to chafe, or altogether to destroy, the blossoms.

Much of the risk which blossoms run of being injured by spring frosts may be prevented by retarding the blooming period. The way to accomplish this is, during the sunny days of winter, and when the sun acquires strength in early spring, to shade them with a sheet of canvas during the whole of the day, and expose them during the night. In this way the wall is kept cool, and the blossoms prevented from too early development.

THE APPLE.

The majority of Apple trees cultivated in the gardens of the cottager or amateur are of the kind termed amongst practical men "dwarf standards." Some also call them "rough espaliers." The latter name is scarcely appropriate, as espaliers are, more properly speaking, trees trained on rails or a trellis. To carry out this dwarfing system, then, by which both the space overhead, as well as below, is economised, a special course of pruning becomes necessary, commencing with the very earliest stages of the grafted plant, and only ceasing when the tree, through age, produces little young spray.

In the present case we must commence with the young graft, and we will suppose that it has just been planted. Whatever length it be, or whether possessed of only one shoot or two, it is absolutely necessary to prune them back to about six or eight buds.

In the second year, if successful, the tree, or rather, bush, will have at least eight or nine young shoots, some well placed, and some crossing each other.

Now pruning as an art truly commences. A selection must be made. The eye should be fixed on about five or six shoots well placed; that is to say, forming a kind of circle, or at least so disposed as to leave a distinctly open space, like a basin, in the midst of the tree, when all are pruned away but these. This being done, and having well determined on a nice form for the future tree, the remainder may be considered waste shoots, and may be instantly cut away, observing to leave nearly half an inch of the base of each shoot. It is well for those not experienced in this matter to tie a bit of thread or matting on each of the shoots to be retained, for fear of error; for, be it understood, we lay much stress on this first selection being made with discretion; on it will depend, in some degree the neatness of form; and we need hardly remind our readers that neatness of form and economy of space are identical. The selected shoots must now be shortened, and, as a general rule, we may say nearly one-half the length may be pruned away this season,—the object being, under a dwarfing system, to cause the lower part of the tree to develope abundance of spurs, or the rudiments of spurs. If the bushes are left without shortening, the sure consequence will be, that some gross shoots will soon take the lead, and some of these would, in due time, assume the orchard character, and the tree would become so unwieldy, as to do away with, or render worthless, all undercropping.

The second year's pruning being thus carried out, the tree in the course of the next summer will have completed its full complement of shoots; and after another selection in the next pruning season, shortening and thinning out will be the principal affair for the next year or two, after which it will suffice to go over ordinary kitchen or baking Apples once in two or three years.

General Maxims.—We may for the present conclude the Apple-pruning, as to young trees, with a few maxims necessary to be observed on all occasions. 1. In selecting shoots to be retained, always prefer short-jointed and brown-looking shoots to those which are pale, succulent, and long-jointed. 2. In shortening back the shoots that are to remain, always cut back to a bud which promises to *extend the tree*, rather than to contract it, unless the tree be of a very straggling habit. 3. Let the shortening back be less every season after the third year's pruning, for the trees by that period will be thrown into shape, and the lower spurs being in a great measure formed, there will yearly be less tendency to produce gross or barren shoots, especially if an occasional root pruning be given.

Pruning and Management of Standard Apples.—As the pruning, &c., of large or orchard Apples differs somewhat from that of the dwarf standard, we deem it necessary to offer a little special advice on that head. This work is mostly reserved for frosty weather, and very properly so, for it may be carried out when other matters, especially spade operations, become stationary. Large orchard trees, when in their prime, require very little pruning; once in three years may then suffice to regulate them. Their pruning will simply consist of a slight thinning out of exhausted or cross boughs, which, situated in the interior of the tree, cannot bring fruit to perfection, and in bearing rob the superior parts of the tree. When, however, the trees become somewhat aged, they require more attention; for when it is found that they cannot bring all the fruit which may "set" to perfection, it becomes necessary to sacrifice some portion, in order to throw strength into the remainder.

As long as the tree continues to bear at all the best fruit will ever be at the extremities of the boughs; nature, therefore, must be followed, or rather, in this case, anticipated. Once in a couple of years the trees should be gone over, and much of their interior wood cut away.

The wearing-out wood may be readily distinguished by its mossy or stunted character, and frequently by its dead points, which are an almost certain sign of the breaking up of the constitution of the tree. There is no occasion to prune the extreme points; the removal of the larger decaying branches will suffice. It often happens, nevertheless, that a good deal of young annual spray grows out of the old branches; such, occasionally, should be trimmed away, or it will decoy the sap from the more important portions of the tree.

The American Blight.—In the course of the month of May this tremendous Apple pest will begin to re-appear, unless fairly exterminated during the winter. Fairly bathing the trees, by means of hand-syringing several times repeated, in a liquor consisting of soft soap, six ounces to the gallon, a good quantity of sulphur, and as much lime as it can carry, adding plenty of urine, has frequently proved effectual in destroying the insects. Should they, however, re-appear in places apply train oil or gas tar by means of a painter's brush; for, although a *wholesale* application of these powerful things is very injurious to the bark of the trees, yet we have often used oil, in *light* cases, without any perceptible injury. When, however, the tree is much infested, oil is out of the question. Nevertheless, mere hand brushing is a great disturber, even with a dry yet coarse brush. Still it is safe practice to use some daubing mixture, which will at least cause them to suspend operations, even if it does not lock them up in their dens. For such a proceeding we would suggest another eligible application at this period. Beat up three ounces of soft soap in a gallon of warm water, add three handsful of flour of sulphur, and then add half a gallon of strong urine from the stables; beat the whole well together, and keep adding pure clay until the whole is a thick paint. This, daubed into their holes, will wedge the insects up in prison long enough for them to be destroyed with the caustic powers of the mixture, and will not injure the trees like oil. Towards the end of the month the Apple trees in fruit will want hand-picking carefully, to free them from the caterpillars. Those amateurs who have only a few dwarf trees ought not to leave on them one of these depredators.

LIST OF SELECT APPLES.

Some kinds like clay soils; some will answer well in sandy soils; and others will succeed in peat, provided it is well drained. Every cultivator, therefore, should keep an attentive eye on the kinds which thrive in his district; or, at least on a soil similar to that of his own garden. Whenever a kind fails, the amateur or cottager should not stand speculating or surmising: let him immediately take steps to graft a kind which *will* answer. By a little inquiry he will soon be able to learn what kinds have paid best for half a century back, and such may be grafted at once at the proper period.

THE APPLE.

DESSERT VARIETIES.

Early Harvest.—Ripens at the end of July and beginning of August.

Margaret.—Ripens about the beginning of August.

Devonshire Quarrenden.—Ripe in the first week of August, and continues in use during the whole of that month, and the greater part of September.

Summer Golden Pippin.—Ripens in the end of August and beginning of September, but does not keep much over a fortnight.

Oslin.—This is a very peculiar Apple, and very little known. It has a flavour and aroma peculiarly its own, and we would advise that it should be grown wherever there is room for half a dozen trees. It ripens in the beginning of September.

Kerry Pippin.—Ripens about the second or third week in September, and lasts till about the middle of October.

Scarlet Crofton.—Ripens in October, and continues in use till December, with a very valuable property of not becoming mealy.

Early Nonpareil, or *Hicks' Fancy.*—In use from October to the end of December.

Pitmaston Nonpareil.—In use from October until March.

Court of Wick.—In use from October to March.

Cox's Orange Pippin.—Ripe in October, and keeps to February.

Downton Pippin.—Ripe in November, and continues till January.

Golden Pippin.—There is a popular error entertained by many people that the old Golden Pippin "has died out." A greater fallacy could not exist; the Golden Pippin is as healthy and vigorous as ever it was, but it requires to be grown on a warm soil and in a sheltered situation, and then it may be had in perfection.

Golden Reinette.—In use from November till April.

Pearson's Plate.—In use from November until April.

Ribston Pippin.

Ross Nonpareil.—In use from November until February.

Wyken Pippin.—In use from December to April.

Boston Russet.—In use from January to April.

Old Nonpareil.—In use from November to May, and may be fairly termed the best dessert Apple in the kingdom in January and February.

Lamb Abbey Pearmain.—In use from December until May or June.

Sturmer Pippin.—From February till June.

KITCHEN VARIETIES.

Keswick Codlin.—In July and August.

Manks Codlin.—In use from July to February.

Early Julien.—It is ripe in the middle of August, and lasts during the greater part of September. It may even be used in the dessert.

Nonesuch.—It is ripe in about the second week in September, and lasts during October.

Wormsley Pippin.—It comes in use in September, and lasts during October.

Cellini.—It is in use during October and November.

Golden Winter Pearmain.—This variety is now pretty well known, and is quite an established favourite. In use from October till January. It is also an excellent dessert Apple.

Beauty of Kent.—In use from October till February.

Minchall Crab.—In use from October until February.

Blenheim Pippin.—November to February.

Bedfordshire Foundling.—In use from November to March.

Dumelow's Seedling.—In use from November till April.

Winter Pearmain.—In use from November till April, and is a good keeper.

Striped Beefing.—It is in use from December till May.

Alfriston.—It keeps till April.

Winter Majeting.—May be kept till May or June.

Northern Greening.—In use from November until May.

Norfolk Beefing.—Will keep until June.

Gooseberry Apple.—It comes into use in December or January, and keeps as late as July or August.

F

THE APRICOT.

Soil.—Apricots do not love a fluctuating character of soil, whether through its dryness, or through the action of spade culture, allowing them to form nice young fibres at one period, only to be destroyed in another. A good sound loam befits them best, one which, although somewhat adhesive or greasy, will yet, by the action of the weather, readily crumble to atoms. Indeed, there are few of our fruit trees but will thrive in a soil of this character. The soil, of whatever kind, must be prepared about half a yard deep; or, if a light soil, let it be two feet. Let a substratum of brick, or other imperishable material, be placed below each tree, according to our platform directions; and see that the soil has some turfy matter mixed with it. As for manure we prefer using a few half-rotten tree leaves, in the proportion of one part leaves to four or five parts soil.

Pruning.—The pruning of this so much resembles the Plum that we need not enlarge on it here, and will, therefore, be somewhat brief. Apricots, like Plums, sometimes produce coarse breast-shoots; these ought to have been pinched in summer, and then there would be no occasion to counsel the winter pruner as to their removal. Blanks must, however, be thought of, and, at times, it becomes necessary to reserve even such rampant subjects, for an improper shoot is to be preferred to a blank. Apricots do not require shortening; indeed, as a maxim, they are better without it; still, cases arise in which the pruner should not be over fastidious. After removing gross and superfluous breast-shoots, observing to leave some short-jointed spray for tying down, the pruner must examine the face of the tree carefully all over, and see if any summer shoots of a late growth, and, consequently, of a barren character, shade the true blossoming spurs. The Apricot, when in proper condition, produces, perhaps, more natural spurs than most of our fruit trees; and although some kinds will blossom and bear on the young wood, yet on the true spurs we must mainly rely, for blossoms from the young shoots most generally develope imperfectly. The pruner, therefore, must, with some precision, cut away cleanly all immature-looking spray which may tend to shade the blossom-buds and produce too much spray in the succeeding summer: this is important. These things done, a parting glance may be cast on the leaders, in order to see if there be one or two too many (which is seldom the case), or, whether, in the event of a large portion of wall being still uncovered, occasional pruning back may be of service.

Young trees, possessing only a few shoots, must be shortened, in order to produce more shoots to fill the wall; and our practice is to shorten the centre portions of the tree, laying in the right and left lower portions at full length. The centre of the tree thus becomes a nursery of young wood for three or four years, and that portion is relieved of its superfluity by continuing to draw the shoots downwards, right and left, until the wall is full, when, of course, shortening may cease, and the very centre of the tree is the last to be complete. Everybody knows the maxim applied to hedges—"Always make the bottom before you make the top," and this applies equally to our trained trees. By this practice it will be found, that by the time the centre is complete, the lower parts, right and left, have become very substantial, from having had the chief appropriation of the sap for two or three years; they, indeed, become so stout by this practice, that no wild centre shoots can ever afterwards "lord it" over them.

February will be found the best month for performing the winter pruning of the Apricot, and at that period the following operations will have to be attended to :—Snags, as they are termed, are frequently produced by these trees, such snags being the remains of the summer's stopping or pinching of the breast-shoots. These generally produce a cluster of buds at their base, which, although not blossom-buds at present, most frequently become such, and must be carefully preserved. All these "snags" must be reduced to the very point where the cluster of small buds here alluded to present themselves; and if no buds appear to be organized we cut them down to the base, unless the part is bare of shoots, when they may be reserved for the production of succession wood. Such snags being removed, the next point is to look over the young shoots of last summer, and determine whether they are wanted in their respective situations. And here we must distinguish between leading shoots and mere side shoots. Of course all leading shoots necessary to carry out and complete the form of the tree will be preserved; and, indeed, any, although not to be considered permanent ones, which are requisite to cover bare portions of wall or trellis. Such being reserved, the remainder may be shortened back to within an inch of their base, in the hope of inducing the development of spurs. And now, as no shortening back is required with the Apricot, unless for some special reasons, the main shoots may be fastened carefully down all over the tree.

No fruit tree suffers more from overcrowded spray than this. Blossoms may form abundantly in this smothered condition, and the tree may, in the ensuing spring, be like a garland; but shortly come complaints of bad setting, which, of course, is attributed to the unusual amount of frost the sufferer has experienced beyond its neighbours. It is good practice, therefore, to pinch liberally betimes, especially during the first three weeks in June. All those breast-shoots of coarse character, not required for covering naked spaces, may be totally disbudded first; and of those remaining, all that are required to form a nucleus for future spurs may have their points pinched off at once. The finger and thumb, therefore, must be kept going all through June and July, after which there is much less tendency than in the Peach to produce late spray. A healthy Moorpark, during the end of July and the early part of August, will produce two or three generations of laterals, stop or pinch how you may; but no sooner does the out-of-doors thermometer descend somewhat below 60° on the average than our hitherto fast friend becomes paralyzed, for Apricots cannot endure a low temperature whilst in a growing state. Every breast-shoot which is not wanted should be pruned to within about three eyes by the third week in August, at latest; for every ray of sunlight after that period is needed to complete and ripen the newly-formed buds on the fruit-spur on the young shoots. If any gross leading shoots are still making way, off with their heads in true Chinese style—let there be no hesitation. All growths made after this period only serve to increase pruning in winter; to waste the true energies of the trees; and to interfere with that high course of concentration and elaboration so essential to tender fruits, and so conducive to a healthily-developed blossom in the ensuing spring.

LIST OF SELECT APRICOTS.

1. Red Masculine.
2. Large Early, or Gros Précoce.
3. Shipley's, or Blenheim.
4. Hemskerk.
5. Breda.
6. Royal.
7. Moorpark.

We have now given a list of all that are truly essential, in the present position of horticulture, whether to the amateur or the cottager. For the amateur who, in a small garden, has room for three only, we recommend Nos. 3, 5, and 7. If four, then take Nos. 1, 3, 5, 7. If five, then Nos. 1, 3, 5, 6, 7. For cottagers, we say Nos. 3 and 7. Above all we would recommend the "Shipley's" to the cottager, as being a hardier and a larger tree, and a much surer bearer.

THE CHERRY.

All the varieties of the cultivated Cherry are budded or grafted on the wild Cherry stock. They are budded or grafted in the same way as Apples or Pears, and at the same period.

In respect to soil less preparation is necessary for the Cherry than for any other fruit tree, as it is not so impatient of indifferent subsoils as some of our other fruits, neither is it so liable to disease; gumming, generally through accidental wounds, being the evil Cherry trees are most liable to. A deep sandy loam suits the Cherry best; such, in fact, as would be considered a good Carrot soil. This should be deeply trenched, and if poor, and no turfy matter in it, any raw vegetable matter may be trenched down.

The system of management adapted to the Cherry is so similar to that which is practised on the Plum, that we shall not here enter at any great length on the subject, but refer our readers to what is found under the head of Plum. The following general rules will, however, be found useful:—

Fan-training is what we must beg to recommend for the Cherry in general; and it is obvious that with the grosser-growing kinds with large leaves, either the first trained shoots in the young tree must be placed a great distance apart, in order that the young shoots, ultimately produced, may be nailed between; or that the first shoots being put the ordinary thickness, much sacrifice of young wood must be made; or they must be tied down on the succession plan. The latter is our practice, and we beg to recommend it. We advise those, therefore, who have the large-leaved Cherries laid in too thickly, to re-arrange them, so that most of the young shoots they have produced may be trained in or tied down upon the older and barren wood as the case may be; for assuredly Cherries of this habit do not produce many surplus young shoots, providing that they are anticipated, and a provision made for their future training. Under such circumstances, most of the young shoots may be tied down, or otherwise encouraged; no two, however, should be permitted to lie abreast of each other. Where two shoots are produced in a parallel direction, within about four inches of each other, one must, of necessity be "spurred back," leaving about one inch at the lower end, which will prove a nucleus for future blossom-buds. No shortening back is requisite with the Cherry in general. The only cases which can justify the practice are, on the one part, crippled or distorted points, and the necessity that exists in young trees to "*prune for wood;*" a practice which signifies an attempt by pruning to cause one healthy shoot to subside into some three or four; for by such means is the desired form of the tree ultimately completed. The rest of the Cherry pruning resolves itself into thinning away cross shoots in standard trees, and those interior shoots which become crowded, and in consequence deprived of a fair share of light. The length of the leaf in each kind may be fairly taken as the distance at which young shoots may be retained, observing in all cases to avoid two strictly parallel shoots; rather choosing a succession, one following speedily on the heels of another.

The Morello.—Here, the foliage being very diminutive, nearly double the number of young twigs may be preserved as compared with even the Duke section. The Morello requires but little "thinning out;" indeed, the avoidance of two young shoots immediately side by side constitutes the chief rule of pruning. Here, again, no shortening back is requisite; indeed, it is positively injurious in the bearing trees, as the principal, and in some cases the only real good wood-bud is at the terminal point; shortening, therefore, must in general be avoided. Through scantiness of the *true wood-buds* on aged trees of this kind, they are apt to lose many shoots; as they increase in age, they die off, or become almost denuded of useful young shoots. Such, therefore, have to be pruned away, or the tree assumes a dilapidated appearance. The pruning these long barren shoots away generally causes a re-arrangement of some portion of the trees, if not of the whole. Now, this is rather a serious item, in point of the time it requires, where people are pressed with business; and, therefore, it may suffice in general to simply cut out the dead shoots annually, and to clear away all the partially barren shoots once in two years.

This two years' examination should be a thorough one. Many long branches will be found with not more than a shoot or two on them. These may be cut clean out at their point of junction with the old limb, unless some favourable shoots, adapted for leaders, appear in the course of their length. It is generally best, in this two years' revision, to untie or unnail the whole tree, and to give it a new arrangement. Of course all young trees, destined to cover trellises of any particular character, must be pruned and trained during the first two or three years with a direct relation to that character, making it a point at all times to secure the most powerful shoots for the lowest situations; for the centre is generally capable of taking care of itself. Indeed, the same may be said as to the walls, and shortening back must be resorted to during the first three years, more or less, in order to produce the requisite number of shoots. It so happens that the younger Cherry trees bear the better, the more prolific they are in wood-buds, and therefore pruning back may be at that period safely practised. This remark applies to the whole family.

The Aphis.—Early in June the Cherry aphis will begin to commit havoc on the trained trees. We cannot hope to dress large standard trees for this pest: but those in a course of close training, or under a dwarfing system, must have particular attention at this period. Before training the young shoots in, whether on a wall, on pales, or trained on stakes, a wash of tobacco-water should be provided. Tobacco-paper, at the rate of 1 lb. to six oz. of strong shag tobacco, will make one gallon of liquor, which will destroy these pests at one dipping. To be sure, the trees may be syringed over; but this requires much liquor, and is, therefore, rather expensive. We prefer dipping the young shoots, which is easily accomplished; a small bowl or basin in one hand, and the other hand occupied in bending the twigs into the bowl, will be found a sure process. The shoots must be dipped fairly overhead in the liquor.

LIST OF SELECT CHERRIES.

Black Tartarian.—Ripens towards the end of June.
Early Purple Gean.—Ripens in the early part of June.
May Duke.—Ripe towards the end of June.
Black Eagle.—Ripe in the early part of July.
Elton.—Ripens in July.
Bigarreau or *Graffion.*—Ripe in the end of July.

Florence.—Much like the Bigarreau, but ripens much later. Wall or standard.
Late Duke.—Ripens during August.
Morello.—Ripens in August and September, and if well protected, will endure until the end of October.
Büttner's October Morello.—Later still than the Morello.

THE CURRANT.

The first year that the cuttings are put out, the Currant commonly produces three or four weakly-developed shoots, of some three or four inches in length. Two or three of the principal of these, placed equidistant, must be selected, and they may have a few of the imperfect points removed, in order to compel, during the succeeding summer, the development of several shoots, from which, at the succeeding rest-pruning, those for the future head may be selected.

On the first formation of the head, of course, much of the future symmetry of the bush depends; and well-formed bushes are ornamental as well as useful, especially in small gardens, or near walks. The circular form is, doubtless, more convenient than any other, and an approximation to it is generally the practice; still the forms we generally find in gardens are but a rude approach to it; and amateurs, and those with small gardens, would do well, in all cases of circular training, to place a strong hoop of the desired diameter, and at the desired height to establish the first formation of the bush or tree. This will insure symmetry, as well as facilitate the ordinary training processes.

A *strong* hoop, of a yard in diameter, will be found exceedingly appropriate; it need not, however, be more than a yard, as it is by far the best to have no interior shoots, but to leave the middle of the bush entirely open. Indeed, if this plan be *strictly* adhered to, thirty inches diameter will doubtless be amply sufficient, as it is needless to waste space which is otherwise so valuable. Three strong stakes may be driven deeply into the ground, at three equidistant points in the circumference of the circle, the top of each being about fifteen inches from the ground, and to the points of these the hoop must be firmly attached by means of copper wire. Those who wish to be very *particular* may choose stakes a foot (or more) longer still, so as to carry another hoop about a foot above the first hoop; and, indeed, this principle may be carried to any necessary extent if requisite. The stakes driven in the ground should, if possible, be good oak; and as for the hoops, we should choose them of thick wire rods;

THE CURRANT.

for although rust is prejudicial to most fruit trees, it could scarcely occur to any serious extent with such slender material. Much care should be exercised in putting down the hoops; the ground must not be trodden into a puddled state, and the operation, should be performed when the soil is tolerably dry. The bush, of course, will be in the centre, either previously or introduced subsequently; and now some intermediate sticks must be used in a temporary way, to lead the young shoots to the hoop. These things will readily suggest themselves, and when the whole has been completed the bush will have the appearance of that shown in the annexed engraving.

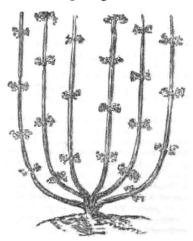

A Tree with Fruit-buds at the Joints far apart.

A Bough of a Tree pruned close each year, and producing a mass of Fruit-buds from top to bottom.

We train them nearly a foot apart, and get very abundant crops; and they certainly ought not to be nearer than nine inches on any account. As a maxim, we say the leading shoots should be so far apart that the *summer spray*, when pinched or pruned back in June, does not meet. This spray we cut back to about four or five inches early in June; and these five inches on each side of two adjoining leaders gives ten inches as the distance from leader to leader. As for the spray-shoots crossing each other previous to the "growth-pruning," that does not signify; it will do little harm.

A Standard Currant tree (leafless) showing its fruit-buds.

Another highly ornamental form which may be introduced is that shown in the annexed engraving. This will be found advantageous in small gardens, where space is limited, and where the crop, being raised on a standard, will admit of an under crop being taken advantage of, which would not be the case where dwarf bushes are grown.

A selection being made of the proper shoots in proper positions, they must be carried along conducting sticks to the hoop, and having been tethered tolerably well at the bottom, may be pruned just as much as will leave a point sticking above the hoops. During the next summer it will be found that the growing shoots will rise perpendicularly with a little assistance.

And now for the pruning of Currants in general (whether by hoop-training or otherwise) when they are well established. As before recommended, the leaders should have a portion of their points cut away at every rest-pruning, in order to cause them to develope side-spurs. If this is not done, and the trees are growing freely, one-half the length of the young leading shoots will be bare of spurs, and thus in such bushes may be seen patches of currants, and bare portions alternately, up the main stems. The object in shortening them is to cause the spurs to be developed in a continuous way; and thus more fruit is obtained in a given space, and room is economized. Nevertheless, if the leaders have been summer-pruned, there may be no occasion for *rest* shortening. Be that as it may, we would never leave above nine inches in length on any account; about seven, indeed, is our average.

The *Red* and *White Currants* bear principally on the "spurs," as they are called; these are produced abundantly on the sides of the main stems, of which there are generally nearly a dozen in a well-formed bush, so that our readers will at once see that the mode of pruning must differ widely from the Black Currant and Gooseberry. These bushes are generally trained, from the first, with a given number of branches, which are not often increased afterwards; if they are, it is on account of the great eligibility as to position that they occupy. The first business of the pruner is to run his knife up these main stems, which will be found studded with spurs—some in groups, others scattered; and from these the future crop must be obtained.

Every lateral spur must be pruned back to about half an inch, as nearly as possible; but whilst making use of the term *every*, which is rather too sweeping, let us observe that exceptions frequently occur. To understand these things our readers must take a close examination for five minutes of these branches and their spurs. They will find that the rule, with strong and healthy bushes, is, to produce abundance of side-twigs, or lateral spray; and that, as an exception, diminutive-looking twigs are produced amid these clusters of spray, which are of a sort of intermediate character, appearing as though nature, in forming them originally for shoots, had changed her mind suddenly, and clothed them with embryo blossom-buds. Such lengthened spurs are generally about two inches in length, and as full of blossom-buds as they can be. Some of the finest fruit will be produced from these, and amid the devastations going on with the knife, they must every one be retained unpruned. Lastly, all the side-spuring being completed, the tops or leaders of the branches must be shortened, in order to cause them to develope side-spurs as they proceed, which long leaders will not do without the pruner's assistance; about six to eight inches each year may thus be left, the other or point of the shoot being pruned away.

The finer White Dutch Currants seldom produce above eight inches in length of extending leader, and from their tame character of growth, as compared with the red kind, they naturally possess a much greater tendency to produce spurs; just as much, therefore, may be pruned away as appears diminutive, shrunk, blighted, or twisted in the wrong direction, for any or all of these evils may befall the shoots; indeed, it generally happens that one or the other does occur.

The Black Currant.—This Currant is somewhat more difficult of culture than the red, or, perhaps, it ought to have been said, more difficult to please with regard to texture of soil.

No soil that does not retain a considerable amount of moisture during dry weather will grow it in high perfection. The fruit is liable to cast, and the whole bush to become severely blighted on hot and hungry soils. It attains a high degree of perfection trained to the wall: and as it both bears and loves a partial shade, is very well adapted for walls contiguous to town or suburban buildings, or such as we frequently find inclosing what are termed back yards, where any aspect would suit it, excepting the north, and there the Morello Cherry would be found to succeed best. Those who try it in such situations should take care to provide a foot in depth of good sound soil, with a border nearly a yard wide, and some sort of edging six inches above the ground level, to retain mulchings, which are of greater benefit to this fruit than any other under culture.

The pruning of the Black Currant is, perhaps more simple than that off most of our bush fruit, being, in the main, confined to thinning out. These bushes, however, vary much in character, according to their age, the previous mode of pruning, and to the soil. Old trees are apt to be of considerable height, and in the attempts made occasionally to keep them within bounds in this respect, it may turn out that much shortening back has to be resorted to, and this has, of course, a tendency to cause the main twigs to branch exceedingly, and by much shading to greatly diminish the bearing qualities of young shoots lower down. In this case the finest fruit is produced upon clean, young shoots, which should neither be excessively long nor stumpy; very long growths generally have great lengths between the buds, and, to say nothing of the character of the fruit, this has a tendency to cause the bush to attain an inconvenient height speedily. Very stumpy wood, the lateral produce of strong branches, pruned back as before observed, is injurious to the successional shoots, which are always springing from below to renew the bush, and these are chiefly the result of cutting back main branches into older wood,—a thing to be avoided. Let the pruner, therefore, prefer wood of a medium character, certainly rather strong than otherwise, and when branches become so coarse and tall as to peril the welfare of the other portions of the bush, rather let them be totally removed than stumped back; thus avoiding the production of those thick bunches of laterals complained of.

And now about shortening. When any portion of the bush is extending beyond the bounds of convenience, I say, reduce it; but only in such cases.

The chief consideration, after admitting the average distance of the young shoots, is to sustain a certain amount of symmetry in the bush, for this of necessity involves a regular supply of good wood from the base to the top. It must be here remarked, that since the Black Currant bears its principal crop on the annual shoots rather than on the spurs, means, of course, must be taken by the pruner to excite and sustain a regular sprinkling of such wood all over the tree; and in this case there is not the same necessity for keeping the middle of the bush open, as in the Red and White Currant and Gooseberry.

LIST OF SELECT CURRANTS.

Red Dutch.
Knight's Sweet Red.
White Dutch.

Ogden's Black.
Black Naples.

THE FIG.

Soil.—Almost any well-drained soil will suit Fig trees, provided that, with its porosity, it also possesses that kind of mechanical texture which, whilst it readily transmits moisture, will also retain sufficient to withstand a hot and dry period in the middle of summer. It is well, however, to lean towards an open, porous character; for if any defect arises through extreme seasons of drought in consequence of the soil being light, a remedy of a very simple character is always at hand in the shape of a good top-dressing and a bucket or two of water. In preference, therefore, to building preventive walls and other matters involving extra expense, we say, so compound the soil for them that they may never grow very gross, neither be liable to suffer from sudden droughts. When the native soil of a garden is too clayey, thorough drainage, and the introduction of a liberal amount of sand, lime rubbish, ashes, &c., with a slight amount of vegetable matter, will in general suffice to make it fit for Fig trees. If the garden soil is too light and porous, some adhesive loam may be added, also old peaty or vegetable matter, or, indeed, anything which may happen to be at hand which is retentive of moisture in its own nature, yet not a "forcing" or rich manure. One thing is requisite: the bed of soil should by no means be deep. We would never allow above half a yard in depth, unless in situations peculiarly favourable to the culture of this fruit, such as occur in our more favoured counties, as Kent, Essex, Sussex, Hants, Dorset, Devon, and Cornwall. These highly-favoured counties form an exception to the rest of Britain.

Management.—To no fruit tree is disbudding of greater importance than to the Fig. Let the soil be ever so carefully constituted to avoid luxuriance, still the Fig, in a trained state, will produce a host of superfluous side-shoots, as well as numerous suckers from the roots. Old worn-out trees, or those which have borne abundantly for years, may prove an exception; but thus it is with the majority. On examining the character of the wood as it springs forth, two or three distinct kinds may be clearly traced; distinct as to the proportion the thickness of the young shoot bears to the length of the internode, or that part between each two joints. This internode, as we have before observed, furnishes by far the best criterion of fruitfulness in nearly all our fruit trees, and should at all times be kept under examination, for it will at once furnish a key to the conditions of the tree, prospective as well as retrospective.

Of the three different kinds of wood, one will be found of an over-luxuriant character, long in the internode, and thick or succulent in substance: a second kind will be found almost as weakly as straws, lanky, and spongy; and a third kind will be found robust, but short-jointed and compact. This last is the kind of wood to reserve for future bearing. This sort of wood does not ramble so fast as the others; and, whereas, the first-named kind may possess internodes of two or three inches in length, the latter will frequently possess three or four joints in that compass.

The present bearing of these remarks refers to disbudding;

implying, thereby, a *selection* of the wood which is to produce the next year's crop. Much allowance must be made for the habit of varieties of this fruit; some naturally produce a grosser shoot and a larger leaf than others; some, as the *Lee's Perpetual* or *Brown Turkey*, seldom produce wood too strong, their bearing properties are so great. As soon, therefore, as the character of the young shoots can be distinguished, so soon should disbudding commence; for, in the majority of Figs on walls, by far the largest proportion of young shoots will have to be stripped away. As this process of rubbing off buds will have to be repeated at intervals through June and even July, it is well to proceed somewhat cautiously at first. In September, when the young shoots have grown coarsely, and have been neglected for a few weeks, they will be found too full of spray of a flimsy and immature character, which proves a serious impediment to the ripening of both wood and fruit. In selecting those to remain, be sure to save the very shortest-jointed shoots; everything depends on a pertinacious adherence to this maxim, which is of equal importance in the case of the Fig as the Vine. It must be remembered, nevertheless, that not too many even of these must be retained: not he who retains the most good-looking shoots obtains the most Figs. We consider that as many shoots may be tied down as will completely clothe the old stems from bottom to top. We speak now of tying down on the main stems, for we hold this the best plan; those, however, who choose to nail them between, can do so, for the difference as to the Fig is scarcely worth contending about, the amount and character of the young shoots reserved being of far more importance. As to number of shoots, that depends, in part, on the distance at which the main shoots are placed. If these are, as we have before advised, a foot apart at least, then there is every chance of laying in a considerable quantity. We would advise the operator to begin at the top of the tree, and commence selecting shoots according to the character heretofore laid down; and when the first is tied down, and *its point pinched off*—of which more shortly—then another may be selected close to the very spot where the pinching of the former took place, and so on downwards, stripping all those away entirely which are considered superfluous. All small, weak, and immature-looking spray of later growth must be rubbed off.

Another matter must receive attention: the root suckers must be thinned out. We need scarcely say that no more of these are to be retained than are necessary to fill the vacant spaces on the wall, or to tie down on the older branches. We may here advise, then, what we consider to be the very best points of practice with this tree.

Firstly.—To train it, if possible, perpendicularly, in order that the main shoots running in parallel lines may always remain in the same position, and be equidistant at all points.

Secondly.—To keep those permanent "leaders" a greater distance apart than is usual; say ten inches in the small-leaved kinds, and fifteen in those of the large-leaved section.

Thirdly.—To commence as early as possible a system of tying down the short-jointed young spray before alluded to, observing to tie down no two young shoots side by side.

Fourthly.—To encourage no root suckers, beyond what are requisite for the above purposes.

Having said thus much about training, selection, &c., we come now to another important part of Fig culture, viz., "stopping." Such Fig trees as we have described as possessing a host of short joints in a very narrow compass, and which are fruitful without interference, need not this process: these, however, are the exception—we have the rule to deal with. It is well, therefore, to stop all those of a doubtful character at the end of August, or the very beginning of September, merely pinching off or squeezing flat the terminal growing point. This will induce the fruit for the ensuing year to commence forming, so as to receive a decisive character. This stopping, however, is a matter of some nicety, and the period of performing it must be determined both by the kind and its condition or habit. A too-early stopping with some Figs, which are not very difficult to fruit, would cause them to develope the fruit for the ensuing year too early; for if they become as large even as a Black Currant berry, they will be almost sure to perish with severe weather in the ensuing winter.

LIST OF SELECT FIGS.

| Brown Turkey. | Black Ischia. |
| Brunswick. | Marseilles. |

The *Brown Ischia* is esteemed by some, and is a very useful Fig, as are most of the *Ischias*. We, however, prefer the Black variety.

THE GOOSEBERRY.

Before entering on the particulars of management of this highly-useful and universally-esteemed fruit, we will state at the outset that our purpose will not be to discuss the merits of what are called "Show Gooseberries," but rather to point out the system of cultivation applicable to the varieties which are generally found most serviceable in the garden of the amateur and cottager.

Planting.—Plant them in the natural ground, about three feet six inches apart; take out the soil, where they are to be planted, three inches deep; make the bottom of the trench quite level with the back of the spade; then put down a stake, or stick, say two feet long, about three quarters of an inch thick; do not leave the stake above six or seven inches above the level of the trench; tie the "bole," or "stem," of the tree to the stake with a little matting (this is done to prevent the wind blowing them about); when you have done this, take all the roots and straighten them, placing a little soil upon them as you proceed; let the roots be placed as uniformly as you can round the trench, taking care one root does not lie over another; then cover the roots one inch and a half deep, including the little you have put on in laying these straight; then lay over this a little spent manure, about one-inch thick; cover this with soil, and they will do without any further trouble till spring. Do not be afraid of making the trench a little wider than the roots extend, as it gives you a little room to extend the roots.

Pruning.—This should be done in December or January, care being taken to leave such branches in the tree as contain good firm buds, and that the shoots which are left should be well ripened. This is easily ascertained by their appearance; for if the shoots are not properly ripened they will look shrivelled, and their buds will be very small and puny. If, on the other hand, the shoots are well ripened, the buds will be strong and firm, the bark of the shoots will have cracked, and a little of the outer bark peeled off. Having selected such well-ripened shoots to be left on the tree, the other shoots may be removed. They should not be cut off close to the branches, but a little of them be left on, so as to form a kind of "spur," say three quarters of an inch long. Shoots that grow erect should all be cut off, unless it be that the tree is not uniform in its branches, in which case, one shoot that may be inclined to grow upright may be left on, in order that it may be trained into the form of the remainder of the branches, of which we shall speak afterwards. Each coarse, thick shoot should be cut off, and that, too, close to the branch on which it grows, as such coarse, overgrown shoots seldom or never produce any fruit: but only, like themselves, coarse and worse than useless shoots. As to the quantity of branches and shoots to be left in the tree, there are a variety of opinions, even amongst men who have had much experience in the culture of prize Gooseberry trees. Some will leave as many as four shoots on one branch; whilst others will only leave one at the end of each branch. He who advocates the former argues "that he is surer of a crop;" but, on the other hand, he is not able to grow the fruit so large as he who has less fruit and less branches for his tree to support. He who leaves only one shoot on each branch says, "If I can only get them *sound* (uninjured by frost), they will grow till the day they are ripe;" but, on the other hand, there is such uncertainty about preventing them from being injured by frost, that we think this is not the most judicious way of pruning, unless protection is given to each bush in the spring, by placing canvas over them during frosty weather, after the bloom begins to show, till about the 17th of May, if the frosts continue so long. We prefer leaving two shoots upon the stronger branches of the tree, and one shoot on the weaker ones. The shoots in all cases must be shortened, leaving them about five or six inches long. If this is done, with proper management afterwards, you will be able, in an ordinary spring, to secure a crop, and grow them large too.

Whether you cut with knife or shears, the shoot cut will, in all cases, die down to the first bud below the wound; and, besides, there is much more ease in cutting with shears than what there is with a knife; not only so, but you are able to cut a tree in half the time.

Those who want to propagate for future stocks should collect carefully the very finest shoots as soon as the thinning is completed. They may be at once named, tied in a bundle, and, "heeled;" or, what is better, trimmed and planted out at once. It is customary with some to put them in a shady place; but this is bad practice, and only justifiable when the cuttings are made late in spring, and scarcely then.

The cuttings should be as strong as possible, and about twelve or fourteen inches long. All the buds should be pruned clean away, with the exception of the topmost four, previously to planting. The cuttings may be put in any time from November to the beginning of February, choosing a shady border for them. They should be in rows a foot apart, the cuttings about six inches asunder. Nurserymen plant thicker; the cottager, however, will do well to have a little more room, for thereby his young plants will be stouter. By the next autumn there will be at least two good shoots on each cutting; two good ones will be enough, and these must be pruned down to about four eyes or buds on each shoot. Unless particularly wanted to plant in their final stations, they should, by all means, remain another season in the cutting beds; they will then be strong bushes, and deserving a permanent place.

Training.—This is done by what we call "hooks and props." These are chiefly made of hazel sticks, varying in length from eighteen to twenty-four inches. *Hooks* are made by cutting them off close to a small branch, immediately below the branch, leaving about one inch and a half of it on to form the hook. *Props* are made by cutting off all the small twigs, leaving the top something like a hay-fork, only the prong should not be above an inch and a half long. The form of the tree to be trained should be what is generally termed a "table trellis." The branches should be trained horisontally from the bole, so that the tree should be as nearly as possible flat on the top. This is done in order that the fruit may hang down on the under side of the tree, without being in danger of being injured when growing, by hanging against the branches, or by coming in contact with the thorns growing on the trees. Great care ought to be exercised in placing the hooks and props, that the buds be not injured or destroyed. When a shoot grows nearly upright, and it is necessary it should be brought down to make it uniform with the others, it should be done by a little at a time; for if done all at once it will be in danger of breaking. This bringing down is effected by thrusting the hook a little further into the ground every now and then, till the shoot is brought to its proper position.

Summer Training is too often neglected, even by men who have had the benefit of long experience. This is done by taking off, with a penknife, the extreme ends of the young shoots that are growing near the bole of the tree, or, in fact, throughout the branches, with the exception of a few of the shoots that are near the extremities of the branches. These should be preserved with all possible care, for in these young shoots are the future hopes of the grower. When the young shoots have grown to a good length, they should be protected from being blown off, by either placing sticks on each side of them, or tying them to a stick with a little bass matting.

Manuring.—This should be done in March (or earlier if the buds begin to swell), and must be performed in the following manner:—Take off the soil round the tree an inch and a half or two inches deep; but the soil must be taken off farther from the roots by six or ten inches, which can be easily ascertained by the size of the tree. As a general rule, the roots will be as far spread as the top, or nearly so. Having taken off the soil, manure must be laid over the whole of the surface from which the soil has been removed, but the greatest weight of it should be placed farther than the roots extend, *as the ends of the roots should find the manure, and not the manure the ends of the roots.*

The Caterpillar.—The ordinary mode of disposing of this pest is to shake the bushes and collect the caterpillars. Some persons use hellebore powder, which is said to be very efficient; others use foxglove, or digitalis, which, at the time the fly prevails, is abundant in our lanes or road sides. This is made into a strong tea by boiling it in water, and the bushes are watered or syringed with it. It is also stated that fresh-slaked lime is completely destructive to the caterpillar, if the leaf is wet at the time of applying it; some persons, we have known to use it as early as three o'clock on a dewy morning. Hunting for the flies and searching for the eggs, are also practised; likewise hand-picking the caterpillars when very small. Prevention, however, is allowed to be better than cure; and we would therefore advise, as a precautionary measure, the opening of a trench one foot in depth at the extremity of the roots, and then scraping or shovelling the surface soil from over the roots for nearly three inches in depth into the trench, in the hopes of burying and destroying the chrysalis, which, probably, are not imbedded much deeper. The paring of soil should be well trampled down, and the occasion may be seized for manuring the roots in the circle or line excavated. Salt and soot might be used to cover the parings before trampling them down, or other strong matters, which are at once fatal to insect life, and a manure to the bushes.

An effectual method for preventing the caterpillar was practised by the late Mr. Robert Hogg, of Bogan Green, Berwickshire, which consists in simply covering the surface of the ground round the bushes with a layer of bark from the tan-yard, either in the autumn or early in spring; and this seems to have such an effect on the insect in its chrysalis state as effectually to destroy it. As we have known this to be successful in every instance where it has been applied we can confidently recommend it.

LIST OF SELECT GOOSEBERRIES.

Warrington.—Hairy Red.

Pitmaston Green Gage. — Green: this is noted for shrivelling in the raisin character on the tree.

Taylor's Bright Venus. — White; also a shriveller.

Coe's Late Red.—Accounted a good late berry.

Champagne Red.—Very rich, and of upright growth.

Champagne Yellow.—Very rich, and upright.

The above we can safely recommend for trellis purposes, or, indeed, for general culture, as dessert fruit.

Rockwood's Early Yellow.—Early.

Leigh's Rifleman. — Red hairy; rather late; great bearer.

Green Walnut. — Green smooth; great bearer.

Whitesmith (Woodward's).—White; good flavour.

Keens' Seedling.—Much like Warrington, and rather earlier.

Roaring Lion.—Red smooth; great bearer.

Glenton Green.—A very good hairy green.

Heart of Oak (Massey's).—Green smooth; good bearer.

NUTS.

Varieties.—The kinds worthy of cultivation may be classed under two heads,—1, *Filberts*; 2, *Nuts*; the remaining portion being for the most part seedlings, not far removed from the wild Nut. Some of these kinds are propagated by grafting on the common Hazel, others are reared by suckers. The *Spanish Cob* is preferred by some, as a stock, on account of the strength, &c.; but we feel pretty well assured that the whole would answer better (as part of a dwarfing system) for small gardens, propagated by cuttings, and trained accordingly.

As special kinds we would cultivate the following :—

The White Filbert—first rate.

The Red Filbert—interesting on account of the pink coating inside, and scarcely inferior to the former.

The Frizzled Filbert—very ornamental.

The Cosford—large, a good bearer, and thin shelled.

The Cobs—very large, upright in growth.

The Nottingham Prolific—a dwarf variety which comes very early into bearing, and very prolific.

Culture.—Nuts, like most other fruits, "run too much to wood." This is to be seen in the ordinary hedge, where Hazels may be found which seldom bear; whilst the uncultivated, unpruned Hazel of the wood is notorious, when in a situation exposed to the light, and possessing some age, for abundant crops.

The cultivation, therefore, of Nuts, is by no means difficult; indeed, they are more likely to be injured by over-cultivation than otherwise. They should, in all cases, be trained to a single stem; for the production of suckers,* or rather, the permitting them to remain, is most injurious to their future success. Suckers will spring up, and they must every year be removed. The stems should be from half a yard to two feet in height, and the head should be formed after the manner of dwarf Apple trees.

It must be remembered that the fruit is mostly produced from the extremities of the shoots; for the Nut loves light as well as most other fruits. After carrying up a clear stem, therefore, the next point is to form a proper head, and this must be accomplished in the same way as in the ordinary Red Currant bush—by selecting four or five shoots which are well placed. Such shoots must, of course, be obtained by heading back—that is cutting them off near to the stem; and in order to obtain a sufficient number, the operation may require to be repeated. The middle of the bush must be kept rather open, for the sake of admitting light to all parts of the tree, or rather, bush, for it should not be permitted to grow above the height of five or six feet in small gardens. The keeping them thus dwarf involves some considerations connected with soil, root-pruning, &c., about which we will presently offer advice. The trees having formed sufficient heads, annual pruning, more or less, must be resorted to; for no fruit tree answers better to judicious pruning than the Nut. This operation must not be performed until February.

The Nut produces both male and female blossoms separately, but on the same bush. The male blossoms are well known by their gay, dangling appearance, and by the yellow dust they shed on being handled; this dust is the fertilizing pollen. The female blossoms, on the contrary, are so obscure as to require a close examination in order to find them. When in full blossom they are of a lively pink colour, and appear like little brushes at the tips of the side-shoots produced by mature wood. The female blossoms do not appear until a few days after the males have opened.

Now, it so happens that trees at a certain age, or under certain conditions of culture, will sometimes produce either almost entirely male blossoms, or otherwise female. Those with the males alone must of necessity be barren for that year; but, if only female blossoms appear, branches should be cut, bearing

* *Suckers*—Shoots from the roots.

catkins of male blossoms, and suspended or tied amongst those possessing female blossoms. Occasionally, too, on a sunny day, a branch of the dusty catkins may be carried in the hand like a rod, and brushed lightly over the tips of the female-bearing bushes.

The fruit is produced, principally, on the former year's wood, and generally from compact side-shoots, the produce of leaders of a short-jointed and mature appearance. Such lateral fruit-bearing branches may be induced in greater abundance by shortening back strong shoots of this character. Thinning out, however, is one of the principal matters; for, unless this be duly attended to, the bush will become crowded with worse than useless spray,—it will also obstruct the light from the bearing portions, as well as hinder the circulation of air. A great deal of small spray will be produced on the inner portions of the branches; and this, although of the character of bearing wood, is generally unfruitful and must therefore be mostly pruned away. Any one who observes the habit of the Nut closely will soon perceive that the shrubs are most disposed to bear at the extremities of the branches, thus evincing their partiality to plenty of light and air. These, then, are the portions of the tree where the eye must be directed as to fruit-bearing properties. The leaders, however, must not be encouraged so thickly as to cross each other; and, in order to prevent the lower portion of the head from becoming naked, a good, strong, well-placed shoot may be occasionally encouraged, heading it back in due time, in order to keep it producing side-branches, &c. After duly thinning away superfluous shoots, the principal leaders should be all shortened. As a general rule, we would say, remove about a quarter of the length; this, as before observed, will cause the tree to produce abundance of side-spray, from which, in the future spring, the fruiting shoots may be selected.

Soil.—Almost any light loamy soil will answer; it should, however, more incline to sand than clay. There is no occasion to use any manure for Nuts when first planted, but merely to dig or trench the ground deeply; and if the soil is turfy, so much the better: the turf may be trenched down nearly half a yard. The main thing in the majority of soils is to guard against over-luxuriance: for such will, in some kinds, cause the production of only catkins or male blossoms. When, however, the trees get old, or become very weak, which is sometimes the case, top-dressings should be applied occasionally, the same as to other fruit trees.

Planting.—Nuts are not always planted in a continuous way in small gardens. When such is the case, if in a single row, about eight feet apart will suffice; if, however, there are more rows than one, and they are side by side, we should place the rows ten feet apart, and the plants eight feet apart in the row.

We have known them succeed to admiration on the marginal borders, alternating with Apples and other fruits. A row of Nut and Gooseberry bushes would answer well if the Nuts were trained with a stem a yard high. They would then assist in protecting the Gooseberries from late spring-frosts.

Root-pruning.—We may here observe, that root-pruning may be practised when the trees are too gross. We have performed the operation ourselves, more than twenty years ago, on a whole line of bushes, which grew in a clayey soil, and produced very powerful rods. This operation was severe, and it brought them into capital bearing in the course of a year: it was accompanied by a severe pruning and shortening.

THE PEACH AND NECTARINE.

As these are neither more nor less than two varieties of the same species, the same mode of treatment is applicable to both, and the same remarks which are made upon the one bear equally upon the other.

Planting.—The station being properly prepared according to our directions on that head, the soil should be flattened a little, or rather, should be formed with a trifling amount of roundness; the highest part of this roundness being where the collar of the tree is to be stationed. Such roundness, however, must be trifling; the only reason for any being that we deem it necessary that the point of every root should incline slightly downwards. Roots inserted with their ends somewhat pointing up will be liable to breed suckers—a thing to be studiously avoided. The soil must not be dug out, but the tree set on the ordinary ground level; for when the newly-made station settles, it will be just of the necessary depth.

The roots must now be spread forth, or rather, trained, with as much precision as the branches, no two touching each other. A barrowful of very mellow loam, and very old vegetable soil, should be at hand, well mixed; and handsful of this will serve to bed the roots in their positions. After some more of the same is scattered over the roots, the ordinary soil may be filled in, but it will be well to have some half-rotten manure, or leaf soil, to blend with this in the act of filling, in order to induce fibrous surface roots.

Pruning.—To understand this operation the better, it will be well to state what are the prime objects, viz.:—

Firstly.—To *thin out*, or remove, superfluous shoots, in order to insure sufficient light and a due circulation of air to the remainder.

Secondly.—To *shorten back*, for the twofold purpose of removing unripe or immature portions, and of inducing plenty of successive shoots lower down the tree.

For illustration, we will suppose an established tree, which has been planted five or six years. The nails being all unloosed, excepting a few to hold the principal shoots, operations should commence at the bottom of the tree, near the collar.* Here it is that a watchful eye must be keenly exercised at each returning pruning season, in order to preserve and continue a due succession of rising shoots from the lowest portion of the tree. It is evident that if the young shoots at this point are not taken care of, the lower part of the tree will become barren, and a part of the wall wasted; besides which, the tree will not be so ornamental. It frequently happens that some of the young shoots in this part are inferior in character; and very frequently shoots which spring from the collar, and reach a yard or so, possess a fine young shoot lower down, which is fitter to become the leading shoot of that portion of the tree than the one already existing. When such is the case it becomes necessary to cut away the older portion; this must be done with a clean cut, and nearly close to the point from which the future leader comes. However, the first point is to cut away any cankered or diseased shoots, and then to shorten judiciously those at the lowest level which can be obtained. It may here be observed, that no fruit should ever be permitted to grow for the space of a foot from the top of the collar on any given shoot. If fruit is produced at these lower extremities, it is always inferior, and only serves to oppress a portion of the tree which ought always to be kept as a nursery for young shoots, to keep the tree well furnished. By "shortening judiciously," we mean cutting back the lowest-placed young shoots *as low as possible*, provided a few good eyes, or buds, are left, and that such shoots are not required to fill existing blanks in the walls.

Such, then, when pruned back, may be considered a guarantee against the tree becoming "naked."

We come now to bearing wood; and here the main point is selection, supposing there are more young shoots than are required. In making a choice, distinguish between the different kinds of young shoots, for there are at least three kinds on many Peach and Nectarine trees, and on most there are two.

We may characterise them as follows:—1st. Perfect bearing shoots; 2nd. Exhausted shoots; 3rd. Barren shoots.

It will here be understood that the above refers merely to the *young* spray.

1. *Perfect bearing shoots.*—These, in general may be known by the majority of the eyes or buds seated on them being threefold, that is to say, in threes. When such is the case, the two outer ones are almost always blossom-buds, and the central one a wood bud. All such is deemed wood of first-rate character, and

* *Collar*—The place where the main stem begins to fork into branches.

it is the aim of the experienced cultivator to secure as much of this as possible.

2. *Exhausted shoots.*—We are not assured that this is the most proper title to give this class of shoots. One thing, however, we do know, that when such shoots begin to prevail generally over a tree, it is a pretty sure sign of what medical men would term a "breaking up of the constitution." These have for the most part a single bud at a joint, and that bud a solitary blossom-bud. Such could not be readily distinguished in early autumn pruning, by a novice, from the next class; and this is a reason why amateurs, who prune for themselves, had better defer it until the early part of February. Wood of this character, if left on the tree, has seldom vigour enough to produce fine fruit. Indeed, such wood not unfrequently "sets" its blossom more freely than the preceding class; and it is by no means unusual, at the thinning period in the end of May, to meet with shoots of this class with a score of fruit on, yet no leading bud or growing shoot. This fruit exhausts the tree much, and eventually falls off.

3. *Barren shoots.*—These, again, possess solitary buds; they are, however, usually late growths, and may readily be known by their pale and unripe character; or they are the production of over-luxuriant trees, and serve to denote a tree of gross condition, or vigour misplaced. The difference between these and the preceding section is at once apparent at spring pruning. The solitary buds of the former become very plump of a sudden, whilst these do not appear to increase at all. Wood of this character, *if ripened*, is frequently of eminent service, inasmuch as it serves to keep up the main fabric of the tree; and although not bearing wood itself, it is capable of producing fine bearing shoots for the ensuing year. Some of this must, therefore, be occasionally reserved, especially if a blank, or space bare of shoots, in any part be anticipated; for, be it understood, much in Peach pruning depends on a far-seeing eye, or skilful anticipations.

We now revert to the pruning. The main business is to reserve a series of shoots all over the tree of class No. 1; and where this class cannot be obtained, to secure enough of No. 3; the No. 2 class may in most cases be considered a last resort. So much for selection. We must now advert to the shortening of the young spray. Only two reasons exist for shortening at all; the one is, where shoots overtake each other, in which case some must be made to retreat, or the tree would soon be all confusion. The other is founded on the necessity of removing unripe portions. The first case any mere tyro can judge for himself; the second requires some care. A little practice, however, will soon teach the uninitiated the difference between the two. The principal criterion is hardness. A practical man would soon distinguish them, although blindfolded, by means of his knife.

Colour has something to do in this matter. Ripe wood is generally of a brownish colour—unripe, of a pale and delicate green. We would advise those who do not understand this to request some gardener to give them a shoot or two of each character; and by the time they have exercised their pruning-knife in cutting these shoots to pieces, they will have learned this portion of Peach pruning. In ordinary cases, about one-third has to be cut

away: nevertheless, it is not easy to lay down a general maxim as to shortening, for it becomes necessary, for the sake of successional wood, to shorten more severely at the lower parts of the tree, decreasing it in amount progressively upwards. We have added a sketch, which may assist in illustrating the foregoing description.

On referring to the preceding sketch, it will be seen that the round black dots denote the lowest shoots on the tree to which we directed attention in the outset. The cross-marks, in like manner, denote the shortenings by the knife; and it must be remarked that these are *by no means opposite each other*, but at different distances. The due observance of this principle in shortening prevents much confusion, tending to keep the young spray about to be produced well divided.

Disbudding.—The first care is to rub off all those coarse-looking young shoots which stand straight out from the wall, and look as though they were ambitious of becoming individual trees. The sooner they are removed the better; nevertheless, when the trees are weak such will scarcely be produced. We consider that their free production is by no means to be deprecated; they merely denote a very healthy root action, not only at the time, but of a retrospective character. All they want is judicious management and a little adroitness, to turn the flow of sap into more legitimate courses or channels.

After slipping such off with the finger and thumb, the next point is to see if any young spray is growing behind the old twigs in a position to become distorted or crushed between the branches and the wall. These, also, may be rubbed off; but, be it understood, such operations are not obliged to be completed in one day; they may be made to extend over a whole fortnight. Another caution here becomes necessary. If any vacant or naked spaces exist on the contiguous parts of the wall, some even of those crooked or gross portions must be retained; for it is better to have a shoot or branch of this character than a barren portion of walling. These things being duly carried out, the next point is to see if even good-looking and well-placed young shoots are not too much crowded. This is sure to be the case if the tree is healthy; and here comes the tug of war; here it is that much discretion and intelligence of a prospective character are requisite. Our practice is to commence at the extremity of every shoot or branch, tracing it from thence downwards. We first remove every side-shoot of young spray which appears likely to enter into competition with the leader; and this will in general cause every young shoot within four inches of the point to be stripped off. No two shoots of young spray should grow side by side if possible; they should, at the ultimate thinning or disbudding, stand in a regular series successively, from the collar to the extremities, all over the tree. Still, as before observed, this cannot be finally accomplished until after the lapse of many weeks.

One point of great importance we here would impress on the minds of beginners in the art of disbudding; and that is, to be sure and reserve all the *lowest-growing* young spray all over the tree. This it is which prevents trees from becoming what gardeners term "naked." Of course, in fan-training, which is the most general mode (and certainly equal to any other, provided the other points of management are based on sound principles), all the branches, by radiating from centres, form a fork like the letter V. Well, then, every young spray which is situated the lowest in this letter V should be carefully preserved, and may, in order to convey a just idea of the ultimate design, be termed a "breeder," signifying that it is in a position to produce, by pruning, young shoots in future seasons to keep up the fabric of the tree.

May Stopping.—The course we are about to recommend is not only requisite as tending to improve the character of the fruit in the *present season*, but the welfare and stability of the tree in succeeding years. Although, at first sight, the process may appear troublesome or expensive, it is, in reality, an economical procedure in the end.

Stopping is practised, in general, for one or other of the following reasons, or for any two or more of them in combination. *Firstly*, to check over-luxuriant shoots. *Secondly*, to concentrate the sap in a given shoot. *Thirdly*, to give room to other competing shoots. *Fourthly*, to check a too late root action.

After a slight disbudding, it will be found, on examining healthy Peach or Nectarine trees, that certain gross-looking shoots thrust themselves forth from various portions of the tree, more especially from young and over-excited subjects. Such shoots very often spring forth just below a branch which has borne a heavy crop of fruit, and which has thereby become somewhat exhausted; in which case there can be little doubt that some degree of constriction, or partial shrinking of the vessels, has taken place. These gluttons, then, if suffered to remain unstopped, will, in most cases, cut away the supplies from the old bearing shoots, and lead to the necessity of their being cut off in a very short period—a process fraught with danger to the stability of the tree, and which, in all cases, may be prevented.

Let us, then, impress on the minds of all those who are taking their first steps in Peach and Nectarine culture, not only the propriety, but the necessity, of pinching off betimes the points of all those gross shoots which show a disposition to shoot into lateral branches. Where such a disposition exists, it will generally manifest itself by the time they are about six inches in length, which will occur, in the main, from the begining of May until the beginning of June; after which, stopping of another kind and for other reasons, will commence.

Autumn Stopping.—One of the last proceedings which we have to recommend, with regard to the summer culture of the Peach and the Nectarine, is a somewhat general pinching or stopping of the young shoots about the first week in August. This is a course not generally practised; and is, when trees are hard worked, or lean in condition, more honoured in the breach than the observance.

Stopping at such a period tends to sustain the full capacity of the principal leaves, and the functions of the tree henceforth become almost entirely elaborative.

SELECT PEACHES AND NECTARINES.

The varieties enumerated in the following list are given under the names by which they are most generally known, and are placed as nearly as possible in the order of their ripening, such only as are truly good and useful being selected.

PEACHES.

Early Anne.—Beginning of August; its earliness is its principal merit.
Acton Scot.—End of August: an excellent early kind.
Pourprée Hâtive.—End of August.
Malta, also called the *Italian*, or *Pêche de Malte.*—End of August, and beginning of September.
Grosse Mignonne.—Ripe end of August and beginning of September. Excellent.
Royal George.—Beginning of September.
Noblesse.—Beginning of September.
Bellegarde.—Middle of September: keeps well.
Late Admirable.—End of September.
Walburton Admirable.—End September, or beginning of October.

NECTARINES.

Violette Hâtive.
Balgowan.
Elruge.
Murrey.
Roman.

THE PEAR.

As it is altogether as a garden and not as an orchard fruit that we intend to treat of the Pear, the instructions contained in the following observations will have reference to the growth of the tree as a dwarf, a pyramid, or as trained against a wall, or espaliers. We shall, therefore before proceeding to the subject of training and pruning, say a few words on the stocks which are best adapted for the purpose.

Stocks and Soil.—Pears are grown on two kinds of stocks— the ordinary Pear stock, otherwise called a free stock, and on the Quince.

The Pear stock produces a stronger and longer-enduring tree; much longer, also, in coming to a bearing state. It will also grow and thrive on soils on which the Quince will scarcely exist. This, therefore, is the most proper stock for ordinary orchard Pears. A Quince stock is notorious for causing the tree to assume a dwarf and bushy character. This is a mere consequence of a much less vigorous root action. For this very reason the trees come much sooner into bearing; but they require a much more generous soil.

It so happens that some kinds of Pears are of delicate growth, or they are such very fine bearers, that it becomes advisable, even under a dwarfing system, to graft them on the free or Pear stock, in order to induce a more vigorous growth.

Almost any ordinary soil, if not too sandy, will grow the Pear on the free stock. We have known them succeed to admiration on both sandy and clayey loams, on soils of a chalkey character, and on shingly or gravelly soils, provided there was some degree of adhesiveness in their constitution. The Quince stock, on the contrary, will never answer on hot or sandy soils; and where the Quince plant (ungrafted) will not succeed, it is vain to think of planting it when grafted. The soil in which, above all others, the Quince will both luxuriate and continue in permanency is a soil which possesses the features of alluvium.* We do not mean that it

---

* *Alluvium* is fine fertile soil, such as is found in valleys, washed down during the course of many years from the higher-lying lands.

must be alluvial soil, but that the well-known texture of that material must at least be imitated.

When it is taken into consideration how small a quantity of soil will maintain a dwarf Pear on a Quince stock, it will readily appear that it is quite practicable so to improve the soil in any small garden as to adapt it to the Quince stock. A compost of this kind may be readily got together. The furrowings of low or clay soils might form the principal staple; in addition to which, abundance of old, rotten vegetables, tree leaves, or even old and spent tan might be added, and a good sprinkling of any fine sand. These materials, collected a few months previously, and turned a couple of times, would doubtless form a proper compost for the Quince. We have even seen ditch scourings in the neighbourhood of trees, which had lain on the bank to mellow for some time, which would alone have been complete or nearly so, for the cultivation of the Quince. A little very old manure would be a benefit, as it is not easy to over-excite the Quince. As to quantity, we should say that six wheelbarrowsful of this mixed soil would be amply sufficient for a tree on the dwarfing system. The holes should not be made deep by any means. Half a yard in depth of soil will suffice for either the Quince or the Pear stock, and this should rest, if possible, on impervious materials, such as stones, bricks, or hard-rammed cinder ashes.

Disbudding and Pinching.—Everybody knows that Pears in general, on the free stock, have a tendency to produce too much breast-wood in June and July, some, indeed, almost up to September. Now, there is really no necessity for *compelling* the free stock to produce so much gross wood. This fault is not in the tree, but in the planter. There is no doubt that many of our stronger-habited Pears would succeed better in a compost one-half of which was stones than in richly-manured soil. Perhaps burnt clay would be a useful thing, nearly in the state of brick. Amateurs would do well to try such an experiment.

The first proceeding which Pears in a trained condition are subjected to is disbudding. This is performed during the end of April. It consists in going over every main branch, and totally removing those gross shoots which may be considered as having a tendency to encourage an over-powerful root action. It may here be understood, that in general, although the removal of such a class of shoots has a tendency for awhile to throw increased strength into those which remain, yet that the same proceeding also has a tendency to check rampant growth, or grossness in the general system of the tree. If any of the trees at this time are very luxuriant, do not hesitate, if time can be spared, to open a trench, and remove a slight portion of the extremities of the root fibres, although this must be done with more caution now than late in the autumn; for we consider that the best period to root-prune bearing trees.

In the very beginning of June it will be found that the young spray on many of the trees has become too crowded to give fair play to either the fruit or the shoots necessary to be reserved, and we deem it necessary to go over and thin them. Some persons may think that such operations necessarily involve much skill or science; but the fact is, any tidy labourer can do it. Let the operator, then, perform this at twice, *at least*, say in the beginning of June and in the end; but in doing so he must *select*, that is to say, he must remove unfruitful-looking spray, and reserve that of the opposite character. Long-jointed shoots, pale and watery-looking, and fast ramblers, are known to be of the former class. Those of the latter, of course, approach an opposite condition; and the difficulty is, since they merge into each other, to distinguish. This is what puzzles our amateurs so much. Ultimately, this reserve wood is chiefly tied down to the main shoots. After these things are done practise "stopping," and this is done at twice; say in the early part of July, and again in August. Our practice is at this period to pinch or stop *all* the points of the young shoots, excepting those which are considered leaders at the extremities of the branches. Young trees, however, just establishing themselves, may be left growing, in order to obtain strength to cover the wall, fence, or treillage in the succeeding year. The operator should first go over the tree carefully, and see what short-jointed shoots can be *tied down*, or otherwise trained, without darkening the spur adjoining them; for all such may be secured. This being done, and their points pinched, he may at once prune back all the rest to three or four eyes, leaving as many leaves at the base as he can without shading the spurs. Let it, however, be remembered, during this operation, that the whole process is carried out merely in order to admit the sun to the embryo fruit-buds of the ensuing year.

Winter Pruning.—If due attention is paid to the summer pruning in the way of pinching, as described above, little will be left for winter operations, except to shorten the terminal and some of the lateral shoots. On this subject it is impossible to give very definite instructions, particularly as regards the length to which these shoots are to be pruned, as that must be entirely regulated both by the vigour of the tree and the habit of the variety. The great object in Pear pruning is to develope as many spurs as possible; and if the shoot is pruned too closely, those buds which were intended to produce spurs will be developed into shoots. The pruner must, therefore, exercise his judgment on this subject, and endeavour to ascertain from the previous year's growth the disposition the tree has for the natural production of these spurs. Should there appear to be any tardiness in this respect, then the shoot should be pruned close; but if there is a free production of spurs, merely remove a small portion from the tip of each shoot. These, and the removal of all misplaced shoots, or such as appear to be overcrowding the tree, will constitute all that is necessary to be done during the winter pruning.

We shall now proceed to notice some of the best modes of training.

Pyramidal Standards.—These are generally purchased from our nurseries with the framework of a pyramid already commenced; that is to say, one perpendicular shoot and a few developed side-branches; the lower extending from six to eight inches, and another series or two narrowing gradually to the point. Such trees, after planting and commencing growth, must have some attention immediately. It will be found that, when luxuriating freely, more shoots will be produced in some portions of the tree than it is expedient to retain ultimately; and as for leaving crowded spray for winter pruning, it is nonsense. The cultivator of pyramidal Pears must, from the first, keep in view the chief objects sought to be attained by this mode, which may be stated as follows:

1st. To grow a complete collection of Pears in a narrow compass.

2nd. To reduce them to thorough control.

3rd. To insure liberal crops.

4th. By uniformity in appearance, and general management, to render them as ornamental as useful, and to convey an idea of system, and the triumphs of gardening skill.

The one great principle on which the pyramidal mode turns as to practical routine is, that the culture shall be so conducted that the advancing tier of branches shall not be permitted to overhang, shade, and render barren the lower tier. In order to carry out such a plan, the shoots should be watched during their most active growth, and the month of June is, of all others, the most important period for controlling irregularities. Of course, the practitioner will desire to extend the base of his pyramid as much as is consistent with fruitful habits; but a limit must be assigned to the extension of rapid-growing shoots, although at the base. As a general rule, we may observe, that as soon as any shoot has extended from eight to ten inches, the point may be removed. This is done for a double reason; first, in checking the most powerful, to throw power into weaker shoots, and thereby contribute ultimately to the symmetry of the tree, and also to induce a degree of maturity or solidification betimes, effecting that great object termed *ripening the wood.* Besides limiting the extension of the lateral and permanent branches, there will, occasionally, spring a host of inferior spray from various parts of the tree; and this, if not required to carry out the trainer's object, must be pinched back as soon as three or four eyes in length; and the probability is that embryo buds will be engendered towards the base, which will ultimately tend to stud the branches with blossom-buds in clusters close to the chief branches, and, of course, from the character and form of the trees, give the most complete control as concerns protecting matters, whether against frost or the depredations of birds, &c.

The Umbrella Mode.—This title expresses that form which consists of one straight stem with the shoots trained downwards from a centre. This mode of training is tolerably well adapted to some kinds, principally those with slender and supple shoots; those of a gross and stiff habit, and inclined to perpendicular growth, are rather inapt; they are constantly at war with this principle. However, we must try and deal with them. A tree of this kind, when selected, should have a clean, strong, self-supporting stem, of from three to five feet in height, according to the taste and designs of the cultivators, and should possess from four to six or more shoots at the summit; but these shoots should be of the last year's wood, or such as will readily bend. Of course, some kind of trellis will be requisite, at least for half a dozen years at first. Many fine trees are trained on supple sticks out of a coppice, such as Oak or Hazel; but it is far better, and looks by far more artistic, to use an umbrella form of wire, such as we have all seen applied to the training of Tree Roses, but, of course, in shape and size adapted to the Pear.

The training rods may radiate from the centre, and in outline may be the segment of a circle. It would, doubtless, however, be an improvement on the old plan to adopt two circles of wire at the top, from the outer of which the radiating lines might proceed. Thus, one circle might be established at four inches from the apex, and another (parallel) at about five inches from that; and from the latter may radiate the downward curving wires. This will, in a measure, obviate the crowding which is sure to take place near the top, owing to the acute angle from which the radiating wires proceed when they start immediately from the apex. The wires may start at about eight inches distance from the outer circles, and by the time they reach the ground, or nearly so, they will be about one foot apart. It is best to let them all terminate on a horizontal rod, at about four inches or so above the ground level; this gives strength and consistency to the whole, and keeps the shoots and fruit from being splashed.

On such wires, then, or bended sticks in a similar form, the first leaders must be carefully trained as soon as they can be handled, getting one on each as soon as possible; but this is not always accomplished in the first year. If there be but a limited number of shoots—say four—they should be divided equally around.

The first training will, of course, take place during the winter pruning; and, if the head is deficient of shoots, one, two, or more, if necessary, of the very strongest shoots must be pruned back to about four or five inches, in order to multiply the leaders for the next year. If the wire circles are established they may be pruned back to the outer circle. Throughout the summer the growing shoots must have attention, more especially during June and July; and in another year or two they will need disbudding, pinching, &c., as other trained Pears.

The Old Trellised Espalier.—This form is now almost out of date in the case of the Pear; at least, in our principal gardens; but there is much merit in the form, if well carried out, as to certain kinds. A young tree should be selected for the purpose, having a good stem, and, if possible, a pair or two of side branches at distances suitable to the lines of the trellis. Trees of this description being planted about twelve or fifteen feet apart, a leader must be preserved until the height of the trellis is reached, when, of course, it must be stopped. The whole business is to get every horizontal rod or rail covered with a main branch as soon as possible; and to this end high culture, by a little extra appliance, may be pursued for a couple of years or so, in order to force developments as speedily as possible; for by such practice it is possible to lay on three tiers of shoots in one summer. This may be accomplished by securing a very luxuriant leader, and by pinching it once, or even twice.

LIST OF SELECT PEARS.

DESSERT.

Citron des Carmes.—July.
Jargonelle.—August.
Beurré Giffard.—Middle of August.
Williams' Bon Chrétien.—August and September.
Beurré d'Amanlis.—September.
Flemish Beauty.—September, should be gathered before it is fully ripe.
Fondante d'Automne.—September and October.
Louise Bonne of Jersey.—October.
Seckle.—It ripens in October.
Beurré de Capiaumont.—It ripens in October.
Marie Louise.—October and November.
Althorp Crassane.—October and November.
Duchesse d'Augoulême.—October and November.
Beurré Diel.—November and December.
Chaumontel.—November to March.
Hacon's Incomparable.—November to January.
Passe Colmar.—December and January.
Glou Morceau.—December to February.
Winter Nelis.—November to February.
Knight's Monarch.—January.
Easter Beurré.—January to March.
Beurré de Rance.—February to May.
Joséphine de Malines.—February to May.
Ne plus Meuris.—January to March.
Urbaniste.—October.
Thompson's.—November.
Zéphirin Gregoire.—Ripe in December and January.

KITCHEN.

Catillac, Gilogil, Verulam.

THE PLUM.

Soil.—A good sound yet mellow loam will suit the majority of Plums. Nevertheless, there must be something more than the mere matter of soil which affects them, for we find the Damson thriving in our north-western counties on clayey soils, on sandy loams, and even on peats, provided such are properly drained. From these facts, we have long since been persuaded that the amount of moisture in the atmosphere has something to do with the question. However, be that as it may, some pains must be taken where the soil is of a very inferior character. As before observed, with regard to Pears, Peaches, &c., it is indeed expedient to make what we have termed "stations" for them.

Pruning.—It must be known to most of our readers, that Plums, like many other fruit trees, vary much in habit; some, as the Washington, Magnum Bonum, &c., if planted in a very liberal soil, producing young wood almost adapted for fishing-rods. Others, again, as the Impèratrice section, being of a very delicate habit, are in age apt to become too weak. Of course there will be an intermediate class, and such may be represented by the ordinary Orleans, although the latter sometimes produces very gross wood when young. Now, there is no fruit tree in which gross wood is more inimical to the proper development of the fruitful parts than the Plum. In trained trees, when young, and the soil unfortunately rich, the trees but too frequently have a tendency to produce these "robbers" in several places between the bole and the extremity of the branches; the sure tendency of such is to interrupt and appropriate the ascending sap, and thus to starve the fruit on the portions beyond them.

The first thing the pruner can do is to remove all those very gross shoots that have unluckily escaped the growth-pruner's finger and thumb—such shoots in the large section as extend a half-yard or so in length. If they are leaders, of course they must be retained; but anywhere along the stem, as side or supernumerary shoots, they may be cut *clear away*, not leaving a morsel behind. In the moderate-growing kinds, what may be termed gross shoots will not be quite so long or so thick, but they may readily be distinguished. This refers to trees in which the "growth pruning" has been neglected; where such has been properly carried out, there will be little for the rest-pruner more than simply a slight thinning out.

Now, in the former case, whether the trees possess any gross shoots or not, if there be too many shoots, it is obvious that some must be removed. The pruner's business in such cases is to first survey his tree to ascertain its strength, whether in parts or in the whole, for it sometimes happens that one portion of a tree is too strong, whilst another is too weak. In thinning out, then—into which process the chief of the labours may be resolved —he must first assume a maximum of strength as to those shoots which are to be retained, and having done this in his mind, he may at once proceed to remove all above this point, which may be considered supernumeraries. On the tying down or succession system—by which term we shall designate it, as soon as we can fasten it on our readers' memories—we make a point of reserving all the short-jointed shoots, if possible, and sometimes in the Plum, if the wood is small, we lay them in so thickly, that the base of one shoot is not more than three inches from the base of another. By base, we mean the point on the leader whence the young shoot proceeds.

The gross shoots having been cut clear away, and the remainder thinned duly out, little remains to be done with old or bearing trees; the leading shoots must be laid in at full length, and all suckers extirpated. If the trees are, indeed, too gross, let the operator at once root-prune.

Trained Plums generally produce some coarse breast-shoots at those points of the branches where, from training circumstances, the branch is made to assume an angle or bend. Such shoots are mostly of the class technically termed "robbers," and, as we have before observed, should be treated as such betimes, stripping them all away, or finishing off their points if eligibly situated for the production of useful succession wood. Beyond such points, nevertheless, healthy trees will produce occasionally such shoots; the main stems, therefore, must be traced through, and this practice carried to the very extremity of the branches. Next to these there will generally arise an order of spray, tolerably eligible for future bearing purposes, but by far too much crowded; such, therefore, may be pinched back, a little while after the "robbers" are removed, to within about three inches of the base, in the hope of inducing the formation of natural spurs at that part, which not unfrequently becomes a nucleus of spurs. If, however, this does not take place, all such spray should be cut clear away at the next winter's pruning. After these things are carried out, the trees will present an equal and moderated appearance, and if care has been taken to thin out or "stop" duly, light will be equally admitted to all parts of the tree. One thing may here be observed: If the trees are old and exhausted, much of the *strongest* young wood must be reserved, especially if towards the extremities of the branches; but if the tree is growing wild, it becomes expedient to remove or shorten the *coarser* shoots in order to tame the tree.

LIST OF SELECT PLUMS.

T. signifies for table use, K. for kitchen, and P. for preserving.

Early Prolific. (T.)—This is the earliest Plum we have, and is a very great and regular bearer.

July Green Gage. (T.)—End of July.

Early Orleans. (K. and T.)—Beginning of August.

Morocco. (T.)—Beginning of August.

Orleans. (K. and T.)—August.

Drap d'Or. (T.)—August. The Green Gage flavour. Should have a wall.

Green Gage.—August and September. Best on the wall.

Royale Hâtive. (T.)—September. Very rich; should have a wall.

Purple Gage. (T.)—September. Would succeed as a standard in most of our counties.

Coe's Golden Drop. (T. and P.)—September. A good bearer, and succeeds well as a standard. The fruit if hung up by the stalk, or wrapped in paper, will keep for a long time.

St. Martin's Quetsche. (T.)—End of September. Will answer as a standard.

Washington. (T.) — September. Will answer well as an ordinary standard.

Jefferson. (T.)—September.

Winesour. (P.)—September. Well known as a good preserving Plum.

White Magnum Bonum. (K.)—September. Does best as a standard.

Victoria. (K.)—End of September. A great bearer.

Saint Catherine. (K. and P.)—September. A well-known preserving fruit; also a good bearer.

Ickworth Imperatrice. (K. and P.)—October. Very valuable for its long keeping, if carefully gathered, and kept in a dry room.

THE RASPBERRY.

Any good sound loam will grow Raspberries well, but we have generally found them in the highest perfection in a rather dark and unctuous soil. It may be taken as a maxim, that where the Black Currant will do well, the Raspberry will succeed well also; and that where our ordinary Cherry trees are eminently productive, neither of the former will be satisfactory. In the preparation of the soil, deep digging or trenching should, by all means, be practised; for although the roots do not descend to an unusual depth, yet it is well to have some deep-seated, in the event of very dry weather during the fruit-swelling-period.

In preparing the new Raspberry ground, some half-rotten manure, weeds, and leaves are introduced towards the bottom of the trench, and, with the top spit, some in a more rotten condition. The ground being now marked out by drawing a drill where the line is placed, stations are marked where the centre of each patch is to be inserted, and a hole opened, by removing about three spades of earth; this is scattered over the ground at random. The operator then replaces that amount in the shape of some old compost, consisting of rotten weeds, charred rubbish, old tan, old linings, or any of these, or all well blended together.

Let the second week in October be the *period for planting* the Raspberry. The plants although not at rest at that period, will then sustain the least injury; and the removal will induce what is commonly termed rest. In favourable weather plantations may also be formed, in winter or spring, but it is not advisable to disturb the roots after vegetation has commenced.

In looking over the stools to provide the new plantation, it will be found that it is very frequently possible to light on a nice little group of suckers; there will generally be about three canes in these, and so united that you cannot move one without disturbing the rest. Let these go together, by all means; let them live and die together. Such may be removed carefully with a large ball of soil. However, these are exceptions, and the majority of canes will be single, and these should be planted three together. One, the strongest, may be cut down to about four feet, a second to thirty inches, and the weakest to little more than a foot. Every possible pains should be taken in removing them with a ball of soil, and plenty of fibrous roots; and it requires a little careful handling on the part of the taker up, who must exercise fully as much care as the planter. The plants ought to be inserted as close to each other as their balls will permit, generally about nine inches apart, and the compost is filled in around them, not, however, quite filling the hollow, for as soon as planted they should be mulched for the year, and watered liberally on the mulch. Some staking will be necessary before they begin to grow in the spring, and care must be taken not to tread the ground when wet. If they are staked immediately, a crop of vegetables may be taken off the ground contiguous, taking care to have all cleared away by the dressing time, which will be in the ensuing May or June, and the ground must be kept clean in the meantime.

Pruning.—It is the practice in June to go over the Raspberry bushes, and thin out the young suckers or rods, for they in general produce so abundantly, that they would become confused, and the character of the fruit would be materially injured. About half a dozen of the best are left to select from, and it now becomes necessary to reduce this number. We think that four good rods are better than more; this, however, depends on the strength of the soil, and more especially its continued moisture, even in summer, which is an essential with the Raspberry and the Black Currant, as we before observed. If any of the stools or parent plants are weakly, they must be allowed a less number of shoots; some three, others only two, and in some *very weakly* roots it is necessary to cut them entirely down, in order to strengthen them for the ensuing year. In selecting the canes, the strongest must in the main be preferred. It is worthy of remark, however, that when they are very gross indeed, some of the canes are liable to produce side-branches during the season they are springing. Such must be cut away, for, although so promising in appearance, they will not produce such nice fruit as those of a reasonable amount of strength, and, indeed, prove of too monopolising a character, drawing too much of the sap into their huge vessels. About five feet is the greatest height to which the Raspberry canes should be cut: it is, however, a good practise to cut the canes at different lengths. Thus, supposing there are four canes on a stool,—cut the strongest to five feet, the second in point of strength to four feet six inches, the third to four feet, and the fourth to little more than three feet. Now, as the top buds grow strongest, it follows, by this arrangement, that the young fruit-bearing shoots, which grow from the canes, are more equally divided and enjoy more room, and, of course, more light. Such completes the winter's pruning, after which the canes must be staked, and the soil about them top-dressed. The top-dressing we consider an important matter in their cultivation.

The Double-bearing Raspberry.—This is cultivated in a different way from the preceding, for it fruits on the annual shoot; that is to say, suckers produced in spring will fruit in the autumn. The canes are, therefore, cut nearly close to the ground in the spring, as soon as root suckers begin to appear. These may be planted at the same period as the others, making similar preparations, and when planted the cane may be left about a foot long, to draw the root into action. When, however, the root-suckers arise, say in June, the old stem may be cut down, and the plants receive a liberal allowance of manure water.

This kind must be kept thin, or it will not prove successful; plant in a single row, using single strong plants, instead of planting in groups like the others, placing them nearly a foot apart. They are exceedingly liable to produce a host of weedy-looking suckers, and are by no means fit to grow near other fruit trees, which they would much annoy with their suckers. Much care is necessary at thinning-out time to keep these under, and a careful selection must be made of the suckers to be retained. We thin them in June to about four inches apart, and in the end of July or beginning of August it will be seen which are the bearing suckers, and all but those showing blossom-buds may about that time be plucked clean away.

This kind of Raspberry might be cultivated to great advantage on a perpendicular rail of about four feet in height, having four rows of horizontal espalier wires tightly strained, and, indeed, the idea naturally occurs, glass might be placed over it; the expense of doing so would be but trifling. It is naturally a precarious crop, and seldom attains its full flavour, which it might be readily made to do under glass.

Varieties.—1. Red Antwerp. 2. Yellow Antwerp. 3. Round Antwerp. 4. Fastolf. 5. October Red. 6. October Yellow.

Of these the Red Antwerp is of vigorous growth, and though not so great a bearer as the Fastolf, is, nevertheless, superior to it in the fine aromatic flavour of its fruit. The Yellow Antwerp is excellent for the dessert, and affords an agreeable diversity in colour, but it is not so robust in growth, and therefore requires more kindly treatment. The Round Antwerp is a new kind, raised by Mr. Rivers, with large red fruit of very superior flavour. The Fastolf is the best summer Raspberry, and an abundant bearer, having the merit of producing a second crop occasionally, and of continuing a fortnight or three weeks longer in use than the Red Antwerp. Whatever other kinds are planted, the main dependance must be placed on these two. The October Red and October Yellow are the best two of their respective colours, the suckers put forth in June, producing an abundance of large fruit, which ripen in September and October; and occasionally in dry autumns their production is prolonged far into November.

THE STRAWBERRY.

Doubtless the best practice in Strawberry culture is a very frequent renewal of the stock. We do not advise a continuance beyond the third crop; for the plants generally wear an exhausted aspect by that time; and, indeed, it is probable that their duration in a state of nature is not often extended beyond that period.

As to the time of making the beds, that is sometimes settled on principle, sometimes on expediency; the latter being more generally the case. As early as the runners can possibly be obtained will be found the very best time. As soon as the plants from which the new plantation is to be made have been determined on, the cultivator should spread two or three inches thick of old vegetable soil, or manure, beneath them in the month of May, or before the runners come forth; and on this the runners will be produced unusually early and very strong. By this treatment nice plants will be obtained a month, or nearly so, before those left to chance. Those who are determined to use every means may watch the development of the runners, and place a stand or a hooked peg on the bine, to make the young runners sit close to the ground. In addition, the extending runners may receive frequent sprinklings of water, and such means being taken runners of a very superior character may be generally obtained very early in July. If these can be planted out where they are to remain finally, so much the better. This is doing all that can be done; but if, through a severe limitation of ground, expedients must be had recourse to, the next best plan is to plant the young runners out in reserve beds until October, or the following February.

Planting.—Some plant in beds, some as edgings, and some in single rows. The last is our practice, as well as that of most good cultivators. In making a new plantation, of course the first year the plants will only attain half their size; we therefore plant them twice as thickly in the row as we intend them ultimately to remain, and in the beginning of August, or when the crop is gathered, we cut every other plant up. This gives the remainder room to ripen a good bud. Three feet we do not consider too much between the rows, and the plants may be ultimately two feet apart in the row, so that by double thickness in the row, they may be planted exactly one foot apart at the first. We are aware that practice differs in distance as well as other things; but this, we believe, will produce the greatest crop of good Strawberries, which, whatever market-men may do, ought to be the aim of every private grower. There must be no drill drawn for the plants. The best way is, after stretching the line, to make a mark with the end of a rod, having a notch in it, so as to ride across the line, and then to pull the line up, and plant by the mark. Care must be taken not to bury the hearts of the plants, which is soon done if the planter is awkward; and in order to avoid this, it is well (if the soil is tolerably dry) to pass the foot lightly down the line before planting.

The runners should be taken up carefully with a trowel, every fibre secured, and, if possible, every little ball of soil secured too, and planted forthwith. No lying about or drying up should be permitted. As soon as planted, they must receive a thorough watering, and this may have to be repeated once every two days for a week or two, in order that no time may be lost. As soon as they are rooted in their new situation, liquid manure may be had recourse to until they get strong, when it may be dispensed with; and by persevering attention the plants will be very stout indeed by the middle of September, and forming a strong bud in the centre of each. Henceforth no excitement need be applied; they will sink gradually into a state of repose. We forgot to say that not a leaf must be cut off on any pretext whatever, from the removal of the runners in July until the following February, or rather, March. Of course the plantation must be kept clear of weeds, and those who have tender varieties, such as the British Queen, will do well to throw a little litter of any kind over them during the hard frosts of winter.

Spring Dressing.—Our practice in respect to this, is to cut closely down all decayed or decaying foliage in the second week of March. Some of the older stock which scarcely form a green leaf, we at once cut close over. And now we run the hand through all the crowns, in order to see if any more runners have become wedged in amongst the stock than we have occasion for. The operator carries an old knife in his hand, and removes all that he deems superfluous. This done, we mulch through them, generally using a half-decayed material from the linings of frames or pits, composed of tree leaves and manure which have generally been reserved in breaking up old beds during the frost, for the express purpose of manuring various culinary crops. This material is chopped to pieces with the spade, and forms an admirable dressing; and those who can procure plenty of soot will do well to strew a considerable amount over the heap of mulch before applying it; the soot, of course, tumbling down and blending with the manure in the act of filling the barrows or baskets.

This we spread between the rows, from two to three inches in thickness, placing it, by hand, amongst all bare portions of the divisions of the crown or parent stock.

After Management.—When plantations are two or three years old, some clearing away of runners becomes necessary between the rows, and such may be done (of course previous to applying the mulch) by deep hoeing and raking, taking care to extirpate every runner between the rows. Thus treated, the plants speedily become covered with new foliage, which can expand freely without hindrance; and about *the commencement of the blossoming period* we place straw, clean new straw, on each side of every row. This straw is drawn out of the bundle quite straight, and divested of all chaffy material, and is laid in bundles lengthways. Each bundle straightened in the hand thus constitutes a kind of cushion, propping the blossoms several inches above the soil; and, indeed, through the intervention of the straw, the berries do not touch the soil at all. Thus enjoying a free circulation of air, they attain a high amount of flavour, and are at all times gathered with facility and perfectly clean.

The next point of good practice is to see that the plantation is thoroughly freed from *weeds*. If not attended to betimes, such fast growers as the groundsel will spring up and produce seed, unperceived, amongst the crowns, the offspring from which is a source of constant annoyance. They should, therefore, be carefully looked over in the early part of April; and, finally, more particularly just before the runners extend, which will be about the end of May.

Watering is another great essential in Strawberry culture; but with the practice here suggested of careful mulching, much labour will be spared in this respect. Our practice is, providing the weather is dry, to apply one thorough watering when the earliest fruits are swelling off. Now, this is no mere sprinkling affair; it is the next thing to irrigation. Our soil, however, is a light, though deep, sandy loam, resting on clean red sand, and constitutes what practical men term a hungry soil. This watering will carry them through nearly a fortnight in the driest of weather, by which time they will require more, if drought continue; and such being the case, we repeat a similar application; after which we seldom give any more.

LIST OF SELECT STRAWBERRIES.

Keens' Seedling.
Black Prince.
Duchesse de Trévise.
Highland Chief.
British Queen.

Carolina Superba.
Myatt's Eliza.
Oscar
Old Pine.
Elton.

THE VINE.

Ripening the wood *thoroughly* is undoubtedly the basis on which to ground all the operations necessary for successful Vine culture; and although to those in our most favoured southern counties this may appear a small matter, it is not found so to others less favourably situated. Whatever plan, then, which will tend to make the Vine short jointed, and to ripen the wood thoroughly, will be found to hasten the ripening of the fruit, which is, indeed, the final point to be aimed at.

Soils.—Any light, sandy, and porous soils are by far better adapted for the Vine than those which are tenacious or clayey; for the latter, through their innate power, as also from their capacity for maintaining a permanent moisture in hot weather, are sure to produce long-jointed shoots. If, unfortunately, the natural soil is of this unctuous character, means must be taken to correct the staple; of which we will speak shortly, as it will be better to say something about subsoils and depth first.

Subsoils.—Whatever be the character of the surface soil, the substratum must be so constituted that no water lodgments can possibly take place. Without securing a dry bottom, it is impossible to obtain success in Vine culture. When, therefore, suspicion exists as to water, a thorough drainage must take place. From six to eight feet in width will amply suffice for the border or bed of earth; and the soil should accordingly be excavated that width to make a complete border. It will be necessary to have at least twenty-four inches in depth of soil; when, however, the situation is damp we would have one-half of the soil above the ordinary ground level. Such being the case, and it being desirable to introduce about nine inches in depth of some rubble or other imperishable material, the depth of excavation must be nearly twenty-four inches. Make a main drain along the front of the border, running side by side with the walk. This drain must be a little below the level of the subsoil surface at the border front, in order to receive and convey the water which filters through the rubbly material, or rises from springs. It will, of course, be necessary to seek a good outlet for this drain; and the mouth of it must be secured from the tread of cattle, and from the entrance of rats, which sometimes do serious mischief in this way.

The soil being excavated, the surface of the subsoil must be rendered even; and if the ground be *exceedingly liable to water*, a cross drain or two might stretch from the wall to the front or main drain. Such are generally formed of the ordinary draining tiles, placed on a sole, for fear of sinking. The sole may be formed of slate or flat tiles, or fragments of any imperishable material; some use alder wood, cleft into flattened pieces, like a portion of broken slate. Indeed, the main drain should also have soles; or, in treacherous subsoils, the whole affair may be prematurely broken up by the oozing out of silt or sandy mud from the mouth of the drain.

The drain or drains having been laid, the whole surface of the subsoil should be covered over with broken stone, brickbats, or the scoriæ from manufactories, or clinkers, nine inches in depth, and if any turfy material can be obtained cover the whole surface with it; turf from road-sides or from waste land will be perfectly eligible. If such cannot be obtained, tree leaves, if fresh, or even some loose litter, may be scattered over the surface.

Soil for the Roots.—One of the most important improvers or correctors of soil is lime rubbish, or the sort of material which is obtained in pulling down old buildings. Those who live in the suburbs of towns may, in general, secure a lot of this lime rubbish; if, however, it cannot be procured, let coarse sand, burnt clay, any charred rubbish, and even a proportion of common cinder ashes be cast over the soil before filling in again; using nearly one-half of such poor-looking materials, if the soil is very adhesive.

A little half-decomposed manure, or a quantity of leaves in a similar state, should be added to the mass before filling in; and a dry period should be selected for the operation. The latter is an important matter. Care should be taken, in filling, that all the materials are equally blended, and the roughest portions should be kept towards the bottom of the border.

Management.—The Vine is late in bursting into leaf. This fact alone points to the high amount of excitability requisite in order to promote germination; and, as it is late in its leafing, it is evident that the leaves which develope themselves earliest are the most important, as being the first to be in a condition to elaborate the true sap, which must feed the fruit of the year, and build up the fabric of the tree for future crops. Hence the severe course of "disbudding," "thinning out," and "stopping," which we must recommend. As we are addressing ourselves to tyros in horticultural matters, we may as well explain the technical terms just named, and which, being in common use amongst practical men, must, we suppose, be tolerated; indeed, the three we allude to have the merit of being peculiarly expressive.

Disbudding signifies the removal of every opening bud, at the period of leafing, which is not needed for the present year's crop, or for filling up some space on the wall which would otherwise remain bare.

Thinning out.—This process consists in going over the Vines again about the period they commence blossoming, and then making a final selection of the shoots to be allowed to remain. Such, indeed, becomes imperative at this period; for, in the omission of it, the Vines would speedily become a confused mass of shoots.

Stopping.—This is pinching off the ends of those shoots which are to remain, and is generally performed at one joint beyond the one bearing the bunch; that is to say, one joint and one leaf only are left beyond the bunch. In cases, however, where more walling or training surface has to be covered, as many joints should be left as may be necessary at the ensuing pruning season to cover such space. The ordinary period for stopping is about a week or so after the young bunch fairly shows what its character will be.

Having thus given a definite character to these necessary operations, we come now to the main purpose of these remarks—a thorough spring Vine dressing. A slight disbudding should be carried out, and, when completed, let the trees be thoroughly examined, and not a shoot left in them but what is either wanted for this year's crop or for securing against vacancies in future years. In performing this do not suffer the Vines to be crammed with shoots; thinning out is in general too niggardly performed. It ought to be borne in mind that leaf should not be permitted to overlap leaf, and, above all, that no growing spray, whether lateral or terminal, should be allowed to shade the principal leaves.

To those who do not know what amount of bunches a Vine should be permitted to carry we would say, as a general rule, leave about one bunch to every square foot of surface. So much, nevertheless, depends on the strength of constitution in the individual plant, that it is not easy to lay down rules in this respect. The Vine dresser must learn to distinguish between healthy trees with a safe root action, and those which are weakly or uncertain in their movements.

Vine Stopping is one of these matters of importance. It will be obvious to every one that, unless some process of this kind is resorted to, the shoots of the Vine in-doors would speedily become confused, and that most of the larger leaves would be shaded by spray of inferior growth.

The principal leaves in our dull climate require the full action of sunlight, in order to elaborate completely those juices on which the flavour and size of the fruit, as well as vigorous constitution of the tree, depend. To throw some light on this portion of the subject, and by way of illustration, we may here direct attention to the fact, that a course of *very close* stopping, persisted in from the first, with young Vines, would for years prevent their attaining that bulk of stem which is necessary in order to carry full crops every season for many years in succession. Indeed, by carrying it to a great extreme the vital powers of the Vine would, doubtless, be seriously injured.

We have observed thus far in order to show that a medium must be followed in stopping processes, and we proceed now to show that the Vine, like most other trees, moves by periodical fits, if we may be allowed the term, even in its annual course, and that the stopping must be made to bear a direct relation to such habits. These peculiar periods, on which, as we have before observed, the amount as well as the stopping necessary must be brought to bear, are—

1st. The development of the bunch.
2nd. The first swelling of the berry.
3rd. The last swelling of the berry.

1st Period: Development of the Bunch.—In order to concentrate as much as may be the energies of the Vine in the neighbourhood of the tiny young bunch, pinch off the point of the growing shoot one joint above the joint from which the fruit proceeds. The reason why one joint is selected is this:—It is found by experience that in a roof covered with Vines in Britain every allowable means must be taken at all times to check the tendency of one shoot to overlap another. Light is the prime object after all; and it must be borne in mind by our young and rising horticulturists, that if the stopping took place two or three joints beyond the "show" there would be no harm, but probably good, all other circumstances bearing a just relation to the proceeding.

2nd Period: the First Swelling of the Berry.—After the young points have been pinched, or, in gardening language, "stopped," in a very few days each joint below the stopping will put forth a side-shoot. These are termed "*lateral*" or "*axillary*" shoots; the frequency of the stopping being determined chiefly by the aggression which occurs in the act of these laterals rambling so far as to overshadow the first made or larger leaves.

The result of this close stopping certainly is to limit the extension of the tree according to its innate powers; this, however, is amply compensated for by increased size in the berry, the powers available being concentrated more in the immediate neighbourhood of the bunch. This stopping, therefore, is performed as often as necessity calls for its repetition until the first swelling is completed, when what is termed the "*stoning*" period commences. During this crisis (which in general lasts some six or eight weeks) the berries appear stationary. The close stopping during the second period having accomplished all it was intended to do, may now for a while cease, at least, in part, and as much spray may be suffered to ramble freely as space can be found for. The leading shoot, above all others, may now be encouraged to ramble freely in any direction open to it. This it is, indeed, which holds by far the most powerful reciprocity with the root. We do not say that stopping of all kinds must absolutely cease during this period; still, in free-growing Vines, some amount will be necessary. It must, however, be *stopping of necessity*. Some of the shoots will begin to cross each other's track, and such must be made to give way by a timely stopping.

3rd Period: the Last Swelling of the Berry.—Now, again, commences another and distinct crisis in the Vine: the fruit acquires flavour, and the buds plumpness and firmness. To obtain the greatest amount of light on *the principal leaves* is henceforth the object of the cultivator; and to accomplish this he must strip away all those laterals which shade in any degree the larger leaves. This done, finger-and-thumb work ceases. The cultivator has done all that was required of him.

Let us endeavour to impress one idea strongly on the minds of our embryo gardeners:—Do not strip away leaves or spray *in order to throw sunlight on the fruit.* This is a very common error. The fruit receives its colour through the agencies of the leaves, and not in spite of them. Sunlight is by no means indispensable to the colouring of the berries, nay, it is prejudicial unless when they are becoming perfectly ripened; then their cuticle (skin) is able to bear it, and leaves are sometimes plucked away from any late Grapes, in order to facilitate the dispersion of damps leading to mouldiness.

Pruning.—There are commonly three distinct methods of pruning practised, namely,—

1st. Spur pruning.
2nd. Long-rod pruning.
3rd. Ordinary pruning.

Pruning on the spur system consists in carrying up one leading shoot to the back of the house, establishing thereon what are termed spurs, or what might, perhaps, be more properly termed snags, from the front to the back, as nearly as possible, at measured distances, and as far as may be placed *alternately* up the stem. About one to every foot is sufficient; perhaps better than more. These spurs are first developed as side-shoots; and in order to insure their due and full development, they are produced during about three seasons. There are those who will run a cane up to the back of the house, and fruit it the whole length the next year; but this is not substantial practice, albeit astonishing those who are not aware of the tendency of this *ruse.* A good cane nearly the length of the roof, and about three quarters of an inch diameter, may be pruned to one-third the rafter length the first year, another third the second, and the remainder the third year. By this plan, supposing the rafter fifteen feet long, there will be about five large bunches the first year, ten the second, and fifteen or more the third; and this will be found to tax the powers of the Vine heavily, perhaps too much. By this mode every side-shoot will be strongly developed, and, consequently, a selection may be readily made. The subsequent pruning simply consists in cutting each of these back annually to what has been termed the "spawn eye," that is to say, the last eye at the base of the young side-shoot, although some leave another eye.

Long-rod pruning has for its object the production of larger bunches; and this it can accomplish, although, perhaps, the berries are smaller. The object here is to establish a stump with three strong branches, or, at least, collars; from each of which, in its turn, a shoot may be made to spring. These, by a regular system of pruning, are worked in successive lengths; the one bearing the whole length of the rafter; the second, half the length; and the third collar (recently pruned back) producing the renewal shoot; indeed, it has been aptly termed the "renewal system." There are other "long-rod" practices, but this is the most systematic one.

Ordinary pruning is such as we very commonly see practised on out-door Vines trained against a house, where the leading shoots are carried almost at random, and, at first, chiefly with a view to get the house covered. Here the pruner selects according to the character of the wood, little heeding its situation; reserving the short-jointed and strong, and cutting away the weak. The shoots reserved are shortened back with reference to the space they have to occupy, say from three to six or eight eyes, as the case may be.

In all pruning it is a maxim to cut an inch or so above the eye, not close to it, and to throw the slant of the cut the contrary way to the eye or bud. All Vine pruning should be performed the moment the leaves have fallen; and we hold it good practice to patch each knife wound with a little white lead immediately. This does away with the possibility of bleeding in the ensuing spring.

LIST OF SELECT VINES.

FOR OUT-DOOR CULTURE.

Early Black July.—This is the earliest and hardiest for out-door culture, as it ripens in situations where the Black Hamburgh and others will not succeed.

Early Saumur Frontignan.—A first-rate white Grape, of much better flavour than the Early Black July, and ripening at the same time. It is also an abundant bearer.

Royal Muscadine.—A most excellent hardy Grape, the one that is so extensively cultivated near Paris. The berries are large, amber-coloured, and of rich flavour; and the Vine is an abundant bearer.

Black Hamburgh.—Sometimes ripens against a wall out of doors in good seasons.

FOR COOL VINERIES.

Black Hamburgh.—The merits of this, as a house Grape, are too well known to require comment.

Early White Malvasia.—One of the earliest Grapes known, ripening, in a cool vinery, in the beginning or middle of August. An excellent bearer, and well adapted for pot culture.

Buckland Sweetwater.—A hardy and excellent sort, with large bunches, and large and well flavoured berries.

Black Frontignan.—Berries small, but with a rich vinous musky flavour. Should be in every collection.

Black Prince.—Berries rather large, very juicy and rich, ripening, and always colouring well in a cool vinery, and, in warm seasons, out of doors.

FOR HOT VINERIES.

Muscat of Alexandria.— A delicious Grape, with a rich muscat flavour, and the berries are of a fine amber colour when ripened to perfection; but to do this, a high temperature is necessary. With a high temperature at the time of flowering, and whilst setting, it may be ripened well in a warm vinery.

Lady Downe's.— An invaluable late Grape, which forces well, and the bunches will hang till March without shrivelling. The Vine is a most abundant bearer.

West's St. Peters.— An excellent late Grape, requiring plenty of heat.

Barbarussa. — Bunches frequently attaining a very large size, and hanging late, without which the berries do not acquire their full flavour.

FLOWER GARDEN.

THE FLOWER GARDEN.

The culture of flowers is one of the most delightful and healthful recreations to which man can devote the powers of his mind and body. Even those who thereby earn their daily bread, may enjoy pleasures that the mere mechanic or artizan is debarred from by the very nature of his labours. The clear light of heaven, the sweet fresh air, and the beauties of the objects of the gardener's care, are all sources of the most unalloyed pleasure; and it is a wise dispensation of the Giver of all good, that those delightful pleasures are within the reach of all. To the lady or gentleman florist, to the gardener by profession, to the amateur and the cottager, the flower garden is, or may be, if the proper spirit is brought into action, an elevating pursuit. We, who have tasted those pleasures, being desirous to increase the taste and instruct the ignorant, purpose, if we can, to make the culture of flowers more general, and the practice more easy; and if our object be accomplished, we shall think our attempt will have been a mite cast into the treasury of human happiness.

There are a large number of individuals who, loving a garden and having leisure time, devote a part of it, very wisely and properly, to the cultivation of flowers. Perhaps a still greater number would enjoy the rational recreation if they had the necessary information how to set about it.

ARRANGEMENT OF THE FLOWER GARDEN.

Walks.—No garden can be said to be even respectably managed where the walks are ill drained, badly defined, neglected, and covered with moss and weeds. If every other part of the garden be kept in perfect order, and yet the walks be even partially neglected, they give an air of desolation to the whole. On the other hand, if the walks are dry, clean, and neat, a stroll in the garden will be endurable, though the grass may be rank, and the weeds rampant in the other parts. We feel, even when in health, great comfort in walking in a garden on a solid dry walk; but to the invalid, this is absolutely necessary. Whenever walks are out of order, proceed with pickaxe and shovel to loosen all the rubbish the walk may be made of. If the walk is not drained, or badly drained, have either some draining tiles or bricks with covers ready. Let all the old rubbish be sifted, and the rough laid in a ridge at one side of the walk. The fine stuff that passes through the sieve will do well to mix with dung to manure the garden with, especially where the general soil of the garden is heavy, or of a clayey nature. Where there is plenty of room to lay the rough rubbish, the whole may be sifted at once; but where that is not the case, the work may be done in lengths of ten or more yards at a time. After the rubble is removed, the next operation is to make and lay the drain, provided the walk is deep enough. To make a thoroughly good dry walk, there ought to be at least nine inches deep of open rubble. The drain should be in the centre of the walk; half of its depth ought to be below the bottom of the rubble. Then lay short drains from the sides of the walk to the centre drain; and upon them, close to the edging, lay four bricks to receive a grating, to take in the top water in heavy showers. Where the walk is pretty level, these gratings need not be nearer to each other than from ten to fifteen yards; but if the walk is steep, or even of a moderate slope, the gratings ought to be much more numerous; perhaps, in extreme cases, as near as five yards to each other. The clay, or earth, under the rubble, should be made smooth and sloping from each side, down to the drain. This will convey all the water that settles through the rubble, to the drain, which drain will convey it to a general drain outside the garden. As soon as the drain is laid and the bottom made smooth, the rubble should be put in carefully, so as not to disturb the drain. This should be put in to within two inches of the level of the edging. If the edging, whether it is of grass, box, thrift, daisies, or even slates, be out of order, in this state of the walk it is a very good opportunity to renew it; but great care must be taken not to mix the earth with the rubble. When all this work is well and duly done, let the rubble be beaten down with a rammer, or well rolled, it is then ready for the gravel. Lay on a coating of rough gravel first, rounding it up in the centre, so that the top of the centre should be as high as the edging, and the sides $1\frac{1}{2}$ inch below it. This rough gravel would be better to lay as it is for a few days, or even weeks, if convenient, so that it may settle, and become in a degree solid. Then lay on the last coat of gravel, which should be moderately fine, the pebbles amongst it not being larger than hazel nuts. This coat of gravel should be laid on pretty nearly level with the edging, and rounded up to the centre. This will, after it has been well rolled and has become solid, allow the water to run to the lowest part of the walk—the sides, and from thence into the drains, through the gratings before mentioned. All the drains ought to have a gentle descent, to allow the water to run off freely. If the walk is steep, it will be necessary to lay the bottom of the drain with slate or flat tiles, to prevent the water working away the substratum, which will soon choke up the drain if this precaution is not adopted. In places where the walks are on a steep descent, it is a good plan to pick out of the gravel, or to procure them on purpose, as many pebbles about the size of hens' eggs as will pave each side of the walk six or nine inches wide, laying them rather hollow, so as to form a conduit for the water in heavy rains. This will prevent the gravel washing away, and will not look amiss, provided it is neatly performed.

THE FLOWER-BEDS.—In placing the flower-beds, we ought to be guided by the manner in which we purpose to lay out the garden. If the beds are divided from each other by grass lawn, they should be placed near the gravel walk. They should be of lengthy forms, rather narrow, so as each plant can be distinctly seen. Those long narrow shapes can be more easily managed than broad heavy masses. Weeds can be removed; the beds hoed and raked; the flowers tied up or pegged down, as they require; water can be applied more easily, and the flowers gathered more readily. Also, by having beds of such forms, there is, in performing the necessary operations, less need to set a foot upon them—a pressure always to be avoided.

Another point to be attended to is, to form the beds of different sizes, some of smaller dimensions than others. The lesser beds will then conveniently serve to receive one kind of flowers, such as groups or masses of Scarlet Geraniums, Verbenas, Petunias, Calceolarias, Heliotropes, and other dwarf flowers, which do not associate well with tall-growing kinds. These small plots of flowers should be placed in such situations as to be well exposed to view. A very good place for some of them is on the parts of the lawn between the shrubbery and the main walk. They may be chiefly of the two beautiful forms—the oval and the circle; these are more graceful than straight-sided beds, and, on account of their size, are equally as convenient to manage as the larger lengthy forms. Flower gardens laid out in this style will allow a large unbroken space of lawn to be seen from the windows, or from the covered seat on the mound; whereas, if the clumps of flowers were placed more in the centre of the lawn, they would lessen its apparent size, breaking, as it were, the ground into two parts, and thus destroying its unity as a whole.

We must now briefly notice the method of designing flower-beds, known as the "French parterre" and "Dutch manner." These are very suitable for villa gardens of small extent; and when well laid out in suitable figures, not too large, of easy curves, or neat straight lines, and kept in good order, they have a pleasing effect. They are formed with gravel walks, box edging, and beds for flowers. Here, again, as in the former method, the sizes of the beds should be varied; the smaller ones for the same kinds of flowers, and the larger ones may either be of a mixed character, or in masses of the taller-growing flowers; yet none of them should be so large as to require the gardener to tread much upon them to perform the necessary operations. These kinds of flower gardens require to be kept exceedingly neat and trim to be effective, and are very proper for the ladies to exercise upon, and keep in order, as the gravel walks will be more frequently in a dry state than the lawn; not but that a garden with grass between the beds may be partially managed by its mistress, as well as the other.

SMALL GARDENS.—Small gardens are generally laid out with a round or oval bed in the centre; a narrow gravel walk, edged with box, round it; and the rest forms a border, in which, as well as in the centre bed, are grown trees, shrubs, and flowers. Now this plan is very simple, and if judiciously planted, and neatly kept, is, perhaps, the best way of arranging such small plots. Some such gardens have a square or round grass plot, with a border round it; but grass, in such a situation, is exceedingly troublesome. If it is not frequently rolled and mown, it soon becomes thin of grass, mossy, and out of order, besides taking up the room which might be occupied with flowers. For small gardens, gravel walks, with beds and borders edged with box, are more suitable, more easily kept in order, can be managed by the occupier, without so much assistance from a day-gardener, and afford more space for ornamental shrubs and flowers.

TRENCHING AND DIGGING.

These operations may be performed in the flower garden, where the beds are empty of flower roots; the plan to do this well and effectually is, to remove all the soil out of each bed, to the depth of sixteen or eighteen inches. If the soil be poor or exhausted, take it all away, and entirely renew the bed with fresh soil. Flowers mostly love a light and rather rich soil. The following compost will suit the generality of flowers, usually grown in masses of one variety, in each bed:—One half of turfy loam from a common, or old hilly pasture (this should be at least twelve months laid up in a heap, and regularly turned over once a month, for that time, before using); sandy peat, one quarter; very much decayed cow-dung and leaves, one quarter; with as much river sand as will give the whole a sandy texture. To make this perfectly plain, we will describe the compost as consisting of two barrow-loads of loam, one barrow-load of sandy peat, half a barrow-load of dung, and the same quantity of rotten leaves, with the requisite proportion of sand—perhaps a bushel of sand, to the above quantities, would be enough, or less would do if the loam and peat are naturally sandy. At the bottom of each bed, put in the rougher parts of the compost, which may be picked out for that purpose. The old soil will be useful for vegetable crops, and may be wheeled at once into the kitchen garden. When the soils of the beds is thoroughly renewed, as above described, it will last for several years, with the addition of a portion of dung, or rotten leaves, annually. The soil in the beds ought to be filled in so high as to allow for settling. When all the beds are filled, if they are on the lawn, let the edges be neatly cut with a sharp edging-knife, and the turf that is cut off taken to the compost-yard to decay. It will make good loam for various potting purposes. The beds will now require no more attention till the time arrives to plant the flowers.

We shall suppose our borders or border are furnished with some flower roots, roses, and shrubs—in fact, a mixed flower garden. Procure a few stout pegs, and stick them in close to each patch of bulbs or roots, leaving about two inches visible above ground. Let all your rose-bushes be pruned, edgings cut, shrubs against walls or paling trimmed and nailed, or tied; clear away all the rubbish, and then, if you have any fresh loam, rotten leaves, or dung, or all three mixed, lay on a moderate thickness all over the border, of those refreshers. If you have none of those good things, do not therefore neglect the digging. Commence at one end of the border by opening a trench, that is, taking up with the spade a row of spadefuls across the border. Put this soil in a barrow, and wheel it to the other end of the border; then take up a spadeful of soil at one side, and turn it upside down, directly before you, in the trench you have opened. If your soil is heavy and strong, break it partially in pieces with the spade; if light, it will not need it. Proceed so with the next spadeful, and so on across the border, in as straight a line as you can, taking care not to injure or disturb the flower roots, &c., that may be in the beds or borders. Fill up the trench at the end with the soil that was placed there at the beginning.

If the beds or borders have not been dug for some time, and you are desirous of making a really good job of it, take up all the roots and shrubs, and lay them in by the heels; that is, cover the roots with earth in some vacant part of the garden; then lay on a good coat of fresh earth and dung; open a trench, as before, at one end, but instead of one spit deep of earth, take out two, and make a trench, half a yard wide, of two spades depth. Wheel this soil to the other end, and then turn the next spits of the next trench of the same width, to the bottom of the first trench; then bring up the next spit to the top, and so proceed trench after trench till the whole is finished. After that, lay on another coat of compost and dig it lightly in. This is *trenching*, and will entirely renew your borders for several years. When all this is finished, the flower roots and shrubs should be immediately replanted. If you have not compost enough to afford a covering to both top and bottom spit, omit the first coat, and apply one to the last turned-up spit, for this is most likely the poorer of the two—and, besides, the roots of the plants will sooner feel the benefit of the application.

MANURES AND COMPOSTS.

In every garden there should be a place set apart for keeping dung, loam, peat, and rotten leaves in; and to those who have composts or heaps of any kind of fertilizers, we would call their attention to the following advice:—The dung and leaves require the most frequently turning over, to prevent their heating too much. Should either appear dry, wet them thoroughly with water, or, what is better, with the drainage of the dunghill, the slops from the house, or, if there is such a thing near, the water from a stagnant pool or ditch. Every time this heap is turned, cover it up with a coating of earth; this will check the escape of the gases, which are the best part of the dung. If you can procure such a thing as a bushel or two of lime, it will materially assist the decomposition of the heap, and greatly increase its fitness for vegetable food. Strive to make this heap as large as you can; it is the riches of your garden. Without it, even with the best management, your flowers, as well as vegetables, will be poor and unsatisfactory; with it, liberally applied, they will be rich in colour, in scent, and flavour. Search, therefore, for materials to increase its bulk, as you would for gold in California. It is a more certain increase of your comfort and wealth than any of those wild chimerical schemes now too prevalent.

Reserve a portion, or small heap of dung and leaves, separate from each other, to be turned over frequently, until they become quite decayed, and fit for potting purposes. Attend to the heap of turfy loam also; expose every part to the air in succession. If you have a large heap of this valuable material—considerably more than is likely to be wanted for plants in pots—separate it into two heaps; and the one intended for use in potting, keep as it is; but the other, mix with lime. You will thus find its good qualities for gardening purposes much increased. Peat earth does not require turning so often as the above-mentioned. If it be turned three or four times a year, to keep down the weeds, it is quite sufficient.

Keep a corner also for the soot out of your chimney, and another for broken bones. These last ought always to be mixed with earth, or they will—if even in so small a quantity as half a bushel—heat violently, and lose the greater part of their fertilizing properties. Lime, for dusting your borders or seed-beds, where slugs and worms are troublesome, or to make lime-water, should be kept in a dry place, in some vessel that is as nearly air-tight as possible : this will keep it quick and powdery, and preserve its pungency.

To preserve sand for striking cuttings, it should be kept in a dry airy place under cover. River or pit sand, to mix amongst compost or soils for out-door purposes, may be laid in any corner, stirring the surface occasionally, after heavy rains, to prevent the growth of moss, &c.

We have thus, at some length, dwelt upon the matters connected with the compost-yard, because we feel satisfied of the importance of the subject, and are convinced our remarks will be of use to a great number of our readers. To such as may not have room, on account of the size of their premises, to keep dung and soils by them, we can only say, we are sorry you cannot have the benefit of such useful, nay, indispensable materials. Of course you may, if you can afford it, always buy from a respectable nursery the soils you may want; but that you will find much more expensive than if you could have them by you in small quantities even, to be ready for use whenever your plants may require them.

LAWNS.

After the borders are raked, pay attention to the state of your lawn. If any part of it is bare of grass, and you can procure some good short turf, spring is a good time to lay it. Remove the old turf, and sprinkle a little fresh earth on the surface; then lay down the new turf, packing it closely, to prevent the joints being visible; beat the new turf well down with a turf-beater, to make it smooth and even. A turf-beater is a flat thick piece of heavy wood, with a handle three feet long—a most efficient tool for that purpose. If you cannot procure turf, proceed as follows: —Rake your plot over, and in the places that are bare of grass, make a pretty strong impression with the rake teeth, so as to leave it rough; then procure a sufficient quantity of grass-seed mixture; sow it rather thickly over the bare places, and then sprinkle some finely sifted soil over it, just enough to cover the seed; level it very gently with the rake, and when it is sufficiently dry, roll the whole plot over with a heavy roller. Nothing more is wanted but warm weather and gentle spring showers, with frequent rolling and mowing, and your lawn will soon be in excellent order, exhibiting that beautiful green so pleasing and refreshing to the eye.

After dry hot weather, the grass-plots will, especially if newly-laid, suffer from want of moisture. If you have plenty of water and plenty of time, let that nourishing element be poured upon the lawn freely. Should any cracks appear, fill them up with some finely sifted soil. Roll previously to mowing—it will save the edge of the scythe or the knives of the mowing machine.

Mow early, if the scythe is used, before the dew evaporates, the grass being then more tender, and consequently more easy to mow; besides, the labour is not so much felt by the operator in the cool morning air. The sound of the scythe should never, in well-managed gardens, be heard after breakfast time. Finish the mowing, then, before that pleasant meal, and return refreshed. Then sweep the grass up, and convey it away either to line a hotbed or to decay amongst soil in the compost-yard. Trim the edges of the walks and flower-beds, and remove all the rubbish into the compost-yard. When this is completed, the flowers neatly tied up, and the beds and borders hoed and raked, your garden will have that freshness and trim appearance, so pleasing to the well-ordered mind.

During the latter months of the year, the lawns, if well kept, are exceedingly beautiful. Mow, sweep, and roll them at least once a fortnight. Fresh turf may then be laid with advantage, as it will sooner take root, and form a compact even surface at that season of the year, than at any other. Make the ground solid in every part alike, or it will settle unevenly, and give you considerable trouble to level it afterwards: in treading it, wherever you find a place softer than the rest, ram that place down very hard with a beetle or pavior's rammer, filling up with soil, and beating it down also very firmly, until the place is even with the rest.

To Renovate a Lawn.—In the spring, at the end of March, if your lawn is too large for turfing, dig your ground even, rake it perfectly level, and then sow it with the following grass-seeds, passing a light roller over afterwards. The quantities are enough for an acre, but you can diminish them in proportion if your plot is less. Crested dog's-tail (Cynosurus cristatus), 6 lbs.; hard fescue (Festuca duriuscula), 20 lbs.; fine-leaved fescue (Festuca tenuifolia), 2 lbs.; wood-meadow grass (Poa nemoralis), 2 lbs.; common-meadow grass (Poa trivialis), 4 lbs.; creeping white clover (Trifolium repens), 8 lbs.; smaller yellow trefoil (T. minus), 3 lbs.

FLOWER GARDEN ORNAMENTS.

Rustic Baskets and Vases.—In flower garden scenes it is sometimes desirable, in order to create a variety, to adopt various modes and objects to attain such a varied appearance as will produce effects agreeable to the eye and taste. A cheap way to accomplish this is to place in proper situations, rustic baskets filled with rich light earth ready to receive suitable plants. Those baskets are easily made: any moderately ingenious carpenter may form them. Having fixed on the sizes you wish for, procure some inch boards, either of sound oak, which is the best, or of well-seasoned elm or deal. Cut them into the proper lengths, and nail them together the right width —they will then form a square. Now, we think the best form is a circle, though the octagon is nearly as handsome. Mark, then, the desired form on this square, and, with the proper kind of saw, cut it into the desired figure. When this is done, you have, as it were, the groundwork of your basket or baskets made. The next thing is to fix upon the depth—this requires some consideration. If too deep, the basket will be a great weight, and look clumsy; and if too shallow, there will be too little earth for the plants to flourish in, so as to produce healthy foliage and plenty of flowers. Now, the extremes, we should say, are twelve inches, which is too deep, and four inches, which is too shallow. Take, then, the medium between the two, and make the depth eight inches, and you will be right. But what size shall we advise? In truth, we had nearly forgotten that. Well, we say the size depends on circumstances and situation. If your garden is moderately extensive, you may have them what we consider the largest size to be manageable, that is, from three to five feet in diameter. If a small garden, this size would be inconvenient, and take up too much room. Yet there is no reason why you should not have two or three of those ornaments. For such a garden, the most proper dimensions would be two feet; and for that size, six inches would be a proportionate depth. Having, then, fixed upon the proper size, and cut them to it, proceed to nail to the circular or octagon bottom the sides. If the shape is round, let the pieces of wood to form the sides be narrow, and bevel inwards the sides, and shape them so as to form the circle; but, if of an octagon form, the pieces will be, of course, of the width of each of the eight sides, and planed to fit at each corner. Fasten them firmly together with nails, and the main foundation and walls of your baskets are complete. But they want something more, to give them an ornamental, finished appearance. On the top of the side put some split hazel rods of sufficient thickness to cover it, and hang over the outside edge about half an inch. Place some of the same kind close to the bottom: then, between the two, cover the plain boards with one of the two things we shall now mention. The first and cheapest is some rough oak or elm bark, so closely fitted as to give the idea that the basket has been cut out of a solid tree. The next is more expensive and troublesome, but certainly more ornamental. It is split or whole (as you may fancy) hazel rods, formed into a diamond, circle, or any other tasty forms. These should fit so closely as to completely hide the material of which the sides are formed. The bark plan will not require anything more doing to it after it is neatly fitted, and securely nailed to the sides, but the hazel rods should have a coating of boiled linseed oil applied. This will preserve them, and give a very ornamental polished surface. We shall devote a few lines to the vases. Judiciously placed near the dwelling-house, either on the pillars of a low wall or on pedestals, on a terrace walk, or one on each side of the entrance to the house, they are quite proper and in good taste, if not too numerous or too large in proportion to the size of the garden or house. Vases to grow plants in can be had of almost any size and form of the different manufacturers of them. Perhaps the largest stock in the kingdom may be seen at the New Road, Marylebone, London. Examples of various kinds and forms, from those in costly marble down to others in humble compo or cement, may be found there ready for use.

PLANTS FOR RUSTIC BASKETS AND VASES.—Having now briefly hinted at these interesting objects, as ornaments to gardens of every grade, we proceed to give a list of suitable plants, premising that they require a rich light soil, such, for instance, as fresh loam, vegetable mould, and sandy peat, in equal parts. If the peat cannot be procured, add sufficient sand to make the whole open so as to let the water from heavy rains pass freely through the drainage and holes at the bottom. You must not forget those two last-mentioned points of culture—the *drainage*, which is best made of broken garden-pots and rough charcoal, mixed, and the *holes* in the bottom of each, to allow the superabundant moisture to escape freely. If these two points are neglected, or not properly attended to, the plants will in long-continued wet weather soon show the effects of bad management. Their leaves will turn yellow and drop off, the flowers will be poor and scarce, and in extreme wet weather the whole will die. But if proper care is bestowed upon the drainage, rainy weather will have a beneficial effect, and the plants will flourish as healthily as their neighbours in the open borders. The plants that are proper for vases are, for one Scarlet Geraniums, edged with that beautiful annual Rhodanthe Manglesii (Mangles' Rhodanthe), with the yellow drooping Moneywort (Mimulus nummularis). For another vase, a *Fuchsia* of a drooping habit in the centre, German Stocks of various colours around it, with the canary-coloured Nasturtium (Tropæolum canariense) as a drooper to hang over the edges. The next vase might have a blue Sage plant (Salvia patens) in the centre, with Clarkia pulchella (pretty Clarkia) next to it, edged with dwarf Fairy Roses, and a Maurandya Barclayana for the weeper. These are for the summer months. In early spring various other things might be employed to fill them with, such as Crocuses, Snowdrops, Wall-flowers, Saxifrages, especially Saxifraga oppositifolia, Wall-cress (Arabis alpina), white and Aubrietia deltoidea, purple. After these early flowers are out of bloom, they should be removed, a little fresh earth added, and the summer flowers put in. A thin coating of living green moss would be ornamental, and would preserve the roots from the too-sudden changes of the atmosphere. In dry weather they will require well soaking with water once a week, and sprinkling every evening. We would remark, previously to leaving this subject, that you may, if you so prefer, fill one or two of your baskets or vases entirely with one sort of plant, such as Scarlet Geraniums, Fuchsias, or dwarf Fairy Roses.

If the vases are fixtures, as soon as the summer flowers are removed you might plant in each any of the following plants, to look green during the winter: Yucca recurva (Recurved Adam's needle); Y. filamentosa, and filamentosa variegata (Thready, and Thready variegated-leaved Adam's needle); Picea canadensis (Hemlock Spruce); a dwarf bushy box-tree, or an Aucuba japonica; any of which would have a better appearance than empty vases. In very severe frost, cover them with an extra thickness of moss. The rustic baskets had better have the earth taken out of them, be well cleaned, and be removed during winter to some dry shed, to preserve them from the weather.

ORNAMENTAL TREES AND FLOWERING SHRUBS.

OF TREES—we would remark that they are useful in such gardens, to shield off in sultry weather the hot rays of the sun; and as villas are generally near a highway, they partly shelter the lower growing flowers from the dust, and serve also as a screen from the passers by. Those trees, then, ought to be planted close to the boundary-fence, and should be kept pruned in, so as not to hang over either way. Deciduous (losing their leaves in winter) trees are most proper. The following we conceive to be the best for this purpose:—the Lime-tree, Laburnum, Platanus, or Plane-tree, and Robinia Pseud-Acacia, or, as it is commonly called, the Acacia. One of each of these will be sufficient. The price depends upon the size; trees from four to six feet high are 1s. each; ten feet high, 2s. 6d. each.

SHRUBS.—We would by no means have a garden, however small, without some shrubs in it. These may be planted between the trees, and to serve as a division between such gardens. In this class is the queen of flowers—the Rose, of which every garden can scarcely have too many; at least, we have no fear that villa gardens will ever be overstocked with this universal favourite. In very smoky parts of towns, such as London, Manchester, Birmingham, &c., we are reluctantly obliged to confess that the Rose will not thrive; but at short distances from such towns, it will do moderately well. Deciduous shrubs may be planted any time in autumn, after the greater portion of the leaves have fallen, or before vegetation commences in spring. Previous to planting let your ground be prepared by digging, in

142   ORNAMENTAL TREES AND FLOWERING SHRUBS.

the manner already described; then plant your shrubs, giving them, if the weather is dry, a good watering at the roots. Evergreens may be planted till April with success, if they are put in with puddle, that is, earth and water mixed together till of paint-like thickness, in the hole where the tree is to be planted. The shrub is then put into this puddle, and filled up with earth, mixing again with water till the hole is filled up level with the ground. We have removed large evergreens in a hot, dry July, and by using puddle they have all succeeded well. Now, as we have proved the great use of puddle in planting large trees and shrubs, it is surely not too much to expect that it will answer as well, or better, for smaller ones.

SELECT LIST OF TREES AND SHRUBS for a villa garden. The expense of these is so moderate as to be within the reach of all amateur gardeners:—

Acacia, Rose, 10 feet.
Almond, Dwarf, Double, 3 feet.
Althæa frutex, 4 feet.
Arbor Vitæ, Chinese, 10 feet.
Arbutus, 8 feet.
Aucuba japonica, 4 feet.
Berberis aquifolium, 2 feet.
Broom, Portugal, 6 feet,
———— Yellow Spanish, 6 feet.
Cistus, Gum, 4 feet.
Cotoneaster microphylla, 2 feet.
Erica, herbacea, 6 inches.
Furze, Double, 3 feet.
Gueldres Rose, 6 feet.

Holly, variegated.
Laburnum, Scotch, 15 feet.
Laurels.
Laurustinus.
Lilacs.
Mezereon.
Pæony, Tree, 3 feet.
Ribes sanguineum, 3 feet.
Syringa, Double, 5 feet.
Rhododendrons.
Spiræa ariæfolia, 3 feet.
Thorn, Scarlet, 10 feet.
———— Double Pink, 10 feet.

Roses are a distinct class of shrubs, and are deserving a separate notice and list. A row of standard roses, not very tall, on each side of the walk, is very desirable. One standard might be planted in the middle of the bed, with smaller ones round it, and dwarf ones, in front, in which case the Tree Pæony must be placed elsewhere. These should not be planted thickly, but at such distances as will allow room for flowers. Some roses may also be planted in the corners of the border, where it is widest.

AS STANDARDS.

Moss Roses, *Celina*, rich crimson.
———— *Crested* Moss, bright rose.
———— *White Bath*, white.
French or Gallic, *Kean*, rich velvety purple.
———— ———— *Oh!*, dark crimson and scarlet.
Hybrid Provence, *Blanchefleur*, white.

Of other Classes, *Chénédolé*, large vivid crimson.
———— ————*Coupe d'Hébé*, deep pink.
———— ————*Paul Ricaut*, rosy crimson.
Austrian, *Persian Yellow*, finest yellow.

These cost from 2s. to 2s. 6d. each, and ten standards, as the above, will furnish a small garden sufficiently. Those we have named are select, good, showy kinds.

DWARF ROSES.

Provence, *White*, pure white.
Moss, *Common*, pale rose.
―――― *Crimson*, light crimson.
―――― *Laneii*, rosy crimson, tinted with purple.
Damask, *Leda*, blush, edged with cherry.
―――― *Madame Soëtmans*, orange white, shaded with buff.
Alba, *Madame Audot*, pale flesh.
French or Gallic, *Boula de Nanteuil*, crimson purple.
―――――――*Transon Goubault*, deep bright crimson.
Hybrid Provence, *La Volupté*, bright rose.
Other Hybrids, *Beauty of Billiard*, scarlet.
――――――*Coupe d'Hébé*, deep pink.
―――――― *Paul Ricaut*, rosy crimson.
―――――― *William Jesse*, purplish crimson, tinged with lilac.
Hybrid Perpetuals, *Baronne Prevost*, pale rose, superb.

Hybrid Perpetuals, *Caroline de Sansal*, clear flesh.
―――――――― *Dr. Julliard*, rose purple, shaded with carmine.
―――――――― *Duchess of Sutherland*, pale rose, very double.
―――――――― *Géant des Batailles*, bright crimson, shaded with purple.
―――――――― *General Jacqueminot*, bright red, velvety.
―――――――― *Jules Margottin*, bright cherry.
―――――――― *La Reine*, rosy pink, tinged with lilac.
―――――――― *Senateur Vaisse*, bright red.
―――――――― *William Jesse*, crimson, tinged with lilac.
Bourbon, *Dupetit Thouars*, bright crimson.
―――――― *Sir J. Paxton*, bright rose, shaded with crimson.
―――――― *Souchet*, deep crimson, purple.
―――――― *Souvenir de Malmaison*, clear flesh, edges blush, very fine.

The above kinds are all very fine. The hybrids thrive best if budded on very dwarf stocks. If the garden is too small to hold the whole number, choose any number you may think sufficient, varying the colours as much as possible.

SHRUBS FOR A WALL.

The first thing to attend to is to prepare the border. The soil should not be rich, as the object is not so much to grow them rapidly or strong as to have a variety of moderately grown and freely-flowered plants. The border need not be wide; if it be four feet it will be quite sufficient. Even two feet will do, and it will be more convenient, as it will allow the operations of nailing and protecting the shrubs to be more conveniently performed. A good compost for them is formed of one-half loam and one-half sandy peat, well mixed, but not made too fine. If the situation is low and wet, it must be drained, and a quantity of brick ends, or broken stones, or clinkers, put at the bottom about four or five inches thick. The depth of the compost need not be more than sixteen inches. Should a walk be next to the border, the drain can be under the walk, and an edging of box planted. The compost should be put in two or three inches higher than it is intended to be, to allow for settling.

The border being made, and the shrubs planted, the next operation will be to fasten them to the wall. The most common method practised is with shreds of cloth and nails. The shreds are generally made of the list, or outer edging, of woollen cloth, clipt into suitable lengths; longer for the thick branches, and shorter for the small ones. This list can be procured from the tailors. Cast iron nails, on account of first cheapness, are mostly used, but hammered nails are the best, and cheapest too, in the end. Another method of fastening shrubs to the wall is by having a trellis of wooden laths set up against and nailed to the wall previously to planting, so as to allow matting or twine to pass under each lath to tie the shrubs to. This plan, when the trellis is neatly made, and painted green, has a very ornamental appearance, but there is an objection or two to it : it is rather expensive, is liable to decay, and harbours dead leaves and insects. The next plan we shall notice is that of having cast-iron nails with an eye to each. These can be driven into the wall at certain distances, between every row of bricks, where the wall is of that material. The plants can be tied to those eye-headed nails, and this will answer pretty well. In our opinion, however, the best plan to adopt for this purpose is that of using long lengths of copper, iron, or zinc wire stretched horizontally along the wall, at about nine inches apart. It can be fastened to the wall with such eyed nails as we have just mentioned, or with iron staples.

The following is a select list of shrubs suitable for this purpose :—Those marked with an asterisk may be used where the extent of wall is moderate. The whole are well worth cultivating where there is room for them.

DECIDUOUS.

* *Amygdalus persica flore pleno.* Double-flowering Peach.
Cercis siliquastrum. Long-podded Judas-tree.
* *Chimonanthus fragrans.* Sweet Chimonanthus.
* *Cydonia japonica alba.* White Japan Quince.
* " *rubra.* Red ditto.
* *Hydrangea quercifolia.* Oak-leaved Hydrangea.
* *Magnolia conspicua.* Showy Magnolia.
* " *Soulangeana.* Soulange's ditto.
* *Punica granatum.* Pomegranate.
Ribes speciosum. Showy Ribes.
Robinia hispida. Rose Acacia.
* *Weigela rosea.* Rose-coloured Weigela.

EVERGREEN.

Berberis dulcis. Sweet Berberry.
" *fascicularis.* Bundle-flowered Berberry.
* " *trifoliata.* Trifoliate Berberry.

* *Ceanothus cœruleus.* Blue Ceanothus.
Cistus ladaniferus. Gum Cistus.
* *Cotoneaster microphylla.* Small-leaved Cotoneaster.
Escallonia macrantha. Long-flowered Escallonia.
Jasminum fruticans. Shrubby Jasmine.
Laurus nobilis. Sweet Bay.
Ligustrum japonicum. Japan Privet.
Magnolia grandiflora. Large-flowered Magnolia.
* " *Exmouthii.* Lord Exmouth's Magnolia.
Photinia serrulata. Saw-leaved Photinia.

CLIMBERS.

Ampelopsis hederacea. Virginian Creeper.
Atragene austriaca. Austrian Atragene.
" *Sibirica.* Siberian do.
* *Bignonia radicans major.* Large Ash-leaved Trumpet flower.
* *Clematis azurea grandiflora.* Large blue Clematis.
" *florida.* Large-flowered do.
" " *fl. pleno.* Double Large-flowered Clematis.

Clematis flammula. Sweet ditto.
,, *Hendersonii.* Henderson's ditto.
* ,, *Sieboldii.* Siebold's ditto.
,, *montana.* Mountain ditto.
Corchorus japonicus flore pleno.
* *Cratægus pyracantha.* Evergreen thorn.
* *Hedera Helix.* Ivy (several varieties).
* *Jasminum officinale.* Common Jasmine.
,, *revolutum.* Revolute-flowered ditto.
* *Lonicera italica.* Italian Honeysuckle.
,, *coccinea.* Scarlet ditto.
,, *flexuosa.* Twining ditto.
,, *grata.* Evergreen ditto.
* ,, *sempervirens.* Trumpet ditto.
* *Passiflora cœrulea.* Blue Passion-flower (rather tender).
,, *Mayana.* May's ditto.
,, *palmata.* Hand-leaved ditto.
Vitis riparia. Sweet Vine.
* *Wistaria sinensis.* Chinese Wistaria.

In addition to the above, the following climbing roses would make a very agreeable variety:

Amadis. Crimson.
Gracilis. Rosy red.
Laure Davoust. Pink.
Ayrshire Queen. Dark crimson.
Boursault Elegans. Crimson purple.
Félicité Perpétué. White.
Spectabile. Rosy lilac.
Madame d'Arblay. White.
Miller's Climber. Purple.
Yellow Banksian.

To fill up the wall until the permanent shrubs cover it, annual creepers should be planted, such as Tropæolum canariense, Maurandya Barclayana, Lophospermum Hendersonii, Rhodochiton volubile, Cobæa scandens, and Eccremocarpus scaber.

Should these not be sufficient to cover the wall entirely, Fuchsias, Scarlet Geraniums, some strong-growing Verbenas of different colours, Heliotropes, Phlox Drummondii, Mimulus glutinosus, and M. puniceus may be planted during the first summer.

PILLAR ROSES.

There is no kind of shrub, however beautiful, that is used to ornament a garden scene, so well adapted to take various forms as the rose. It can be used as a dwarf tiny plant to fill the smallest bed; as a bush to plant amongst other shrubs; as one to plant in beds of larger dimensions in groups; as a tall standard, to form avenues of roses on each side of a noble walk; standards can also be planted in groups on a lawn. These also are often planted in the centre of a large circular bed, with half standards around them, and dwarfs in front, thus forming an amphitheatre of roses, which, when in bloom, is one of the finest sights in the flower garden. It can also be used to cover naked banks and dry rocks, and as a climber to ornament the amateur's villa, or the more humble abode of the cottager; also to plant against naked walls or palings, and to form drooping shrubs when grafted on high standards, to wave gracefully their boughs, laden with fragrance and bloom, in the warm gales of summer and autumn. All those forms are very beautiful; but amidst them all, elegant though they are, there are none that show off the beauty and grandeur of the rose with such effect as training it up pillars or poles. The poles, when single, ought to be pretty stout, and set firmly in the ground, or they may be blown down by strong winds. More slender poles may be used if placed in a triangular form, about three feet from each other at the base, and the ends brought together at the top. Tie them together with some strong tarred cord, or with stout copper wire. They will, in this form, stand the strong gales much better than when planted singly. The best kind of poles for this purpose are young larches—the thinnings of plantations—they last much longer than any other kind. Should you adopt the triangular pillar, you may either plant three roses of the same variety, or have three different kinds—planting one at the foot of each pole. This being a matter of taste, we may leave the choice to the cultivator. Train the roses from pole to pole, so as to completely hide them when in full foliage and flower; they will then form a beautiful tall pyramid of flowers. Our cottage friends may easily have pillar roses, as in the country such poles may be had almost for nothing. It is true that larches do not grow everywhere; and, in the case of there being none near you, other kinds of poles may be used—such as oak, ash, or hazel. These will last a considerable time if the ends that are in the soil be charred, and then dipped in pitch while warm. Set them in the sun some time till quite dry previously to using them.

To return to iron pillars. Our amateur friends willing to be at the expense of erecting such, may easily ascertain the cost from any respectable ironmonger. These may either be formed of a single upright rod, or with four rods at about nine inches distant from each other; thus forming a square pillar, fastened with cross pieces of strong wire. The rose may be planted in the centre, and the branches as they grow be trained to each corner rod, and small shoots trained between them. Bring all the shoots to the outside, and do not allow any to twine round the rods, but tie them to each with bass matting or small twine. These can then be easily loosened from the pillars whenever they require painting, an operation that must not be neglected, as the iron will soon rust, and thereby injure the plants, and be very unsightly. Previously to planting the roses, make the soil very rich, as you require those roses to grow quickly in order to flower freely, and cover the pillars, arches, and festoons as soon as possible.

We shall place them before our readers in their several classes or sections, so that the cultivator may choose such as will suit their situation and taste.

CLIMBING ROSES.—*Boursault.* This is quite a distinct section, very gorgeous, of rapid vigorous growth, blooming in large clusters. To prune them rightly, thin out the branches severely, but do not shorten much those you leave.

Amadis, or *Crimson*—Deep purplish crimson, large and semi-double, cup-shaped flowers. *Blush,* or *De l'Isle*—Blush, rose centre, very large and full, globular. *Gracilis*—Bright rosy red, large and full.

AYRSHIRE ROSES.—These may be properly termed "running roses," being of a free and rapid growth, and will thrive in rough wild situations, such as rocky banks, or climb up old or dead trees. For these purposes there are none to equal the Ayrshire varieties. They also form beautiful drooping objects, if budded upon tall standard wild briars.

Ayrshire Queen—Dark purple crimson, large and semi-double, cup-shaped. *Queen of the Belgians*—Creamy-white, small and double, cup-shaped. *Ruga*—Pale flesh, large and double, globular.

EVERGREEN ROSES.—These are a valuable section, blooming in very large clusters of from ten to fifty flowers in each. They retain their fine shining foliage the most of the winter, are free growers, and very hardy. Like the preceding, they form beautiful weeping heads if on tall standards. Prune them so as to leave the largest previous year's shoots, which will flower in the extreme ends.

Felicité Perpetué—Creamy-white, small and double, of a compact form. *Flora*—Bright rose, full. *Myrianthes*—Blush, edged with rose, small and double, cup-shaped. *Spectabile*—Rosy lilac, large, double, and of compact shape.

BANKSIAN ROSES.—Like the last, nearly evergreen, requiring a warm wall and dry border. They should be trained with long shoots, to bloom on the short branches these shoots make, and will then flower very freely and beautifully. The older they are the more flowers they will produce. Any long, strong, extra shoots they may produce, that are not wanted, should be cut away towards the end of June.

Banksia Alba—White, very sweet, in clusters of small elegant flowers, cup-shaped. *Banksia Jaune Serin*—Yellow, equally fine as the last, with large flowers, and cup-shaped. *Banksia Lutea*—The old yellow, very small and double, cup-shaped.

HYBRID CLIMBING ROSES.—These, on account of their decided climbing habit, are separated from their proper sections. The first two are varieties of *Rosa multiflora* hybridized with other kinds. The last named is a variety of the *Musk Rose*. They require pruning the same way as the Boursaults.

Laure Davoust—A most desirable rose, pink, changing to blush, and very double, of a compact shape. *Russelliana*—Strong grower, dark crimson, and double, of a compact form. *Madame D'Arblay*—White, blooming in large clusters, very showy.

ROSA MULTIFLORA (*Many-flowered Rose*).—The varieties of *Rosa multiflora* are rather tender, requiring a warm sheltered situation, and a very gentle use of the knife in pruning. "The seven sisters" is a splendid variety when it has proper treatment.

Grevillii (Seven Sisters)—Blush, changing sometimes to a deep red, double, and compact form. *Elegans*—Blush and white, small, double, and of a compact shape. *Triomphe de Bayeux*—White-centred, straw-coloured flowers, in corymbs, or flat heads of bloom.

All the above are truly climbing roses. If the garden is small, select one only out of each section. There are a large number of hybrid China summer-blooming climbers; for autumn-blooming, hybrids of Bourbons, Noisette, and Perpetuals, are proper.

Though there are several vigorous growing roses amongst the Provence, Damask, and French kinds, yet they are scarcely fit for training up pillars; we shall, therefore, select from the Hybrid-China, Noisette, and Bourbon varieties, together with Boursault, Ayrshire, Hybrid-Perpetuals, Hybrid-Bourbons, and Noisettes; all of which contain some excellent kinds, well adapted for pillars.

Blarii No. 2, blush pink, very large and double. *Brennus*, deep carmine, very large and full. *Chénédolé*, light vivid crimson, very large and double. *Coupe d'Hébé*, rich deep pink, large and very double. *Frederic the Second*, rich crimson purple, large and double. *General Jacqueminot*, purplish crimson, large and full. *Madame Plantier*, pure white, full. *Madeline*, pale flesh, edged with crimson, large and double. *Paul Perras*, pale rose, very large and full. *Vivid*, rich vivid crimson.

BOURSAULT ROSE.—*Amadis* or *Crimson*, deep purplish crimson, large and semi-double.

This variety, having strong vigorous shoots, is one of the very best to form a pillar of roses: it frequently has shoots six or seven feet long, which the following summer break at nearly every bud, and are covered with flowers all their length. They should be suffered to hang loosely, in order to display all their beauty.

AYRSHIRE.—*Dundee Rambler*, white, edges pink, numerous small flowers, and double. *Miller's Climber*, bright purple, semi-double.

HYBRID CLIMBING ROSE.—*The Garland*, nankeen and pink, changing to white, very showy, semi-double.

HYBRID PERPETUAL.—The strong vigorous growers of this class of roses are excellent for pillars, and have the advantage of blooming through the autumn months. On that account we advise the greater number of roses for this purpose to be selected from the following names:

Alexandrine Bachmeteff, bright red, large and full. *Duchess of Sutherland*, pale rose, large and very double. *General Jacqueminot*, brilliant velvety red, large and double. *Dr. Julliard*, rosy purple, shaded, large and very double. *Gloire de Rosomènes*, brilliant carmine, showy, large, and semi-double. *Louise Odier*, fine bright rose. *Louis Chaix*, bright red, shaded with crimson. *Madame de Cambacères*, rosy carmine, large and full. *Madame Rivers*, clear flesh, large and full. *Pius the Ninth*, crimson purple, large and full. *Souvenir de Reine d'Angléterre*, bright rose, large and full. *Triomphe de l'Exposition*, beautiful reddish crimson, large and full. *William Jesse*, crimson, tinged with lilac, very large and double.

BOURBON ROSES are peculiarly autumn roses: they are also free and constant bloomers, with fine foliage, bright colours, and in general finely shaped flowers.

Acidalie, blush white, superb, large and full. *Empress Eugénie*, rose purple, edges large and full. *Glorietta*, deep red. *L'Avenir*, bright rose, large and full. *Marquis Balbiano*, rose, tinged with silver. *Sir J. Paxton*, bright rose, shaded with crimson, large and full. *Reveil*, cherry, shaded with violet. *Souvenir de Malmaison*, clear flesh, edges blush, very large and full.

NOISETTE ROSES.—These bloom generally in large clusters throughout the summer and autumn. They are free growers, and fragrant.

Caroline Marniesse, cream white. *Du Luxembourg*, lilac rose, deep red centre, large and very double. *La Riche*, pale flesh, very large. *Madame Massot*, pure white, flesh centre. *Triomphe de Rennes*, canary, large and full.

PRUNING.—Pillar roses should receive a kind of temporary pruning about November. At that time shorten-in the long straggling branches only. In the beginning of March, prune-in the side shoots, to three or four eyes, and tie-in the leading ones to nearly their full length. Take away all coarse, strong, gluttonous shoots—those robbers of the strength which ought to be husbanded to nourish the flower-bearing branches.

INSECTS.—The rose caterpillars* will soon begin their destructive attacks upon the leaves and young buds of the rose. No application of any liquid that we know of will destroy these insects. The only way is to crush them with your finger. "The worm i' th' bud," alluded to by Shakespere, is this insect. In the bud, then, you must look for it; but too often the effect is discovered before the cause; or, in other words, the buds containing the flowers, are eaten by this caterpillar before you perceive its presence; but this is the effect of want of observance. We advise you, therefore, earnestly to be diligent every day in examining your rose bushes, and crush the enemy before he has destroyed your rose buds, and thus made of no avail all the pains, cost, and anxiety you may have bestowed.

ROSES FOR BEDDING.

We have often been surprised at the demand for flowers for bedding purposes, that is, for flowers of distinct colours, of one kind, for each bed. "Anything *new* for bedding?" is the perpetually recurring inquiry. Every nurseryman that has customers for plants for this purpose is often puzzled how to supply novelties; many things have, in consequence, been recommended, and made use of for one season, that have utterly failed to please, either on account of the fewness of their flowers, or the want of decided colours, or a succession of bloom. The passion for such new things has in some degree prevented the use of others of decided merit, and of none more so than the flower with which we have headed this paragraph. We have

* The caterpillars attacking the leaves and buds of roses are those of more than one species of moth, but the most common are those of the *Argyrotoza Bergmanniana* or *Tortrix rosana*. The moth is very small and beautiful, and is often very numerous in gardens and about hedges, late in July and early in August. The caterpillar draws the young leaves of the rose together by its web, and pierces with numerous holes the mass thus formed. The caterpillar is about half an inch long, of a dark flesh-colour, with a black head. The remedy is to open the leaves attacked, and to destroy their assailant.

had frequent inquiries as to what are the best roses for bedding-out purposes, and shall therefore endeavour to give a few names, with their colours and season of flowering.

The rose, by reason of its beauty, clear colours, fragrance, fine bright foliage, and capability of taking any form, either upright or prostrate, is peculiarly well adapted to plant in masses of one colour and one kind in each bed. Roses are classed first into two grand divisions, summer-blooming and autumn-blooming; these are again divided into several sections. We will just give the names of each,—

1st Grand Division.—Summer Roses, flowering from May to July. Sections:—1, Provence; 2, Moss; 3, Damask; 4, Alba (white); 5, Gallicia (French); 6, Hybrid Provence; 7, Hybrid Chinese, Bourbon, and Noisette; 8, Scotch Roses; 9, Austrian; 10, Sweet-brier.

2nd. Grand Division.—Autumnal Roses, flowering from July to November. Sections:—1, Perpetual Moss; 2, Perpetual Scotch; 3, Damask Perpetual; 4, Hybrid Perpetual; 5, Bourbon; 6, Noisettes; 7, China, or Monthly Roses; 8, Tea-scented China.

Some readers will no doubt be surprised that there are s many classes of these beautiful flowers; yet there is good reason for thus dividing them, as it enables collectors to choose such as will suit their various wants and purposes, and to select them also to bloom at any particular time of the year those flowers may be wanted.

Roses suitable for beds are kept in pots by most nurserymen, and, therefore, can be had at the time the beds are ready for them. The seventh and eighth sections of the autumnal roses are the China (Rosa indica); this group contains the greatest number of kinds for the purpose. We have seen dark China roses planted in a bed, and then a wire trellis placed over it, raised about six inches from the ground in the centre, and brought gradually down to the grass at the edge of the bed. To this trellis the branches of the roses as they grew were tied down; in the course of a short time the ends of each shoot turned upwards, and produced abundance of roses. The bed then presented the appearance of a large bouquet of those splendid richly-coloured flowers, forming a truly magnificent spectacle. We strongly recommend this method to our readers, and assure them, if they give it a trial, having the soil right, the plants strong, and a moderately fine season, with the requisite attention to tying down, weeding, and watering, the display of beautiful flowers will be agreeably surprising.

CHINA ROSES SUITABLE FOR BEDDING IN GROUPS.

White—Madame Plantier (Hybrid China); Mrs. Bosanquet; Madame Bureau; Duchess of Kent.

Yellow—Jaune (Tea-scented); Eliza Sauvage (ditto).
Rose-coloured—Adam; Goubault.
Red and Scarlet—Fabvier; Baronne Delaage.
Crimson—Fulgens; William Jesse.
Dark Crimson—Cramoisie Supérieure.

The *Fairy* roses both white and red are excellent for small beds.

The *Bourbons* contain some of the finest roses blooming in autumn. They are free and constant bloomers, with fine foliage, bright colours, are very hardy, and of free growth. *The Noisettes* are fine roses, blooming in large clusters throughout the summer and autumn; some of them scarcely cease blooming for six months together. We shall arrange them in colours, commencing with.

NOISETTES FOR BEDDING.

White—Aimée Vibert, Miss Glegg. *Yellow*—Lamarque, Solfaterre. *Rose*—Du Luxembourg. *Dark crimson*—Pourpre de Tyre.

BOURBONS FOR BEDDING.

White—Acidalie (there are no yellow Bourbons). *Rose*—George Cuvier, Leveson Gower. *Red* and *scarlet*—Emilie Courtier. *Crimson*—Souchet, Paul Joseph.

PERPETUAL ROSES FOR BEDDING.

White—Perpetual White Moss. It is a somewhat singular fact that this beautiful autumnal rose is the only clear white one in this class, the darker colours seeming greatly to preponderate. *Yellow*—It is equally extraordinary that there are no yellow perpetual roses. *Rose colour*—Celestina, Comte d'Egmont. *Scarlet*—None strictly of this colour. *Crimson*—Lee's Crimson or Rose du Roi, Louis Buonaparte, Madame Laffay, Dr. Marx. *Dark crimson*—Louis Philippe, Mogador, Antinous, Edward Jesse.

This class of roses is very rich in the two last mentioned colours. Any of the kinds named will answer admirably to plant in beds; the collector may choose which he pleases, and he is sure to obtain a rich coloured, very double, and free-flowering rose.

AUSTRIAN ROSES.—*Persian Yellow.*—This is the very finest of hardy yellow roses; it is of a rich orange yellow, very full, large, and superb; it opens its flowers much better than the yellow Noisette, and is altogether a very desirable rose; it is also a free bloomer, and has a neat foliage, with the scent of the sweet-brier. To succeed in growing and blooming it well, you must place it in a good loam, mixed with peat and leaf-mould. In pruning, all that is required is to thin out the shoots pretty freely, and not shorten in the remainder, but peg them down to the ground their full length, or very nearly so; if the shoots are very long and rather weak, you may take off four or five buds from the end. By this method of pruning, each bud will break and produce flowers on short upright shoots, nearly the entire length of each of the long shoots; the bed then will be truly gorgeous.

Roses for Grouping in Beds.—There is so great a number of kinds of roses that answer admirably for bedding purposes, that we feel almost at a loss which to recommend in preference to others equally as good. We shall give three more that are needful for moderate-sized gardens, and which are really good for the purpose. Our readers, consequently, need be at no loss which to have and which to reject.

White Damask—Madame Hardy.
White Provence—Unique.
Rose-coloured—Common Moss. A bed of roses all of this kind, when in flower, is one of the finest sights the kingdom of Flora exhibits. The delicious fragrance and lovely hue of this beautiful rose, half shrouded, as it were, with a veil of green mossy spray, renders it peculiarly attractive and desirable. To grow it to the greatest perfection, you must take some pains; and before we describe the proper management it requires, we will observe that the same treatment will suit all the strong growing Provence, Damask, and Gallic (French) roses, when grown on their own roots as dwarf roses.

In the first place, the soil should be of a good loamy texture, made rich with very rotten dung. The plants should be put in early in autumn, and a covering of short dung spread all over the bed. The first year they should be pruned to three buds of the previous year's growth. In the autumn of the following year, fork the bed over, and lay on a fresh coat of rotten dung; then in the spring, early in March, procure a few hooked pegs, and peg down a sufficient number of the strongest shoots to cover the bed completely, shortening them in a few inches from the extremity of each shoot. Cut off the shoots that are not wanted, to the same length as you do the spring previously. The shoots thus pruned, and those pegged down, will send up short shoots, and each will have a bunch of fine flowers. Though the first year's bloom will produce some tolerable flowers, the second will be by far the finest. To prevent the bed being entirely bare of flowers in the spring, some patches of Crocuses and Snowdrops might be planted amongst them without any injury to the roses. In the autumn, after the roses have done blooming, cut off all the decayed flowers, and plant a few low growing annuals, such as Nolana prostrata, Nemophila insignis, Leptosiphon androsaceus, and others. These will serve to make the bed look gay when the glory of the rose has departed.

ANNUALS.

Annuals, notwithstanding their real beauty, are now too often considered as mere weedy things. The short time during which many of them remain in full perfection is one reason why they are less used than formerly. The little care taken of them, allowing them to remain in a mass unthinned and uncared for, is another cause of their decaying popularity.

A garden cropped with well-grown annuals is a treat: few things are more beautiful, when seen at their best. Just think of beds and rows of different coloured Candytufts! What is there among the finest bedding-plants that will beat them? Come a few inches lower down, and what more lovely than the Nemophila insignis, and its sister species, macalata and atomária? Rise a foot or so higher, and what more pleasing than groups of Godetia Lindleyana, roseo-alba, and masses of Pholx Drummondi, Chrysanthemum carinatum, Viscaria oculata, and even the Erysimum Perofskianum? For low-growing compact beds, we need scarcely mention the Saponaria calabrica, the Sanvitalia procumbens, and the different kinds of small Lobelias, because these are pretty well recognised as fit for bedding or edgings, from lasting the most of the season through.

There are two modes of keeping up a *succession of bloom in an annual bed:* first, by preventing the plants seeding. By merely cutting and stripping off the seeds, we have had beds of Œnothera Lindleyana fine from May to October. The same mode has been adopted with Eschscholtzia, Erysimum, various kinds of Lupines, &c. Frequently, pieces of the stems would be cut off altogether, and then a top-dressing and a good watering would carry the plants on for a month or two. Other things will hardly admit of this treatment, as the labour would be so excessive, such as in the case of the Candytufts, the Nemophilas, the Collinsias, especially the beautiful C. bicolor, but by sowing and planting these rather thinly in rows, early in spring, say by the middle of March, we have seen a good succession kept up by sowing between them in the beginning or towards the end of May, and thinning out the first gradually, to give the young ones room. We once had a fine bed of Collinsia bicolor from the end of May to the end of October, by sowing in September, in May, and July, and the bed never looked bad, though twice during the summer, for a few days at each time, it was rather seedy, before the old plants were all pulled up and the younger ones had taken their place.

By keeping a large reserve garden of annuals sown in pots, or on thick pieces of turf, with spaces scooped out for fine soil and seeds, a bed of annuals might at once be cleared away, the ground dug, and a similar, or a different colour of annual or annuals planted. Much could be done in this way, in small gardens, where freshness and frequent changes are desirable, and where labour is an item never complained about.

In using annuals for beds and these different purposes, we have tried three plans, and if there were conveniences we would prefer the last for obtaining abundance of early flowers. The first is, sowing the seeds in small patches, in the middle and towards the end of March, and covering each patch with a flower-pot until the seed is up, and then at night, and in cold weather, for some time longer, and afterwards carefully thinning out the young plants. The second mode is to sow in poor soil, over a stiffish clayey loam, in September, and protect with a few green boughs in winter. The seedlings are lifted with a trowel, in small patches, in March, and planted in ground well dug and pulverised for them. Most of the Californian annuals answer well by this treatment, as also all the varieties of Candytuft, Sweet Alyssum, Virginian Stock, &c. In severe winters however, unless well protected with snow, there will not be many plants, remaining. The third mode is to prepare a slight hotbed with leaves, &c., about the middle of March; on that place a little rotten dung, next a couple of inches of rough soil and rough leaf-mould, and then an inch of fine soil, and on this sow the annuals in rows, to be transplanted out in little patches when from one to two inches high. If these can be covered with a glass sash, so much the better; if not, hurdles or mats will do. For want of a slight hotbed, we have done the same on a warm border, and protected a little with what we could get, until the plants would stand the weather, and then they were lifted in little patches, and planted according to their height and mode of growth, from a few inches to twelve inches apart.

But though even the hardiest annuals will not dislike the above treatment, there are many suitable for groups which will not do much good without as much, or even more heat than such a slight hotbed; and in the following short list, the letter A will designate those which particularly require such treatment, while the letter B will designate those that will be most likely to bloom the whole season without any extra care, it being understood that the others will not do so without successions, or preventing the seeding process from being completed. If it were not for the labour, almost every annual would keep on blooming if the seeding were wholly prevented, and top-dressings and waterings given.

Those marked with an asterisk * may be sown in the open ground.

ABRONIA *umbellata*—A B, lilac; trailing.

AGERATUM *mexicanum*—A B, lilac blue; two feet in height. This would be better sown in a hotbed and hardened off.

ALONSO *Warszewiczii*—A B, scarlet; eighteen inches in height; treatment as last.

ANAGALLIS of kinds—A B, blue; chiefly one foot high.

ANTIRRHINUM—A B, sown in spring, will bloom in the summer and autumn.

ASTERS, Chinese, German—A B, in addition to these, sow on the open border, in well-mellowed ground.

ANNUALS.

*BARTONIA *aurea*—A B, orange; one foot; if not sown in the ground, should be sown in pots, as it does not transplant well. A rough-looking plant, singular foliage, but the flowers large, and the stamens long and numerous.

BRACHYCOME *iberidifolia*—A B, whitish-blue; nine inches high; compact habit; neat and pretty.

CACALIA *coccinea*—A B, scarlet; one foot high.

CALANDRINIA *umbellata*—A B, red-crimson flowers, about six inches in height; plant compact and close to the ground; sow in pots, as it transplants badly; very neat for a small bed.

———————— *discolor*—A B, rose-colour; one foot.

———————— *speciosa*—B, purple.

CALCEOLARIA *pinnata*—A B, yellow; one-and-a-half feet; sow in pots, and cover thinly.

———————— *chelidonoides*—A B, sow this also in pots and cover slightly, though it would come freely enough in the border. Both of these will want the seed-pods to be removed, to keep up a continuance of flowering.

*CALLIOPSIS *atrosanguinea, Drummondi, coronata, grandiflora,* and many more, will continue to the end of the season if the seeds are cut off, and will be more regular if raised and then planted; all of them are well furnished with fibry roots, and most are from two to three feet in height.

CAMPANULA *carpatica, Lorei, pentagonia,* &c.—low growing plants, with blue and purple flowers. The first is a perennial, but will bloom the first season if treated as an annual.

*CANDYTUFTS (*Iberis*)—a well-known class; valuable for early blooming.

*CHRYSANTHEMUM *carinatum*—A B, one-foot-and-a-half high; showy for large beds. There are several very handsome varieties.

CHRYSEIS, or ESCHSCHOLTZIA *crocea,* orange; *californica,* yellow. These are best sown in the ground, though they transplant pretty freely, and few things are more dazzling than a yellow or orange bed.

CENIA *turbinata*—A, white, like camomile flowers; a few inches high.

*CLARKIA *pulchella,* purple; and *alba* white; A. These are well known, and for a month or six weeks few annuals will beat them. They generally stand the winter well; about twelve inches in height.

*COLLINSIA *bicolor,* lilac and white; and *grandiflora,* pink and blue. The first from a foot in height; the latter more trailing, and also more lasting. These do well sown in autumn, and also as A. The variety *candidissima* is an excellent pure white.

CLINTONIA *pulchella*—A B, pretty, party-coloured, low plant, suitable for beds and vases, should be sown in a pot in a hotbed, and then hardened off.

COBÆA *scandens,* with large purplish flowers; is well adapted for covering palings and unsightly objects. Sow on a moderate hotbed, and plant out in May in a warm situation.

*COLLOMIA *coccinea*—B, one foot high, flowers bright scarlet.

*CONVOLVOLUS *minor*—A B, varieties; from one to two feet; splendid when the sun shines; *major*, a climber.

*ERYSIMUM *Perofskianum*—A and B, if seeds pruned away; stands the winter when sown in autumn; fine orange; from one-and-a-half to two feet.

*EUCHIRIDIUM *grandiflorum*—A, purple; one foot. Excellent for small beds.

*EUTOCA *viscida*—A, and nearly B, blue; one foot high; very pretty for beds.

*GILIA *tricolor*, and others—good for early-blooming and very pretty.

*GODETIA *Lindleyana*—pale rose with a red blotch in the centre of each petal; *rubicunda*—rose with red centre; and *roseo-alba* rose and white,—from one to two feet high, do well sown in autumn as A, or in the open ground. The flowering will be over in the end of July, unless the plants are pruned, and seeding prevented.

GYPSOPHILA *elegans*—A, whitish-purple; nine inches.

HAWKWEEDS—yellow, white, and purple; have had them almost B, with a little picking; about one foot.

HELIOPHILA *araboides*—blue; and several more; one foot; will be A B, in a shady place; plant thickly.

*HIBISCUS *africanus*—A, yellow and brown; one to one-and-a-half feet.

ISOTOMA (*Lobelia*) *axillaris*—A B, purple-blue; one foot; best sown in a pot, in a hotbed, and hardened off.

*KAULFUSSIA *amelloides*—blue; nine inches; A B.

*LARKSPURS of sorts.

*LEPTOSIPHON—*densiflorus*, pale purple; *luteus* and *aureus*, yellow; are all low-growing, and may be sown in autumn, spring, or as A.

LINUM *grandiflorum*—A B, scarlet; one foot,

LOBELIA *erinus speciosa*, four inches, bright blue; and *ramosa*, one foot, deep blue. The former is the best of all the varieties for bedding, and makes beautiful edgings. The latter may also be employed for beds out of doors, but is better adapted for pot-culture in the conservatory; A B; make beautiful beds, edgings, &c.; as the seed is small, should be placed in pots covered with a dusting of silver-sand, and get a little more heat than A.

*LUPINUS, *nanus*, white and blue, and *Hartwegii*, *mutabilis*, *Cruickshankii*, &c.; will all answer to A B, if seeds are removed; *nanus* is about one foot, and the others from two to five feet; the annual blues, roses, and yellows, will also bloom long, if the seed is removed as soon as the pod forms.

*MALOPE *trifida grandiflora*—dark crimson; good for large, tall beds, either treated as A, or sown in the ground.

*MARIGOLDS of sorts— A B.

*MIGNONETTE.

MIMULUS—A B, good for early summer and autumn.

*NEMOPHILA *insignis, maculata*, and many varieties—A, or in the open air; none of them stand the heat of the end of July well, though few things are more splendid in early summer.

*NASTURTIUMS of sorts.

NOLANA—A B, from six inches, bluish, and should be sown in pots, if not sown where to grow at once, as they do not transplant well.

PENTSTEMON—perennial kinds, treated as A, will bloom after Midsummer.

PETUNIA—*white* and *purple*, A B.—These can always be procured, and white and purple beds are thus often better procured from seeds than from cuttings of the best kinds, as they are so apt to go off in some grounds.

*PRINCE'S FEATHER—though not continuous, a small bed of this would have no bad effect.

PHLOX DRUMMONDI—A B.—Many varieties of this are easily procurable by seed, and a bed will generally stand the whole season; while a bed procured from cuttings of the best kinds will generally go off after the dog-days.

PORTULACA—A B, would only be worth trying in very dry and warm positions, where *Thellusoni* and *splendens* are very ornamental.

RHODANTHE *Manglesii*—the same as the last.

SALPIGLOSSIS—A B; very ornamental; should have rather more heat than A to start them.

SALVIA *patens*—this never does better than when treated as an annual. It would be well to sow the seeds by the beginning of March, and in a hotbed, taking them out into a cooler place as soon as they were up.

SANVITALIA *procumbens*—A B, orange and black; trailer; has often been recommended.

*SAPONARIA *calabrica*—A B, pink; this has already been recommended. It is beautiful for beds, edgings, and rockwork.

*SCHIZANTHUS of sorts.

SILENE, *pendula, compacta, Schafta*—low plants, with pink and rose flowers.

SULTAN—purple and yellow; A, or open air; nearly B.

SWEET ALYSSUM, open air, or A B, white and sweet; one foot in height; always in flower.

*SWEET PEAS of sorts.

SPHENOGYNE *speciosa*—A, and nearly B, neat, compact, yellow-orange; one foot.

STOCKS of kinds—A.

TAGETES *signata*, A B, yellow; one to two feet.

*VISCARIA *oculata* and *oculata alba*—rose and white; from one to one-and-a-half feet; A, and nearly B; if the seeds are removed will keep on well to the end of the season.

WHITLAVIA *grandiflora*—a dwarf annual; something like the Eutocas, A.

TROPÆOLUM *canariense*, yellow; *majus, minus*, orange and crimson—make showy beds, when the leaves are to a great extent removed to show the flowers. The Tom Thumb varieties in particular make excellent beds.

*VIRGINIAN STOCK.—This pretty little annual may be had all the summer by sowing in September, the middle of March, and the end of May.

VERBENA *venosa*, purple; and *Aubletia*, bluish-purple—will make good beds in summer and autumn if the seed is sown in a slight hotbed; and so will any of the Verbenas, though you will not be able to depend upon the colour, A.B.

XERANTHEMUM and HELICHRYSUM, A.B.—There are yellow, white, and rose varieties, and from two to three feet in height. Many cultivate them for the flowers which are used in winter nosegays, and for similar purposes, being what are called everlastings.

ZINNIA of varieties, A B, but either more heat should be secured, or the seeds should not be sown until the middle of April, under glass. The goodness of beds of these beautiful flowers greatly depends on the plants never receiving a check; and, therefore, the middle of April will generally be early enough for sowing, as it will not be safe to plant out before the beginning of June, or after the first week is past.

All those alluded to as blooming early will make fine pot-plants for greenhouses. Few things will rival Nemophilas, Collinsias, Schizanthus, &c., when thus grown.

SOWING HARDY ANNUALS.—Should the weather be favourable in March—that is, warm and dry, and you have got your beds and borders nicely trimmed—you may venture to sow some of the hardiest annuals, such as those marked thus*. Proceed to sow them as follows:—With a small rake draw a portion of soil from the places where you intend to sow, commencing at the furthest side of your borders, or in the centre of the beds. Make as many of these hollows as you can conveniently reach to sow at once, without unnecessarily treading upon the ground; for the less it is trodden upon, the better your flowers will thrive. For large seeds, such as Sweet Peas, Lupines, and the like, make the hollows fully an inch deep; for smaller seeds, a quarter of an inch will be a sufficient depth. Having made as many hollows as you think right, then take two papers of the tallest annuals of different colours, carrying also with you as many short pieces of wood as you judge there may be patches of flowers in the two packets of seeds. The two sorts may be sown near to each other. Sow of large seeds from four to half a dozen seeds, and of those that are smaller from 12 to 20 in each place. Stick one of the short pieces of wood in the midst of the seeds, leaving them uncovered till the whole of the tall kinds are sown. Then with the rake cover them in, and put out all footmarks, making the ground neat and level. Proceed then to open other hollows with the rake, and, if your beds and borders are not very wide indeed, you may with this second batch finish the sowing for this time. If your soil is heavy and wet (which it ought not to be, if you have been able and willing to follow the instructions previously given), you had better, for the small seed especially, have some light soil sifted moderately fine, and cover those small seeds with it. Do not forget to leave spaces for the half-hardy annuals you are raising in your frame or pit.

BIENNIALS AND PERENNIALS.

Biennials are those plants which, being sown in one year, flower and then die in the next. Perennials are sown in one year and flower in the next, but although they die down in winter, the roots remain alive, and the plants spring up again every year.

BIENNIALS.—The best time for sowing is in the beginning of June, in an open situation, in moderately rich soil; sow thinly: there is nothing gained by sowing thickly. Water gently in dry weather every evening. In July prepare a bed in some open part of the garden, by digging and raking, to transplant them into. By transplanting them whilst young they will make nice bushy plants close to the ground; and will, in such a condition, be more able to endure the frosts of winter. The soil into which you transplant them should not be enriched with any manure. If it is of a heavy nature, a coating either of quicklime or of some finely sifted coal-ashes would be of great use. Your biennials should be planted thinly, to allow them room to make stocky plants. It is much better to have one dozen of good plants than twice as many middling ones. Should any of them grow up with a single stem, and show no tendency to branch out near the ground, nip off the centre shoot near to the ground. This will cause them to branch out freely, and make plants that will, when the flowering season arrives, send up numerous spikes or heads of flowers.

These directions being attended to, the plants will, in August, be bushy and fit for planting out in the places where they are to flower next year. Should they, in consequence of moist weather, be growing so strongly as to become crowded in the nursery beds, and the situations you wish to grow them in are yet occupied with other plants, it will be advisable to transplant them again, so as to give a check to their too luxuriant growth. Unless they actually touch each other, it will not be necessary to plant them wider apart, for the mere lifting them will give them a sufficient check. Attend to these suggestions, or your plants, should the winter be severe, will be all, or nearly all, destroyed.

In February, if the weather be open and mild, biennials may be removed out of the bed into which they were transplanted last autumn. Plant them in the borders where they are to flower, placing the tall growers at the back of the border, and the dwarfer kinds in front. They generally consist of—

Anchusa italica, 2 feet.	Scarlet Lychnis, 2 feet.
Canterbury Bells, 2¼ feet.	Stocks, Brompton, 3 feet.
Catananche bicolor, 9 inches.	,, Queen, 1¼ feet.
,, coerulea, 9 inches.	Sweet Rocket, 1 foot.
Foxgloves, 4 feet.	Sweet Scabious, 1½ feet.
French Honeysuckle, 2 feet.	Sweet William, 1 foot.
Honesty, 2½ feet.	Valerian, 1 foot.
Humea elegans, 4 feet.	Wall-flowers, 2 feet.
Indian Pink, 6 inches.	

PERENNIALS.—There is no better time for sowing seeds of all hardy perennials than from the middle to the end of May, when there is plenty of time to look after them till they are past nursing and can take care of themselves. The best and cheapest way for sowing is to dig up a spare border, or any piece of light ground, to rake the surface as fine as possible, then give it a good soaking of water, and next day it is fit to receive the seeds; small, narrow beds are best, the seed to be sown rather thin, and a barrow load of fine, dry, sifted mould to be at hand for covering them, so that each kind may be covered according to the size of the seeds; generally, a quarter of an inch is a covering thick enough for any of these seeds, but if the very small seeds are just covered it will be enough. If this miscellaneous assortment is sown in the usual way, like so many cabbages or lettuces, and "raked in," as we say, the chances are that one-half of them are too deep, and the other half not so deep as they ought to be, as they cling to the little lumps of soil on the surface, or go after the teeth of the rake. There is no better way of covering flower seeds than by hand from a heap of sifted soil, and when the bed is well watered before the seeds are sown, there will be no danger of the surface "caking," as no more watering will be necessary before the seedlings are up, unless the weather is very dry indeed. Where the ground is liable to cake after watering, a little sifted leaf-mould put all over is the best preventive. A reel of white cotton run across, or along the bed, and fastened to little sticks, will keep off the sparrows and other birds, if anything will. The after treatment will be the same as in the case of biennials.

PROPAGATION.—The large families of *Phlox, Pentstemon, Campanula, Delphinium* (Larkspurs), *Chelone, Dianthus* (Pinks),

&c., may be propagated in June by cuttings under hand-glasses, placed in a shady situation. If struck and potted separately they make fine plants for the following season. A number of plants of this description produce bottom shoots that will not flower the same year; these make excellent cuttings or slips, as they are sometimes called. Take these off carefully with a sharp knife, and treat in a similar manner to the more woody cuttings; like them they will make strong plants for the following year. *Hepaticas*, and all similar early blooming plants also, may now be divided, and planted in a border shaded from the sun; they will there make fresh roots and nice tufty plants, to be planted in the borders in autumn, to produce their welcome flowers in the early season of spring. The general mode, however, is to wait until the plants have finished blooming; cut down the flower-stalks, the plants will soon begin to push afresh, and then early in autumn the plants should be raised, and divided into pieces, and planted in light, rich, sandy soil, into nursery rows. Each of these will generally be a nice strong plant before spring, when they should be thinned out, and placed in their blooming quarters. *Phloxes, Pæonies, Potentillas,* and *Delphiniums,* may be moved whenever they have done blooming and the leaves are withered. Some of the tender kinds are most safely divided when growth is just commencing in spring.

SPRING-BLOOMING PERENNIALS.

Adonis vernalis (Spring Adonis), 6 in. Yellow.
Alyssum saxatile (Rock Madwort), 6 in. Yellow.
Anemone apennina (Mountain Anemone), 6 in. Blue.
Arabis saxatile (Rock Wall-cress), 6 in. White.
Aubrietia deltoidea (Triangle-leaved Aubrietia), 4 in. Purple.
Cardamine pratensis, flore pleno (Double Cuckoo-flower), 1 ft. Purple.
Cheiranthus alpinus (Alpine Wall-flower), 4 in. Yellow.
Corydalis nobilis (Noble Fumitory), 6 in. Yellow.
Dodecatheon giganteum (Giant American Cowslip).
Gentiana acaulis (Dwarf Gentian), 4 in. Deep blue.
Helleborus niger (Christmas Rose), 1 ft. Pink.
Hepatica triloba alba (Common Hepatica), 3 in. White.
Hepatica triloba cærulea (Blue Hepatica), 3 in. Blue.
Hepatica triloba rubra (Red Hepatica), 3 in. Red.

Iberis sempervirens (Evergeen Candytuft), 9 in. White.
Iris persica (Persian Iris), various colours, 4 in.
Iberis gibraltarica (Gibraltar Candytuft), 1 foot.
Linum flavum (Yellow Flax), 4 in.
„ *narbonense*(Narbonne Flax), 4 in. Blue.
Orobus vernus (Spring Bitter Vetch), 1 ft. Purple.
Phlox divaricata (Early-flowering Phlox), 1½ ft. Blue.
Phlox verna (Spring Phlox), 6 in. Pink.
Phlox setacea (Bristly Phlox), 6 in. Rosy.
Phlox subulata (Oval-shaped Phlox). Pink.
Phlox nivalis (White Phlox), 4 in.
Phyteuma orbicularis (Round-headed Rampion), 1 ft. Blue.
Primula vulgaris alba plena (Double-white Primrose), 3 in., double. White.
Primula vulgaris sulphurea (Double sulphur-coloured), 3 in. Yellow.

Primula vulgaris violacea (Double crimson), 3 in. Crimson.
Pulmonaria virginica (Virginian Lungwort), 1 ft. Blue.
Pulsatilla vernalis (Spring Anemone), 1 ft. Blue.
Sanguinaria Canadensis (Canadian Blood-root), 6 in. White.
Saxifraga oppositifolia (Oppositeleaved Saxifrage), 3 in. Red.
Tussilago alpina (Alpine Coltsfoot), 6 in. Purple.

SUMMER-BLOOMING PERENNIALS.

Achillea ptarmica, flore pleno (Double Sneezewort), 1½ ft. White.
Anthericum liliastrum (Spiderwort), 1 ft. White.
Antirrhinum majus (Larger Snapdragon), 1½ ft. Various colours.
Aquilegia vulgaris (Common Columbine), 1½ ft. Various.
Aquilegia, Skinneri (Skinner's Columbine) 1½ ft. Scarlet.
Bellis perennis, flore pleno (Double Daisy), 4 in. Various.
Betonica grandiflora (Large-flowered Betony), 1½ ft. Purple.
Caltha pelustris, flore pleno (Double Marsh-marigold), 1 ft. Yellow.
Campanula carpatica (Carpathian Bell-flower), 6 in. Blue.
Campanula glomerata alba (Clustered Bell-flower), 1 ft. White.
Campanula grandis (Large Bell-flower), 1½ ft. Spotted.
Campanula persicifolia (Peach-leaved Bell-flower), 1½ ft. Blue.
Campanula trachelium (Throatwort), 2 ft. Blue.
Centaurea montana major (Larger Mountain Centaury), 18 in. Blue. Plant this in quantities, as it is very pretty, growing under trees, and flowering abundantly and early.
Chelone Lyoni (Lyons' Chelone), 3 ft. Purple.
Convallaria majalis (Lily of the Valley), 6 in. White.
Coreopsis lanceolata (Lance-leaved Coreopsis), 2½ ft. Yellow.
Delphinium Barlowii (Barlow's Larkspur), 3 ft. Blue.
Dianthus aggregatus, flore pleno (Double Sweet William).
Ficaria ranunculoides, flore pleno (Double Ranunculus-like Pilewort), 6 in. Yellow.
Gentiana septemfida (Crested Gentian), 6 in. Blue.
Helianthus multiflorus plenus (Double many-flowered Sun-flower).
Hemerocallis cœrulea (Blue Day Lily), 1 ft.
Hemerocallis flava (Yellow Day Lily), 2 ft.
Hemerocallis rutilans (Red Day Lily), 6 in.
Hesperis matronalis, flore pleno (Double Rocket), 1½ ft. White.
Iris graminea (Grass-leaved Iris), 18 in. Blue.
Iris germanica (German Iris), 2 ft. Blue.
Iris sambucina (Elder-scented Iris), 2 ft. White.
Lathyrus latifolius (Everlasting Broad-leaved Pea). This plant is very ornamental, and will answer well to plant against palings, walls, or the stem of a tree.
Lupinus polyphyllus (Lupine), 3 ft. Blue.
Lysimachia verticillata (Whorled Loosestrife), 18 in. Yellow.
Pœonia albiflora (White Peony), 2 ft. Various kinds.
Pœonia officinalis (Common Peony), 2 ft. Various kinds.
Pentstemon gentianoides (Gentian-like Pentstemon), 3 ft. Purple.
Pentstemon coccinea (Purple Pentstemon), 3 ft. Purple.
Phlox brightoniana (Brighton Phlox), 2 ft. Red.
Phlox candidissima alba (Whitest Phlox), 1½ ft. White.
Phlox omniflora (Many-flowered Phlox), 1 ft. White.
Phlox elegans (Elegant Phlox), 1 ft. Purple.
Besides the above there are numerous fine hybrids which greatly excel the original species in the size and beauty of the flowers.
Potentilla Macnabiana (Macnab's Cinquefoil), 2 ft. Fine crimson.
Rhodiola rosea (Rosy Rhodiola), 6 in.
Saxifraga retusa (Retuse Saxifrage), 3 in. Red.
Saxifraga pedatifida (Foot-cleft Saxifrage), 3 in. White.
Spirœa trifoliata (Three-leaved Spirœa), 1½ ft. White.
Trollis europeus (European Globe Ranunculus), 1 ft. Orange.

AUTUMN-BLOOMING FLOWERS.

Anemone vitifolia (Vine-leaved Anemone), 2 ft. White.
Anemone japonica (Japan Anemone), 2 ft. Pink.
Aster amellus (Italian Starwort), 1½ ft. Blue.
Aster elegans (Elegant Starwort), 2 ft. Blue.
Aster Novæ-Angliæ (New England Starwort), 5 ft. Purple.
Aster pulchellus (Handsome Starwort), 6 in. Purple.
Aster pulcherrimus (Handsomest Starwort), 1½ ft. Blue.
Aster spectabilis (Showy Starwort), 1½ ft. Blue.
Chrysanthemum arcticum (Northern C.), 9 in. White.
Liatris squarrosa (Round-headed Liatris), 2 ft. Purple.
Matricaria grandiflora (Double Wild Chamomile), 1 ft. White, double.
Œnothera serotina (Late-flowering Evening Primrose), 3 ft. Yellow.
Phlox tardiflora (Slow-flowering Phlox), 1½ ft. White.
Phlox Wheeleriana (Wheeler's Phlox), 3 ft. Red.
Pyrethrum uliginosum (Marsh Feverfew), 4 ft. White.
Rudbeckia hirta (Hairy Rudbeckia), 2 ft. Purple and yellow.
Rudbeckia Drummondi 3 ft. Yellow and brown.
Rudbeckia Newmanni, 1½ ft. Yellow.
Rudbeckia purpurea (Purple Rudbeckia), 3 ft. Purple.
Solidago lanceolata (Lance-leaved Golden-rod), 3 ft. Yellow.
Solidago altissima (Tallest Golden-rod), 3 ft. Yellow.

The above is a selection of plants that are perfectly hardy, well suited either for the amateur or cottager's mixed flower-border; and which, if planted judiciously, will furnish flowers during the whole of the season. In planting them, put in one that flowers in spring, then one that flowers in autumn, then one that flowers in summer, then an autumn one, next one of the spring-flowering, and then one of the summer-flowering. Mix the colours in the same manner. The border will by this method always present, taking it as a whole, a fair display of flowers.

HARDY BULBS.

Hardy Bulbs, of which Hyacinths are the chief, are very numerous in varieties, and make gay spring flowers from April to the end of May. Deep sandy loam is what they prosper in for years: it should be worked twenty inches or two feet deep, and not a particle of animal manure added to it, unless in the shape of liquid manure, and of that, if the season is dry at the time they are pushing up their flower-stalks, they take large quantities; decayed leaf-mould is also good for them, and very decayed cow-dung, placed eighteen inches below the bulbs, will give stronger bloom for a season or two, but in our climate the bulbs soon die off if rich dung is used for them.

EARLY TULIPS.—The varieties of these are endless, beginning with the single and double *Van Thol*, which begin to open about the 10th of April in the open beds, and others follow on in succession till the middle of May. There are three most beautiful yellow ones of the same size, which come into bloom on the 10th and 12th of April. A dozen of each in a bed near the house would make a fine variety. Their names are *Canary Bird, Yellow Prince,* and *Prince du Ligne.* They would make a nice edging to a mixed bed of early tulips. The yellow shades are different; therefore, if planted in a row as an edging, they would look better if two of a sort be not planted together. For a red bed *Purpur Kroon* is a fine purplish red, and double; *Claramond,* rosy red; and *Areste,* a reddish yellow. These three correspond in height, in their time of flowering, and agree better than one would think from the description of their colour. *Vermilion Brilliant,* is a very effective scarlet; *Royal Standard,* single, red and white, is a fine one for a bed by itself; and so are *Duchesse de Parma,* orange crimson, margined with yellow; *Golden Standard,* single, red and yellow; *Annie Laurie,* red and yellow, and *Parragon Guldebloem,* white feathered, and striped with rosy lilac. The four latest are *Marie de Medicis,* yellow and rose; *Chineuse,* cherry and red; *Pæony,* rose; and *Cato,* reddish. *Rex Rubrorum* is the best of the early double tulips for a bed, a large and very dark red flower; *Marriage de ma Fille,* a variegated one, is the next best; and nearly equal to it is the *Tournesol,* orange and yellow; these three would make a fine bed of themselves. One singular feature in these early Tulips is that there is hardly a good white flower amongst them all; *La Candeur* is but a dirty greenish white; *White Pottebakker* and *White Van Thol* are tolerably pure.

Now, these notices are chiefly intended for those who have some knowledge of the subject. For such as know nothing of these things, by far the best way is to buy the cheapest mixtures that one can meet with, plant them altogether in a bed or border, and make notes of their height, colour, and time of flowering, so as to have them better arranged next time; and, lastly, there are three or four called *Parrot Tulips,* with great loppy flowers, but they make a variety in the spring. From a penny to threepence each you may buy all these; but taking them by the gross, they seldom cost more than ten shillings the hundred.

The early Tulips will flourish in any tolerably good garden soil, that is not too heavy. Where it is likely to be so, the addition of leaf-mould to it will both lighten it, and be agreeable to the growth and vigour of the bulbs. They do not require any fresh manure, but will succeed best where the soil has been kept in tolerably good heart, by the manuring of previous crops. In planting they should be placed about five inches apart, and about three inches deep.

The NARCISSUS TRIBES furnish a large assortment of spring flowering bulbs. Those called *Polyanthus Narcissus* are very numerous; and amongst the best for rows, patches, or beds, are *Grand Monarque,* one of the best whites, and *Soleil d'Or,* the best yellow.

The old CROWN IMPERIALS, which one may see in every cottage garden all over the country, have run into ten or a dozen varieties, and all of them are useful for borders in the spring; and then the *Turban Ranunculus*—what is more beautiful than a bed or an edging of the scarlet Turban? Moreover, there is a yellow and a black Turban, which are not quite so bright as the scarlet ones. If these are set a couple of inches deep they will do very well, but there should be two plantings of them, one in November and one in February. This will prolong their blooming season in the spring.

The large double scarlet *Anemones* may also have the same treatment; and where is there a finer spring flowering plant? Whether in single rows, along the side of a border, or only in patches here and there, they make a very showy appearance, and a full bed of them near the windows is gayer than any other.

GLADIOLUS.—Excepting the common Gladiolus communis, and perhaps G. byzantinus, the different varieties ought to be planted in a bed by themselves. To succeed well in blooming them the soil should have an extra care bestowed upon it; there ought to be a large proportion of peat earth (heath mould) mixed amongst it, as well as a considerable quantity of vegetable mould; the proportions should be two parts loam, two parts vegetable mould, and three parts heath mould, with a portion of river sand, say, one-eighth of the whole. The situation of the bed ought to be open and airy, and provision made for sheltering them when in flower with an awning of canvas. We do not recommend planting in the open bed before the middle of November; if they are planted earlier they might spring up, and the young shoots be destroyed by severe frost.

TULIPS for blooming should be planted about the 10th of November; and when that planting is finished, then immediately plant your Gladiolus bulbs. The larger kinds of Narcissus, such as *Grand Monarque, La Soliel d'Or, Grand Primo,* and *States-General,* may either be grown in pots a little larger than those for Hyacinths, or will do very well planted in beds of deep rich soil in the open air. If in pots, manage them exactly the same as described for the Hyacinth among "Florists' Flowers." *Van Thol,* and other kinds of early Tulips intended to bloom in pots, should be placed from three to five in a pot 4½ inches wide, proportioning the number to the size of the bulbs. Always allow them time in a level place to form roots, previously to placing them in heat to bring them into flower.

JONQUILS.—These sweet-scented flowers are very desirable to grow either in pots or in the open beds or borders; manage them the same way as the Crocus.

PERSIAN IRIS.—A beautiful dwarf variegated flower, sweet-scented, and suitable for pot culture. It does not thrive well excepting in a warm sheltered border in the open air. The roots, unless preserved with great care, are very apt to perish after the first year. Their native dwelling is in the hot sandy plains of Persia, the difficulty of imitating which is no doubt the great cause why we do not succeed in preserving them. Pot them in November in a light, sandy, peaty soil, and place them in a cool, dry frame to form roots. They do not force well, but will flower beautifully in the months of April and May, as it were naturally.

BULBS IN BEDS.—The best arrangement for planting bulbs will depend on the shape and size of the beds, and their connection one with another; but we will give a few hints as to the cheapest and most useful kinds, so that every one may suit his own means. We would, however, particularly wage war against indiscriminate mixtures, unless in mixed herbaceous borders, when the various sorts may be planted in patches wherever there is room for them, observing always, however, to keep the dwarf kinds to the front of the beds, and the taller kinds nearer to the back. In a geometrical garden, where the beds are numerous and comparatively small, it will be better, in a general way, not to introduce more than two kinds into any one of them; that is to say, one dwarf kind round the edge of the bed, and a mass of some taller species in the middle; these two should contrast in colour, but should accord in season of flowering. When it is desired to prolong the beauty of the beds, two pairs, or sets, of flowers should be planted, one to succeed the other; in this case the two dwarfer things may be mixed together round the edge, and the taller ones mingled in like manner in the central mass.

We will suppose a border, by a walk-side, some eight or ten feet wide, as this would include a very complete series, which will be found in the following list of fifteen sorts. They may be planted in as many single or double lines, or those sorts which are connected with a bracket may be mixed together, thereby reducing the number of stripes to six. This list will enable every one to make a selection according to the size and arrangement of their beds or borders.

No. of Line.	Name.	Colour.	Height.	Season.	Distance apart to be planted.
			feet.		inch.
1	Tall late Tulips—*Tournesol, Rex Rubrorum*, and *Marriage de ma Fille*.	red, yellow	1½	medium. April, May	8
	Tall mixtures	..	..	.. .. ..	..
2	Lilium candidum (the Common white Lily)	white	3	late. June, July	18
3	Hyacinth	red	1	medium. April	8
4	Crocus..............	white	½	early. Feb., March	3
5	Narcissus (tall mixtures)	cream. yell.	1¼	medium. April, May	6
6	Iris xiphium (mixed)	blue, white	1½	late. April, May	12
7	Hyacinth	white	1	medium. April	8
8	Crocus	yellow	½	early. Feb., May	3
9	Tulips—Gold Standard, Royal Standard & Yellow Pottebakker	red yellow	1	medium. Apr., May	8
	Medium mixtures ..	..	..	.. .. ..	..
10	Snowdrop	white	½	early. Jan., March	2
11	Narcissus (dwarf mixtures)	yel. white.	1	medium. Mar., April	6
12	Hyacinth	blue	1	medium. April	8
13	Crocus..............	yellow	½	early. Feb., March.	3
14	Tulip—Double, Van Thol............	red, yellow	¾	medium. April	8
15	Winter Aconite......	yellow	¼	early. Jan., March	2

Such small bulbs as Crocuses, Snowdrops, Jonquils, some Narcissuses, &c., intended to be planted in patches amongst shrubs, or the mixed flower border, should have the places, previously to planting, where they are to be grown, enriched with some very rotten dung. Dig out the earth first, put in the dung, and mix it thoroughly with the under stratum of earth, then level up the place, and plant the bulbs immediately. Mice are very fond of Crocuses. To prevent their ravages, chop some furze (gorze or whin), and cover the bulbs with it. The sharp thorns will prick their noses, and effectually protect the roots.

Mixed herbaceous borders may be rendered very gay in spring by introducing patches of the above; and for the same purpose we will add a list of other kinds, which are either not exactly suitable for lines and masses, or are too expensive to be used wholesale; for it is useless to recommend things which not one in a thousand can afford to purchase.

Anemones, single and double, are beautiful for patches, and by planting or sowing at different seasons they may be had in flower nearly all the year round.

Amaryllis belladonna and *A. formosissima* stand in the open borders in the Channel Islands and the south of England, but in less favourable localities they require the protection of a south wall.

Anomatheca cruenta, Crinum capense, C. album, and *C. revolutum, Nerine sarniensis* (Guernsey Lily), *Pancratum illyricum,* and the Yellow Amaryllis, *Sternbergia lutea,* are all very beautiful, and come under the same general rule as the *Amaryllis belladonna.* They are all well deserving of a place where they can have a little protection. *Ixias, Sparaxis, Babianas, Ferrarias,* and many other very early-flowering Cape bulbs, require very similar conditions of cultivation and protection, for which their beauty is an ample recompense. The rest of our remarks will be confined to bulbs which require no artificial protection.

Bulbocodium vernum. — A very pretty little, dark-purple, Crocus-like plant, flowering at the same season.

Colchicums (Autumn-flowering).—The well-known Meadow Saffron, or Autumn Crocus. There are four varieties, the common, pencilled, white single, and a double variety.

Dog's-tooth Violets are more beautiful in their foliage than in their flowers; the prettiest way in which we have seen them used, is as an edging along the inside of a stone-curbing, to which they give a very agreeable relief.

Hyacinths.—Feathered, Grape, and Musk (Muscari), are pretty for patches; the Feathered, or Monstrous, requires support, as its great head holds the moisture in damp weather, and becomes top-heavy

Fritillarias are curious dusky-looking plants, and appear best when they are on a level with the eye, as amongst rockwork. There is also a white variety.

Iris.—These are all very useful plants. We have included the best bulbous-rooted species in our arrangement; and of the kinds which grow from tuber-like under-ground stems. There are many very useful for borders or rockwork, as their stiff, spear-like leaves contrast agreeably with plants of different habits. *I. tuberosa* is a very pretty dwarf species from the Levant, which, on account of its shyness of flowering, is not cultivated so much as it deserves to be; the fault, however, is not in the plant, but in its being taken up too often. Its best place is at the foot of a wall, where it should remain till it flowers.

Jonquils are beautiful border flowers, of bright golden colour; the large double is the most showy variety, but the single one is the most fragrant.

Lilies.—We have recommended the Common White for a line, and it is truly beautiful as such; the Bulb-bearing (*L. bulbiferum*) would make an excellent line in front of the white, as it does not grow quite so tall, and retains its foliage better. All the species and varieties are good, and as most of them grow very tall, they are well adapted for planting in open spaces amongst shrubs and in the back of mixed borders.

Narcissus.—These are all excellent, and they are all suitable for lines. We have mentioned only a few of the best.

Ranunculus.—These are often, we may almost say always, grown in beds, but we think they would give greater satisfaction as lines or patches; they are amongst the most beautiful of bulbs. The Turban Ranunculuses are the hardiest and easiest of management.

Scillas are lovely little bulbs, after the way of our common wild Hyacinths. *S. sibirica* and *præcox* are the earliest of those generally cultivated.

Tulips are too well known to need any comment, and we merely mention them that they may not be forgotten. The Sweet-scented Florentine is a variety we would draw attention to as deserving of more general cultivation.

Zephyranthes candida is as hardy as a Crocus, and not unlike a white one in flower, only that the leaves are more like those of a Jonquil; it flowers from May to October, preferring deep sandy soil. The Argentine Republic and the River La Plata are so called from the silvery hue of its flowers on the banks of the latter.

There are also some really beautifully early flowering hardy bulbs, of which we recommend the following for borders :—

Anemone nemorosa fl. pleno (Double Wood Anemone), 6 in., white.

Cyclamen coum (Round-leaved Sow Bread), 3 in., red.

Erythronium dens-canis (Dog's-tooth Violet), 4 in., red and white.

Hyacinthus racemosus (Raceme-flowered Hyacinth), 6 in., blue.

Narcissus bicolor, 1 ft., yellow and white.

„ *bulbocodium* (Hoop-petticoat Narcissus), 6 in., golden yellow.

Narcissus minor, 6 in., yellow.

Scilla bifolia (Two-leaved Squill), 2 in., blue.

„ *alba* (White Squill).

„ *peruviana* (Peruvian Squill), 1 ft., blue.

„ *alba* (White Peruvian Squill), 1 ft.

„ *sibirica* (Siberian Squill), 6 in., blue.

BULBS.—Masses of Winter Aconite, Wood Anemones (especially the white double), Snowdrops (single and double), and Crocus of all colours, may be taken up from the border as the shoots appear above the ground; also, Tulips, Narcissus, Jonquils, Dog-tooth Violets, Bulbocodiums, Hyacinths, &c., if potted in October, placed in a dry place, and covered up with ashes, if there is a small forcing pit, may be brought into bloom about

Christmas. If taken, after being well-rooted, to the greenhouse, they must not be expected to bloom until February and March, if no other heat is given them. Those recommended to be raised out of the border will not stand anything like forcing, but must have pretty much their own way, though they will be more forward in the house than out of doors. Though not bulbs, yet in company with them in the greenhouse, may be placed the beautiful tribe of Cyclamens, which, when pushing, should be top-dressed with rich compost. Lachenalias and other bulbs will follow in the spring.

THE FERNERY.

SITUATION OF THE FERNERY.—In small gardens, in the suburbs of towns, the habitation for ferns should be in some retired part, the south side of it, to be shaded either with a north wall or shrubbery. Several species of fern will grow well in shady plantations, without any further care than planting, occasionally stirring the ground around them, and clearing away anything likely to smother or otherwise injure them. They may also be successfully cultivated in pots.

In gardens of large extent, the situation of the fernery should be some retired place, with a dense shrubbery or plantation to the north of it. An arbour made of rustic materials might either be formed in the bank of ferns itself, or be placed in the plantation to face the rockwork, so as to have a view of it. Those who will be at the trouble and expense of forming such a scene will not only be delighted with the effect themselves, but will find it give great pleasure to all their friends and visitors.

SOIL.—The soils suitable for ferns are of very various kinds. Such ferns as are found in moist shady woods, require a mixture of heath-mould and rotten leaves. Those that grow on mountains will thrive in gravelly loam, while those that flourish in peaty bogs require a peaty bog soil, and such as are natives of heaths or crevices of rocks do best if planted among sandy heath-mould. With those different soils most kinds of ferns may be successfully cultivated.

FERNS IN POTS.—Like Alpine plants, ferns may be satisfactorily cultivated in pots, plunged in coal-ashes, under a wall facing the west, where they will thrive very well. The larger-growing species, however, do not send up such fine fronds as they would do if they were planted out in a proper situation, and in the right soil. Some of the more delicate kinds do exceedingly well in pots, in a compost of peat-earth, light loam, and sand, mixed with very small pieces of broken garden-pots. The larger pieces can be used for drainage. Those delicate kinds are such as grow naturally in the crevices of rocks in exposed situations. Should the rains fall ever so abundantly and frequently, the roots of those ferns are never over-supplied with moisture, if the drainage in the pots is so perfect that the superabundant water will readily pass off from the plants. Of course, those that are found in low moist places do not require so much drainage. In fact, if there be one piece of broken pot, or an oyster-shell, over the hole of the pot, it is quite sufficient.

Ferns in pots should never be allowed to become dry. The fibres of the roots are so small and delicate, that drought soon destroys them. They should be sprinkled over-head every morning and evening from April to August, excepting on rainy days. In the autumn and winter they require no care but removing from them the decaying fronds and weeds. Mosses and lichens may be allowed to grow, as they will assist in protecting the roots from the severe weather of winter.

The following list of British hardy ferns, divided into their several localities, will materially assist the cultivator in placing them in his fernery:—

I.—Such Ferns as grow on exposed Rocks and Crevices of Walls.

Adiantum capillus—veneris. True Maiden's-hair Fern.
Allosorus crispus. Rock-brake.
Polypodium calcareum. Smith's Polypody.
Woodsia ilvensis. Ray's Woodsia.
  ,, *alpina.* Bolton's do.
Cystopteris montana. Wilson's Mountain Fern.
Polystichum lonchitis. Holly Fern.
Lastrea oreopteris. Mountain Lastrea.
Lastrea rigida. Rigid Fern
  ,, *recurva.* Recurved do.
Asplenium lanceolatum. Lance-leaved Spleenwort. (Also on Sea-cliffs.)
Asplenium Adiantum — nigrum. Black Spleenwort.
Asplenium Ruta—muraria. Wall-rue Spleenwort.
Asplenium germanicum. Alternate-leaved German Spleenwort.
Asplenium septentrionale. Forked Spleenwort.
Asplenium trichomanes. Common Spleenwort.
Ceterach officinarum. Scaly Spleenwort.
Lycopodium annotinum. Interrupted Club-moss.
Lycopodium alpinum. Alpine, or savin-leaved Club-moss.
Lycopodium selaginoides. Selago-like Club-moss.
Polypodium vulgare. Common Polypody.
Polystichum aculeatum. Prickly Polystichum.
Scolopendrium officinarum. Hart's Tongue Spleenwort.
Scolopendrium, var. *undulatum.* Wavy do.
Scolopendrium, var. *augustifolium.* Narrow-leaved do.
Botrychium lunaria. Moonwort.
Lycopodium clavatum. Club-Moss.
  ,, *selago.* Fir do.
Ophioglossum vulgatum. Common Adder's-tongue.

II.—Such as grow on shady, moist Rocks, near Waterfalls or Ditches.

Lomaria spicant. Spiked Lomaria.
Polypodium vulgare, var. *cambricum.* Welsh Polypody.
Polypodium phegopteris. Beech Fern.
Cystopteris fragilis. Brittle do.
Asplenium viride. Green Spleenwort.
Asplenium fontanum. Fountain's Abbey do.
Trichomanes speciosum. Bristly Fern.
Hymenophyllum tunbridgense. Tunbridge Filmy Fern.
Hymenophyllum Wilsoni. Wilson's do.

III.—Such as grow in moist, shady Woods.

Polypodium dryopteris. Oak Polypody.
Polystichum angulare. Angular Polystichum.
Lastrea spinosa. Spiny Lastrea.

Lastrea multiflora. Many-flowered Lastrea.
Lastrea filix—mas. Male Fern.
Athyrian filix—fœmina. Female Fern.

IV.—Such as grow on Hedgerows, open dry Heaths, and old Pastures.
Athyrium filix—fœmina, var. *Smithii.* Smith's Lady Fern.

V.—Such as grow in Boggy Heaths.
Lastrea thelypteris. Marsh Fern.

Lastrea cristata. Crested Lastrea.
Osmunda regalis. Royal Fern.
Lycopodium inundatum. Marsh Lycopodium.

VI.—Sea-side Ferns.
Asplenium marinum. Marine Spleenwort.
Asplenium lanceolatum. Lance-leaved Spleenwort.

ALPINE PLANTS AND ROCKWORK.

ALPINE PLANTS.—Many of the plants that grow in mountainous regions, and are known as Alpine plants, are very beautiful, and may be successfully cultivated in gardens, either in pots or on artificial rockwork—the latter being the least trouble, and the plants in the most natural situation. As we wish to make the amateur and cottager's gardens as interesting as possible, we strongly recommend our friends to attempt the cultivation of those interesting plants. Rockwork may be formed with flints and scoriæ, or, as they are commonly called, clinkers. Where it is plentiful, rough pieces of natural stone may be employed, or all three may be tastefully mixed, and a few rough roots of dead trees can always be used, here and there, with good effect. First, a bank of any kind of earth must be thrown up in the intended form, which should be of irregular outline; then place the flints and other things so as to leave vacancies between the stones; those vacancies should be partly filled up with a compost of leaf-mould, loam, and sandy peat, in equal parts. The aspect of the rockwork, if convenient, should be to the north, as Alpine plants are, in their native countries, during the winter, covered with snow—and consequently, in our artificial rockery, should have as little sun as possible in the cold months. The best time to plant them is in spring, as then they will be well established before the winter sets in. These elegant plants may be successfully cultivated and brought together, so as to bring their beauties under our observation without having to travel to seek them in their native wilds. They may be grown, and very well too, either in an artificial imitation of rock, or alpinery, as it may be termed, or they may be cultivated in pots. Upon the latter method we will dilate a little, for this reason, that some of our friends may not have the materials to form this aerial habitation for them, or may not choose to go to the expense. Still, some who have not the convenience of a rockery, may wish to have a few of these admired plants, if they only knew how to manage them. We will endeavour to supply that knowledge. To cultivate Alpine plants in pots, three things are necessary,—the proper soil, the right sized pots, and good drainage.

SOIL OR COMPOST.—Whatever kind of plant we attempt to

cultivate, we ought to learn as correctly as possible what kind of soil is natural to it. Now, the soil in Alpine situations we may easily conceive to be of a poor, gravelly nature, formed by the decay of rocks and mosses and other small plants. This soil may be imitated by using heath mould, rotten leaves, and broken potsherds; of the two former two equal parts each, and of the latter one part; in other words, two bushels of heath mould, two bushels of rotten leaves, and one bushel of potsherds, or pieces of broken flower-pots. The whole to be well mixed with one-eighth of coarse white sand.

Pots.—Alpine plants in nurseries are generally grown in small pots, about five inches in diameter. The proper size to grow them fine in, is a pot nine inches across at its top. It should be rather shallow, about seven inches deep, and be pierced with holes to admit air to the soil. These pots may appear rather large for such small plants, but such as are of a creeping habit, as many of the Saxifrages, for instance, will soon cover the top of the pot, and such as do not creep may have three or four plants put in one pot. The reason why we recommend pots of the above size, is to have fine specimens. We have seen them grown in such pots, and they were so fine, both in growth and flower, as to appear almost like gigantic varieties of their puny brethren, as grown in small pots; in fact, quite equal to the finest plant on the best-managed rockery.

Drainage is the third important article in the culture of Alpine plants. Unless the pots are well and perfectly drained, the plants will soon turn yellow and die. The way to drain them is to place over or against each hole in the pots a piece of a broken pot with its hollow side downwards. Then put in as many large pieces as will cover the bottom of the pot one inch thick; upon this stratum place another inch of fine broken pots, the dust being sifted out (the fine sifting will answer well to mix with the compost), and over this second layer place some of the rough fibrous parts of the soil; the pot is then ready for filling with the compost and receiving the plants.

Situation.—There is an advantage in having these plants in pots, so that they can be removed according to the season. During hot weather the best situation for them will be on the north side of a low hedge or wall, but in the early spring or late in autumn, the east side of the garden will be the place for them. During winter, a bed covered with hoops and mats will be a good habitation for them.

Watering.—Whilst the plants are growing, they should be watered freely, but should be kept pretty dry during winter. All these minute particulars may appear to the practical man to be too precise, but to the uninformed we are conscious such instructions cannot be too explicit; and we are so much delighted with Alpine plants, when well grown, that we should like to infuse the same feeling into every amateur and cottager in the kingdom.

We now subjoin a short select list of those interesting little gems of the Alpine region:—

Ajuga genevensis (Geneva Bugle). Purple.
Alyssum saxatile (Rock Madwort). Yellow.
Alyssum saxatile variegatum. Variegated.
Arabis saxatilis (Rock Wall-cress). White.
Arabis lucida variegata (Shining-leaved Variegated Wall-cress). White.
Arenaria verna (Early Sandwort). White.
Aretia Vitaliana (Vital's Aretia). Yellow.
Aubrietia purpurea (Purple Aubrietia). Purple.
Campanula nitida alba (Shining Bell-flower). White.
Campanula pumila alba (Dwarf ditto). White.
Campanula pulla alba (Russet ditto). Blue.
Chieranthus alpinus (Alpine Wall-flower). Yellow.
Cornus canadensis (Canadian Dogwood). White.
Cortusa Mathioli (Mathiolus, Bear's-ear Sanicle). Red.
Coronilla minama (Least Coronilla). Yellow.
Dianthus alpestris (Rock Sweet-William). White.
Dianthus Hendersonii (Henderson's ditto). Bright Red.
Draba aizoides (Aizoon-like Whitlow-grass). Yellow.
Erinus alpinus (Smooth Alpine Erinus). Purple.
Erodium Reichardii (Reichard's Heron's-bill). White.
Gnaphalium dioicum (Diœcious Everlasting Flower). Pink.
Gypsophila prostrata (Trailing Gypsophila). White.
Linaria alba alpina (Alpine Toad-Flax). White.
Linaria cymbalaria variegata (Variegated Cymbal-leaved Toad-Flax). Rose-colour.
Myosotis rupicola (Rock Scorpion-Grass or Forget-me-not). Blue.
Phlox divaricata (Early-flowering Flame-flower). Blue.
Phlox nivalis (Snowy ditto). White.
Phlox setacea (Bristly ditto). Red.
„ *verna* (Early ditto). Purple.
„ *procumbens* (Trailing ditto). Lilac.
Potentilla repens, flore pleno (Double-creeping Cinquefoil). Yellow.
Primula auricula alpina (Alpine Bear's-ear Primrose). Various.
Primula farinosa (Mealy Bird's-eye ditto). Lilac.
Primula nivalis (Snowy ditto).
„ *marginata* (Margined ditto). Rose.
Primula ciliata purpurea (Fringed ditto). Purple.
Saponaria ocymoides (Basil-like Soap-wort). Pink.
Saxifraga granulata plena (Double-grain-rooted Saxifrage). White.
Saxifraga muscoides (Moss-like ditto). Yellow.
Saxifraga nivalis (Snowy ditto).
„ *oppositifolia* (Opposite-leaved ditto). Purple.
Saxifraga pedatifida (Bird's-foot ditto). Purple.
Saxifraga pyramidalis (Pyramidal ditto). White.
Saxifraga retusa (Close-sitting ditto). Purple.
Saxifraga recularis (Rose-shaped ditto).
Saxifraga stellaris (Star-like ditto). White.
Sedum dasyphyllum (Thick-leaved Stonecrop). White.
Sedum monstrosum (Monstrous ditto).
Sedum rupestre (Rock ditto).
„ *Sieboldii* (Siebold's ditto).
Sempervivum arachnoideum (Spider Houseleek). Red.
Sempervivum globiferum (Globe-bearing ditto). Red.
Sempervivum tectorum (Roof ditto). Red.
Sempervivum Webbianum (Webb's ditto). Red.
Sempervivum montanum (Mountain ditto). Red.
Silene acaulis (Stemless Catchfly). Pink.
Silene quadridentata (Four-toothed ditto). White.

Soldanella alpina (Alpine Soldanella). Purple.	*Veronica montana* (Mountain Speedwell). Blue.
Soldanella alpina minima alba (Smallest White ditto).	*Veronica saxatilis* (Rock ditto). Blue.
Thymus corsicus (Corsican Thyme). Purple.	*Veronica taurica* (Taurian ditto). Blue.
Thymus serpyllum (Wild ditto). Purple.	*Vinca herbacea* (Herbaceous Periwinkle).
Thymus azoricus (Azorian Thyme). Purple.	*Vinca minor rubra pleno* (Lesser double Red ditto).

THE AQUARIUM.

Of all the ornaments used to embellish a garden, there is none that has so pleasing an effect, especially in the warm days of summer, as water. On a large scale, when we can have so much of it as to afford space for islands, planted with weeping willows and other suitable trees, together with water-falls, rocks, and secluded and open walks, rustic bridges, boat houses, and rustic seats, we have then a power to please the eye and delight the senses to the highest degree. In happy England there are many such scenes, but with such grand specimens of the power of water to embellish scenery, these pages have nothing to do. Yet in the garden of the amateur, if not in our cottage gardens, small pieces of water may be used with very good effect; that is, wherever there is a supply of that beautiful and useful element. The extent of the collected water ought to be proportioned to the size of the garden, that is, of that portion of the garden devoted to the lawn, flower garden, and shrubbery. Its form may either be ornamental or natural. By ornamental, we mean formed with masonry, either round or oval, surrounded by a gravel walk or the lawn. A natural piece of water is of an irregular form, the points of which may have a few rough stones so placed as partly to hide the hollows, with a weeping willow or two planted amongst them. If a walk is carried on one side of it, a shrub or two should be planted to hide the extent of the water; and on the opposite side a shelving pebbly walk, with a small bed of shrubs here and there, would make pretty small views and shadows in the water. To preserve the water from wasting away, or making the ground wet about it, the bottom and sides ought to be well puddled either with well wrought clay, or fine sifted earth; we have used both for large reservoirs with equal success. If the ornamental form is adopted, the stones should be well built with Roman cement, and the bottom flagged and covered with the same. This water being exposed to the air will imbibe portions of it, and will, in consequence, be greatly improved for the purpose of watering the garden, plants in pots, syringing, &c. This water will also afford an opportunity and a good situation for growing aquatic plants, a considerable number of which are exceedingly handsome. We possess in this country one plant, an aquatic, of which the foliage and flowers are surpassed by scarcely any exotic water plant. We allude to our own lovely Water-lily, a plant whose beauty attracts the admiration of every one.

Gold and silver fish may also be kept in the water, the only thing to attend to in keeping them being to have a corner of the water protected from frost, to allow the fish a breathing place. This may easily be accomplished by having a few pieces of wood laid across one end of the pond, and placing upon them some twigs of fir trees, or a thick straw or rush mat.

SELECT AQUATIC PLANTS.

Alisma plantago (Water Plantain). Pink and White.
Alisma ranunculoides (Ranunculus-like do.). Purple.
**Butomus umbellatus* (Umbel-flowered Flowering Rush). Pink.
*Calla palustris (Marsh Calla). White.
Caltha palustris, flore pleno (Double-flowering Marsh marigold). Yellow.
Caltha asarifolia (Asarum-leaved ditto). Yellow.
**Hottonia palustris* (Marsh Water-violet). Flesh-coloured.
Lobelia dortmanna (Dortman's Lobelia). Blue.
Menyanthes trifoliata (Three-leaved Buck-bean). White.
Myriophyllum spicatum (Spiked Water-milfoil). Red.
Myriophyllum verticillatum (Whorled ditto). Green.
Myosotis palustris (Forget-me-not). Blue.

Nuphar lutea (Yellow Water-lily). Yellow.
Nuphar advena (Strange ditto). Yellow and Red.
*Nymphæa alba (White Water-lily).
Polygonum apmhibium (Amphibious Polygonum). Pink.
Potamogeton fluitans (Floating Pond-weed). Red.
Sagittaria sagittifolia (Arrow-head). White.
Sagittaria latifolia (Broad-leaved ditto). White.
Teucrium scordium (Water Germander). Purple.
Trapa natans (Floating Water-caltrops). White.
Trapa quadrispinosa (Four-spined ditto). White.
Villarsia nymphoides (Nymphæa-like Villarsia). Yellow.
Villarsia cordata (Heart-shaped leaved ditto). White.

Where the extent of the water is small, those marked with an asterisk (*) are the best. Most of them are natives of this country. The double marsh marigold is a fine species, and should be planted close to the bank.

PLANS OF FLOWER BEDS.

PLAN No. 1.

This plan (183) is very accommodating; it may stand either in front of a villa, next the road, or nearest the country. The front door, or the centre of the house, may be opposite 1-1, or opposite 2-2; or it may be a distinct feature in a part away from the house. 1-1 and 2-2 would be one of the best arrangements for Herbaceous Plants, and the middle figures for gay bedders. Or, if the house stood behind 1, the opposite 1 might be of Dahlias, or with Dahlias and a row of the best Hollyhocks behind them. The same with the 2-2. No one can go up straight to the middle of this garden; and this is always a wise arrangement, particularly in plans of limited extent. Again, 1-1 and 2-2 might be made the "Rosary," surrounding the flower garden, with rose arches thrown over the four corners; and if so, pillar-roses, or high standards, ought to run along the centres of each long bed. Those who object to tall standards, would have pillar-roses about seven feet high, or the height of the rose arches, and festoons from pillar to pillar, joining the arches. For any of these suggestions, the long beds would need to be at least six feet wide, and eight feet would be better, particularly for the roses, as we must suppose a good pillar rose to be at least two feet through at the bottom, and the festoons will need as much room as the bottom of the pillars, to allow them to swing about with the wind. Then with an eight feet bed we have only room for three rows of dwarf-roses on each side of these beds, and hardly that. Once more, if these long beds were only three or four feet wide, and raised six inches above the general level, and filled with florists' flowers, the best late Tulips would do in the one farthest from the house; the best early Tulips, being dwarfer and earlier, next the house; and the side ones might be filled with Hyacinths, bordered with Turban or some common Ranunculus. In the summer, all the long beds, being planted with Roses, might be edged with the white Campanula pumila, at six inches from the sides, or the white C. carpatica at nine inches—the plants standing nearly close to each other in the row. Last of all, the two No. 1 beds might be planted with variegated Geraniums and rose-coloured Verbena, plant for plant; or the one next the house this way, and the opposite, with Verbena venosa, and the old variegated Scarlet Geranium. For the middle beds 3-3 ought to have plants a little taller than 4-4 and 5-5, and the dwarfest plants should occupy the four centre beds. If the front door or the drawing-room window stood opposite 2, then 4 and 5 ought to be of one colour; and if a different plant is used for each, their heights and mode of growth ought to be as much alike as possible. The same colours should be repeated in the opposite 4 and 5; the plants being either straight across or corner-wise—that is, the plant in 4 to be repeated in the 5 at the opposite corner, or just across in the other 4. On the other hand, if the door or window is opposite 1, then 4-4 should be of the same height and colour, and 5-5 may be of quite a different colour, and the plants a little higher than in 4-4, as they are farther from the eye. For the same reason, the colour in 5-5 should be brighter, or more telling. If 1 is of the variegated Geranium and pink Verbena, we have a strong pink on a white ground; and no blue, lilac, purple, or white should stand in 3 in front of it. We would put the Kentish Hero Calceolaria in this 3, and a bright yellow Calceolaria in the opposite 3. We would plant 5-5 with two good purples, or light rose-coloured Verbenas or Petunias, and 4-4 with pink or dark-bluish flowers; or, say the right-hand 5 was full of deep pink Petunias, and the left-hand 4 was filled with Saponaria calabrica, then the right-hand 4 with pink Ivy-leaved Geranium, and the left-hand 5 with a rose-coloured Petunia. But any other plants of similar sizes and colours would do just as well. It is the firm opinion of the best planters, that matching the height of plants is as essential as the disposition of the colours, if not more so; also that to suit the height to the size of a bed is of first importance: thus, a circle ten feet in diameter, quite flat, and planted with Tom Thumb Geraniums, all of one size and age, though brilliant in the extreme, would still be bald. The same Tom Thumbs, planted in a circle not more than four or five feet through, would make a perfect gem. We have the plants and colours so disposed of in the rest of the plan that you cannot possibly mar the effect or add much to it. We would plant the four beds with scarlet and white—either Verbenas or Geraniums—or with four shades of the former. Or we would keep them for any of whatever were our pet plants, as no colour will much affect that part of the garden. The little blue Lobelias and yellow Œnothera prostata would do there. All the beds might be large enough to allow these centre ones, in proportion, to be three feet on the sides; in that case, two of them with Saponaria calabrica, the other two of Sanvitalia procumbens, would look very well indeed; but then there should be none of the Saponaria in the plan.

Plan No. 2.

Is a very useful figure for a flower-garden (184), with the names of the flowers planted in it. The Rose bed in the centre will be very gay, if the centre of it is raised considerably above the sides, so that the Duchess of Sutherland does not overtop the Géant des Batailles. Bed No. 10 would do with Calceolaria Amplexicaulis, and a crimson Calceolaria would make a contrast for a border. Mangles' variegated Geranium will make a good flowering edge for 4. To balance 3 with 2, or 12, the only two legitimate ways, 3 ought to be planted with a bright scarlet Verbena; the only difficulty will be in 6, the white Petunia, which is too high for the size of the bed. 6, 7, 8, and 9 ought to be as nearly as possible of equal height. One great advantage of this style, however, is that all the beds may be planted differently every year, except the centre one, so as to have a change of soil for the different plants without altering the fundamental arrangement.

The oval centre bed is filled with Roses; Géant des Batailles being in the middle, encircled by Duchess of Sutherland, and outside this Mrs. Bosanquet.

1 White Verbena.
2 Rose-coloured Verbena.
3 Scarlet Verbena.
4 Scarlet Geranium, edged with variegated Geranium.
5 Heliotrope, edged with Ivy-leaved Geranium.
6 Deep purple Verbena.
7 Crimson Verbena, with violet eye.
8 White Petunia.
9 Nierembergia gracilis.
10 Yellow Calceolaria, edged with crimson Calceolaria.
11 Scarlet Geranium, edged with white Verbena.
12 Scarlet Verbena.
13 Convolvolus minor.
14 White Verbena.

The walks between the beds are gravel, three feet wide, and edged with Box.

PLAN No. 3.

This is a geometric garden for a small space behind a house, by placing it lengthways, as shown (185); or for a front garden, between the house and the road or street, by putting it crossways, and doing away with the two centre circles (2-2) going up to the front door, and squaring the ends of the long beds at the top and bottom of the garden.

If the plan is laid longways from the house, the six circles, marked 2, are the best of places for six pillar Roses. The beds marked 1 are for dwarf Roses and herbaceous plants, Mimuluses, Violets, Pansies, Poppies, Anemones, and all manner of things. Nos. 3 and 4 are for early spring Tulips, as the Van Thols, Golden Standard, Royal Standard, Rex Rubrorum, Marriage de ma Fille, and twenty others besides, if one can get them. The beds 5, 6, 7, 8, to be of Crocuses of sorts, surrounded by Snowdrops, Snowflakes, Turban Ranunculuses, and indeed any of these good old common flowers that come on in the spring, and, at least, one of the squares to be with bedding plants in summer. The two beds, 7, should be of Tom Thumbs, bed 8 yellow Calceolarias, and bed 4, the centre bed, all white; the white Variegated Alyssum would be the best, or rather the second best. Mangles' variegated Geranium is certainly the best for that bed, but a white Verbena will do.

Then, by looking down on these from a back bedroom window every morning, and again in the afternoon, when one went up to dress for dinner, and as often at other times as it might be necessary to proceed up stairs, the eye would soon become accustomed to symmetry, and regular arrangement of colours and flowers, under various lights and shades, from the state of the weather; so that we should soon overcome the vulgar prejudice of scarleting the centres of our flower gardens for everlasting.

Another great step would be gained by the use of such simple figures so planted. We would shame those who plant in such abominable-shaped beds as stars, triangles, kidneys, pears, oak-leaf shapes, and goodness knows how many more shapeless beds besides.

Her Majesty, in all her gardens, has not a single flower-bed of better shape than any in this simple arrangement, nor better planted either.

This plan may be repeated so as to occupy a much larger surface, as were the blocks of which the Crystal Palace was formed.

Plan No. 4.

This geometrical figure (186) is after a celebrated model which we have often seen planted. We could not alter one plant in it without lessening the value of the rest.

The beds are edged with native Heather eight inches from the grass, with the exception of the centre one, which is so edged fifteen inches. The beds Nos. 1, 3, 6, 9, 12, 15, and 17, are encircled by white sand; the others, with dark lime-rubbish put through a sieve.

The numbers on the sketch refer to the plants we would plant, and are as follows:—

No. 9. Geranium, Flower of the Day.
Nos. 3, 6, 12, 15. Geranium, Tom Thumb.
„ 5, 13. Purple Verbena.
„ 8, 10. Verbena Purple King.
„ 4, 7, 11, 14. Calceolaria Amplexicaulis.
„ 2, 16. White Verbena.
„ 1, 17. Bright Scarlet Verbena.

Plan No. 5.

This is a very good geometric plan of a flower garden (187). The grouping is in double groups, and each group in double pairs. The four beds round bed 8 make the first group; and the four round 13 a corresponding group. Each of these groups have corresponding ones in the other half of the garden, and it is a matter of taste whether, in planting, the colours in the group, No. 8, are repeated in the corresponding one round 18, or in cross corners round 21. If the whole garden is on a level, across from the house's side, all the plants in the beds might be just of one height, supposing that could be, without prejudice to the style of planting terrace gardens, or geometric gardens on a dead level. But if the garden falls either to or from the house, the lowest side or the lowest end ought to be planted with taller plants—still keeping to the corresponding colours. As, however, it is not possible, or desirable, to have all the plants of one height for these uniform-sized beds, the tallest kinds ought to be planted on the side

PLANS OF FLOWER BEDS. 181

farthest from the house, unless the situation of the garden is several feet below the level of the front door or drawing-room windows. When a garden is seen from a height, or a bird's-eye view, as it is called, the relative heights of the plants are of very little moment as compared to the proper distribution of the colours and shades. All these are points or principles which are equally applicable to every geometric flower garden, in which the principal beds are balanced as they are in this garden.

What we mean by being balanced is this:—If we look across the centre of the garden from the front-door, we have two rows of principal beds on each side, and of equal size throughout; and if the garden were turned, so that the centre of one end pointed to the front-door, the whole would be equally balanced on each side of the centre walk in the same way. On the whole, therefore, we consider this a very good design to teach the fundamental rules for designing geometric or terrace gardens, and also how to plant them according to the present style of arranging them. We hold it to be far more desirable to be able to understand the rules or principles by which a given design of a flower garden ought to be planted, than the kinds of plants to be used for doing so, and for this reason: If principles are true, they never alter; and if not true, they are not principles, although we might call them so.

1 Geranium Lucea Rosea
2 Lobelia ramosa
3 Tropæolum canariense
4 Rose-coloured Verbena
5 Cuphea elegans
6 Oak-leaved Geranium, pink
7 Gazania elegans
8 Salvia patens
9 Scarlet Verbena
10 Salmon-coloured Verbena
11 Eschscholzia
12 Phlox Drummondii
13 Dahlia Zelinda
14 Scarlet Geranium
15 Nemophila insignis
16 Rose-striped Verbena
17 Calceolaria amplexicaulis

18 Convolvolus major
19 Scarlet Geranium
20 Crimson-violet Verbena
21 Salvia fulgens
22 White Verbena
23 Heliotrope
24 Anemone japonica
25 Yellow Calceolaria
26 Variegated Geranium
27 Lobelia gracilis
28 Tropæolum canariense
29 Bright scarlet Verbena
30 Ivy-leaved Geranium, white
31 Fuchsia
32 China Roses
33 Lobelia fulgens
34 Mixed plants

Plan No. 6.

This plan (188) is on a parallelogram of grass lying on the south side of a house, and is seen usually from an elevation of five feet. The dimensions are about 34 yards by 18 yards. The size of beds 1, 2, 3, 4, &c., is 9 feet 6 inches by 5 feet 6 inches. A 7-feet wide gravel-walk goes round the whole, with a mixed border outside that. No. 2 bed is 8 feet 9 inches, and No. 1 bed is 7 feet 6 inches from the walk. Take the following for an arrangement of colours:—

13. Flower of the Day, with edge of Lobelia ramosoides.
3. } Crimson Calceolaria, edge
18. } of Cerastium tomentosum.
1. Calceolaria, Kentish Hero, edge of Cerastium tomentosum.
20. Calceolaria viscosissima, edge of Cerastium tomentosum.
4. Geranium, Tom Thumb, edge of Cerastium tomentosum.
2. —— Pale salmon-scarlet, edge of Cerastium tomentosum.
17. —— Cerise Unique, edge of Cerastium tomentosum.
19. Geranium, Commander-in-Chief, edge of Cerastium tomentosum.
9. } Smith's Superb.
25. } Purple Petunia.
10. Blue Verbena.
15. Purple Verbena.
12. Scarlet Verbena.
14. Verbena, crimson and violet.
11. —— purple and lavender.
16. —— White.
5. }
24. } Diadematum Geranium.
6. }
8. } Shrubland Rose Geranium.
23. }
7. }
22. } Pale blue Lobelia.
21. White Ivy-leaf Geranium.

Looking down, then, on the garden, and across it, from the usual point of view, a nice balance is observed between the chief predominating colours—the grass green, and the colours which are placed upon it. This is considered absolutely essential, though too often a neglected point.

On descending to the garden level, and standing at one end, in order to view the plan lengthways, the colour is found to be broken into three sections, each of which is distinct in its effect. The middle one, consisting of seven beds (among which 9, 13, 25, but especially 9 and 25, produce the effect peculiar to this section), is as gorgeous as it is possible to imagine—gold and purple, heightened by silvery-white, predominating; while, in the remaining two sections of nine beds each, scarlet is conspicuous, sufficiently toned down by neighbouring colours—in one, by pink and white, in the other by blue and white.

PLANS OF FLOWER BEDS.

Plan No. 1.

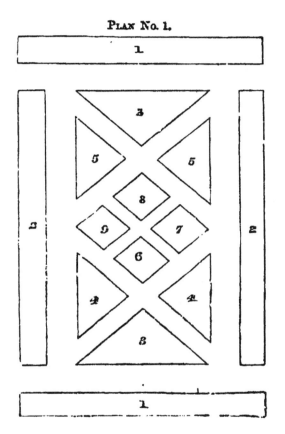

PLANS OF FLOWER BEDS.

Plan No. 2.

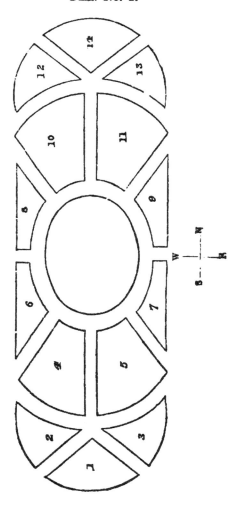

PLANS OF FLOWER BEDS. 185

Plan No. 3.
KITCHEN GARDEN.

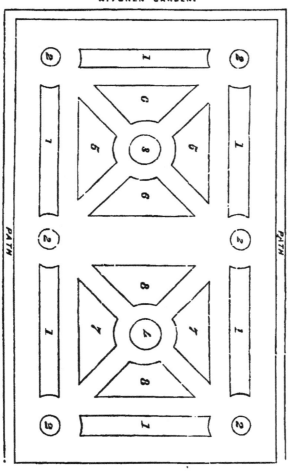

PLANS OF FLOWER BEDS.

Plan No. 4.

Plan No. 5.

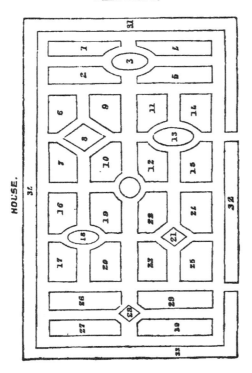

188 PLANS OF FLOWER BEDS.

Plan No. 6.

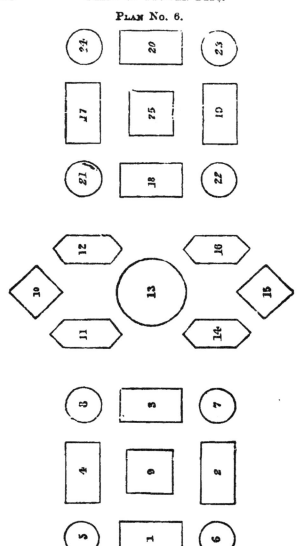

FLORISTS' FLOWERS.

FLORISTS' FLOWERS.

FLORISTS' FLOWERS are those flowers which by their beauty, power of producing permanent varieties, readiness of propagation, and easiness of cultivation are so largely in demand as to be especially worthy of being grown by florists as articles of commerce.

We will treat of them in alphabetical order.

ANEMONE.

Properties of a Double Anemone.—The blossom should be from two and a half to three inches in diameter, consisting of an outside row of stout, large, well-rounded petals, called the guard-leaves. These should spread out horizontally to the edges, which latter should turn upwards slightly, so as to present a saucer-like appearance. Within these guard-leaves, and at a little distance from the edges, there should be such a number of long, small petals, longest at the bottom, and gradually shortening to the centre, as to form a half ball. Self-coloured flowers should have the colour clear, bright, and distinct, whether it be blue, crimson, or scarlet. If variegated, that is, the interior and exterior petals striped, the colours should be very distinct, for even cloudiness, or irregular broken stripes, are objectionable. The stem should be elastic, yet stout enough to bear the flower erect, and should be, at least, from eight to nine inches high.

Soil and Situation.—The Anemone requires a pure loamy soil, well mixed with sand, such as sometimes is found on the sides of rivers naturally mixed with the sand. Choose a situation that is open, but sheltered from violent winds, or strong twisting currents of air; then dig out the soil a foot or more, according as the situation is high or low. If high, it may be dug out three or four inches deeper; but if low and wet, a foot will be sufficient. Mix the soil with sand if it requires it, and fill in the bed again to within six inches of the level of the surface; then level it, and lay on it a thin covering of thoroughly decomposed hotbed manure or cow-dung; the latter is to be preferred. Mix this well with the soil below. Upon this mixed, enriched soil place as much of the pure sandy loam as will raise the bed an inch or two above the walk. No dung must be among this top stratum of soil, because dung causes the peculiar disease called *mould* to attack the bulbs that come in contact with it.

Planting.—The best season is from about the middle of October to the first week in November; the bulbs then form roots before severe frosts set in. Should the planting be unavoidably delayed, the bed must then be covered with fern or straw. Choose a time when the soil is moderately dry, and the day fine. Draw drills across the bed two inches deep and five or six inches apart, and plant the tubers five inches apart in the rows. For choice varieties, a thin layer of sand scattered under and around each tuber will be useful. As soon as the bed is planted, cover the tubers with sandy loam from a basket or wheelbarrow. Take care that the tubers are placed the right side up, by observing the side that has the old small fibres on it. That side place next to the bottom of the drill. When all are planted and covered up the right depth (two inches) then level the surface with a garden rake.

After-management.—If the plants have any kind of covering, and the weather prove mild, the covering should be removed, and replaced on the likelihood of a return of frost, and when the spring sets in remove the shelter entirely. Should the weather prove dry in spring give a thorough watering now and then. The bloom will be greatly prolonged if an awning of canvas, or even garden mats, be stretched over the bed, upon a frame of hoops, to shelter the flowers from the sun, from high winds, and heavy splashing rains. All weeds must be plucked up as they appear, and a diligent watch kept for snails and slugs.

Taking up and Storing the Roots.—In wet summers it is difficult to have the plants sufficiently at rest for taking up and storing. This for the single, common varieties, is not of much consequence, especially if they are planted in patches in a mixed border, but the fine double varieties should be taken up annually. To induce a perfect state of rest, the bed should be covered, as soon as the general bloom is over, with canvas or mats, to keep off the rains that may fall whilst the leaves are decaying. As the foliage decays the real roots will decay also; the tubers will then gradually mature. When the leaves are quite yellow, take up the tubers, cut off the leaves close, and place the tubers in a dry, cool room to dry gradually. Just before they are perfectly so they should be looked over, and any soil, decayed stems, or leaves removed. If this is delayed till they become hard and brittle there will be great danger of breaking off some parts of the roots, and the broken part would be in danger of being attacked with mildew. If the double varieties are named, they should be kept in separate drawers or paper bags, correctly named or numbered. Examine them occasionally to see if there is any appearance of decay or mildew on any of the roots. Roots so diseased must immediately be separated from the stock, cleaned, and fresh dried, and afterwards put into separate bags to prevent infection.

Propagation: by Seed.—For double flowers save seed only from semi-double blooms, with well-formed flowers, and bright, distinct colours. As the seed ripens at different times, and is downy, it is in danger of being blown away with the wind; therefore it must be carefully gathered daily as soon as it is ripe. Spread the seed on a sheet of paper, lay it in a window facing the morning sun for a few days until it is perfectly dry; then put it in a bag, and keep it dry till the sowing season.

The common single Anemone seed may be sown, immediately it is ripe, in a prepared bed in the garden; but seed saved carefully, as described above, is deserving of a little more trouble. Have a one or a two-light box, according to the quantity of seed saved; take out the soil, and prepare the bed exactly the same as directed for the full-grown roots; make the surface very smooth. Let this be done about the middle of December. Place the lights on, giving air every fine day till the surface is moderately dry; then prepare the seed for sowing by rubbing it with the hand for a considerable time amongst some dry soil. This should be done until the seeds are divested of their downy covering, and separated from each other. Then choose some fine, mild day, about the middle or end of January, and sow the seeds evenly and carefully on the bed of earth in the frame; then have a fine sieve and some rather dry light soil ready; sift a very thin covering evenly over the seeds, not above the thickness of a shilling, give a gentle watering with a very fine-rosed garden pot, shut up the frame, and let it be kept close, excepting during bright sunshine on mild days, when a little air may be given. *The surface should never be allowed to become quite dry.* In hot sunshine, in addition to giving air, shade this seed-bed with a mat until the plants have made two or three leaves. As the season advances give more air and water, and afterwards expose them daily to the full light and sun; but as long as there is any danger of frost shut them up at night. Keep them duly supplied with water until the leaves decay; then sift two inches of the surface through a very fine sieve, and carefully pick out all the young small roots. Plant them early in September in the open bed, and treat them afterwards exactly like the old roots until they flower, which will generally happen the second or third year.

By dividing the Roots.—Anemones are easily increased by breaking off one or more of the little knobs of the full-grown tubers. These may be planted and managed exactly like the old-established roots.

ANTIRRHINUM.

The characteristics of a perfect flower of an Antirrhinum have not been defined by any florist excepting Mr. Glenny. He says:—

"1. The plant should be dwarf; the flowers abundant; the mouth wide, and the more the inner surface turns up to hide the tube the better. 2. The tube should be clear and pure if white, and if any other colour it should be bright; and the mouth, and all the inner surface, should be of a different colour and texture (?), and form a contrast with the tube. 3. The petal should lap over at the indentations, so as not to show them; the texture of the tube should be like wax or enamel; the inside surface, which laps over, should be velvety. 4. When the flower is striped or spotted, the marking should be well-defined in all its variations; the colour should be dense, whatever that colour may be. 5. The flowers should form spikes of six or seven blooms, close, but not in each other's way; and the footstalks should be strong and elastic, to keep them from hanging down close to the stem, which they will if the footstalks are weak."

Propagation: by Seed.—The Antirrhinum may be sown in the open border of the garden. Procure a few of the best sorts in cultivation, grow them one year, and save seeds from them, keeping the seed of each variety to itself.

The time for sowing is about the second week in April. Prepare a bed in an open part of the garden, by manuring it well in the autumn, and digging in the manure at the same time, leaving the surface rather rough for the frosts to act upon. When the sowing time arrives, fork the surface over, breaking it as fine as possible. Choose a time when the surface is moderately dry for this operation. Have a sufficient number of wooden labels ready, having on them the names of the varieties from whence the seed was gathered, and so proceed till all the parcels are sown; then rake the bed smooth to cover the seed. Should the weather prove dry afterwards, a very gentle watering in the evening, now and then, will help the seeds to vegetate.

When the seedlings have attained an inch or two in height, dig another larger bed, and transplant the seedlings into it, planting them five inches apart every way, keeping the sorts still separate. Here they may remain till they flower. Then compare each, as they come fully into bloom, with the properties as before given. All that are deficient in form, colour, and size may either be thrown away at once, or planted in the front of shrubberies if good in colour.

Propagation: by Cuttings.—It may, to a limited extent, be increased by division, but that mode is slow and uncertain; whereas cuttings strike so easily that the grower need not resort to any other method.

There are two ways by which cuttings may be rooted; first, in pots, placed in heat; and second, under a handlight in a shady border.

If for growing in heat, prepare a cutting-pot, four or five inches in diameter, by well draining it; place a large crock over the hole at the bottom of the pot, then a few smaller potsherds over that, and upon them at least an inch of still smaller ones, covering the whole with a thin layer of moss to prevent the soil from choking up the drainage; the whole to occupy fully one-half of the depth of the pot. Upon this drainage place as much roughly-sifted light compost, formed with equal portions of loam, leaf mould, and sandy peat, as will fill the pot to within half an inch of the rim, give it a gentle shake down, but do not press it hard; then fill up the remaining space level with the rim with rather moist, fine white sand, stroking it off level with a straight-edged stick. The best cuttings are the short side-shoots produced below the spike of flowers, or weak shoots growing from the sides of the plants. Avoid strong, coarse shoots. Dress off all the lower leaves, leaving only three or four if they are small, then give a clean horizontal cut at the joint. It is advisable always to make the cuttings very short If cuttings are plentiful, then fill a pot with one kind only, placing the label in the centre, and the cuttings close round the side of the pot, just allowing room enough between the leaves of each cutting. As a general rule, half an inch between each is ample space. When cuttings are scarce, and not sufficient to fill the pot, then insert a label between the varieties, so as to distinguish them at the time of potting. Give them a good watering, and as soon as the leaves are dry place them in the frame, or in the propagating house. Shade from the sun, and keep the sand moderately moist. They will soon bear the sun's rays for an hour or two in the morning and afternoon; and every cutting ought to be rooted in a fortnight or three weeks. The season for putting in these cuttings may be from April to August, but the best time is about the middle of July.

Immediately they are rooted they should be potted off singly into three-inch pots in the same compost. Nip off the tops as soon as potted, to cause them to make bushy plants. Place them, when potted, in a cold frame, shading them from the sun till fresh roots are made; then give air, moderately at first, and more freely as they can bear it; they will then be ready to plant out in the blooming-bed, or, if very much valued, they may be kept in the pots in a cold pit till spring.

To strike them under handlights, prepare the border for them (behind a low north wall) in the same manner as described for the pots, with the exception of the drainage, unless the border is wet, then it will be advisable to drain it also. Raise the border two or three inches above the ordinary level; make the sand smooth, and place the handlights upon it, to make a mark to show where the cuttings are to be planted; make the cuttings exactly as described above for those in pots; then, with a small stick, insert them in rows within the space marked by the edges of the handlight, and when all are planted, give a gentle watering, leaving the handlights off till the leaves are dry; then place the handlights over the cuttings, and they will need no more care till growth takes place, when the hand-glasses should be lifted off for two or three hours every morning, and finally removed when the cuttings no longer flag with the exposure. In a month's time they may be transplanted where they are to flower.

Culture in Pots.—Soil.—Obtain turf from an upland pasture, taken off about two or three inches thick, and keep it in a heap for a year, to cause the grass roots to decay and to mellow the soil. Chop it and turn it over four or five times during the year—it will then be in finer condition for use. Of this loam take three parts, and of well decomposed leaf mould one part, or of hotbed manure well decomposed, in fact, reduced to a fine black mould; and of sandy peat one part. A small portion of old lime rubbish, slightly sifted, will be of service to the plants if mixed amongst the compost. Being duly mixed in sufficient quantity, let the compost be brought under shelter to dry some time before the potting season.

Pots.—Antirrhinums may be grown and bloomed very tolerably in what are called large 48's, which are five inches and a half in diameter; but for exhibition purposes, or to grow them finely, they ought to be planted in eight-inch pots; and the pots should be of the deepest size made.

Potting.—The proper time for this is early in March, when the plants are beginning to push up three or four strong shoots from their base. These are to produce the flower-spikes. Drain a pot well, then fill the pot high enough for the ball of the plant to be nearly level with the rim of the pot. Turn the plant out of its present pot, and remove the old drainage carefully out from amongst the roots. Open these out without breaking them, and work the fresh soil amongst them. Fill the soil up round the ball level with the rim, covering the ball about a quarter of an inch, and then shake the soil down by striking the pot smartly on the bench. When all are finished give a good watering, and place them in a cool pit or frame. Protect them from severe frosts by a covering of mats or some other material; but open the frames every day, as early as the weather will permit, to keep them cool. This is a grand point; for if the plants are drawn up into weak growth there will be no fine bloom. Should any of the plants produce one or two strong shoots, these ought to be stopped, to cause them to produce more shoots. Every plant should have at least five shoots for bloom. When these strong shoots have made some progress, and have a fair proportion of leaves, then all the small, weak shoots should be cut off. They make the very best cuttings.

After-culture.—The plants must be well supplied with water, and when the pots are filled with roots, a weak solution of dung-water will be serviceable. The great object is to produce a strong, healthy, bushy plant before the flower-spikes appear. It may be necessary, where the shoots of any variety are weak, to place small green sticks to support them, though they should never be used except in cases of necessity. Some varieties cluster their shoots together, and, in such a case, sticks must be used at an early stage. Place a stick to each shoot to spread them out, leaving the tallest shoot in the centre.

As the season advances the plants should be placed in the open air, on a bed of coal ashes, in a situation sheltered from the wind. Just before the blooms begin to open cover the plants with an awning, to shelter them from the sun and heavy rains. To produce a number of fine blossoms at once, nip off the very tip of each spike whilst they are growing.

General Management in the Border.—To grow Antirrhinums in the border, it should be prepared early in the autumn. Choose an open situation, but sheltered at a distance from the north and west winds. Mark out the bed three feet wide, and if the situation is low and wet, let it be well drained. Throw out the soil on each side of the bed, and place a layer of brick rubble at the bottom, three or four inches thick; upon that place a covering of the most convenient material on hand; thin turf, the grassy side downwards, is the best, but old thatch, or strawy litter, or even small twigs of trees, would answer the purpose, which is to prevent the soil choking up the drainage. Then mix the soil, if tolerably good, with some well decomposed manure or vegetable mould, and some road scrapings and sifted lime rubbish; the materials to be added amounting altogether to about one-eighth of the soil. When duly mixed, then cast it into the bed, using as much as will raise it six inches above the surrounding level.

Choose a dry day for the operation of planting, and take care to have the plants tolerably strong at the time; then place them on the bed in their separate sorts, allowing six inches square to each plant. Have some kind of labels to each sort. When all are planted, level the bed between the plants, and they will require no further care till the spring. As soon as the winter is passed, press any down that the frost may have lifted up; clear away all weeds, and stir up the surface of the soil with a small fork. As the plants advance in growth it will be necessary to thin the shoots when too numerous. This thinning must be in proportion to the strength of each plant. Weak plants should only have two or three flowering shoots left, but strong ones may have four or five. Just before the blooms expand, each spike should have a stick placed and tied to it, to prevent the winds from breaking it off. When in full bloom a covering of hoops and canvas, if handy, would greatly prolong the bloom.

If it is desired to have a long season of bloom, cut down the first flowering spikes before seed is formed, then fresh flower-spikes will push forth from the base of each plant, and there will be a succession of bloom.

The finest flowers will always be produced on young plants; therefore, whoever wishes to excel in blooms should renew his bed and plants annually.

AURICULA.

Terms used in describing an Auricula :—*Thrum*, the stamens showing beyond the throat. *Pin-eyed*, the pistil showing beyond the throat. *Paste*, white circle next to the tube in a florist's flower. *Ground colour*, circle next to the paste, being the distinctive colour of the variety. *Edge*, outer circle or border. *Pip* is a single flower. *Truss*, a number of flowers on a common flower-stalk; it is desirable there should not be less than seven.

Characteristics of a good Flower.—The pip should consist of four circles, formed at equal distances round a given point. The first, the *tube*, round, of a yellow colour, the thrum rising a little above the eye, or paste. The *paste*, pure white, dense, and round. The *ground colour* should be dense and distinct, perfectly circular, next the paste, slightly feathered towards the edge. The *edge* should be distinct in colour, whole, and circular, instead of starry in outline. The whole *pip* should be round, flat, and smooth at the edges. All the pips in a *truss* should show boldly, without overlapping. The *stem* should be strong, and the foliage healthy.

Propagation: by Suckers.—These are generally removed at potting time, because the plants are thus dressed at once. Those rooted should be placed in small pots in proportion to their size, or two or three in a pot. Those not rooted should be placed two or three inches apart round the sides of a pot, in rich, sandy soil, and kept under a handlight in a shady place until they are rooted, when, according to their strength, they may be potted separately in small pots, or, as will generally be preferable, kept in store pots all the winter, and shifted early in spring.

By Seed.—When the flower fades, and the seed-pod is swelling, more air and exposure may be given. Cut off the seed-vessels as they become brown, about the beginning of July, and place them in a dry sunny place, on a sheet of paper, until they open. When this takes place, the seeds may be sown at once on rich, light soil, under a handlight, or better still, in a box that may be protected, and easily moved under cover in winter. Seed from which good flowers may be expected should be sown in February or March, as in that case the plants attain a good size before they encounter the first winter. The seed, in either case, should not be covered more than the eighth of an inch. On this account it is well to sow in pots, plunging them in a gentle hotbed, covering each pot with a square of glass, and shading until the seedlings appear, when light and air must be gradually given. This would secure a more uniform vegetation of the seed. As soon as the seedlings can be easily handled, they should be pricked out into a bed, about five inches apart, supplied with a frame, so as to be wintered there, and many will show bloom the following year, when the good ones may be potted and placed with the florists' flowers, and the others transferred to the border.

Soil.—Take one part of two-year-old, dry, rotted cowdung, collected from the pastures in summer, when it is dry and caky; place it in a dry shed, so that the wind may whistle through it, and thus banish all the worms. By the time specified it will be flaky and light. Add to this two parts of rotted turf, from which all worms have been driven, and half a part of silver sand, or other clean sand. If the cowdung has come from stall-fed animals, a less quantity will be sufficient. Very rotten hotbed dung will answer equally well, if well dried and sweetened before use. The same may be said of leaf mould. If no rotten turf is to be had, obtain a little sweet mellow loam from a roadside. You will find it safest rather to underdo your compost in richness. You may communicate strength by manure waterings. These, however must consist of old cowdung in solution, and, if at all fresh, it must be mixed a long time before being used. All strong manures, and especially if of a hot nature, are dangerous.

Time and Mode of Potting.—If a plant has defective drainage, or is sickly, pot or examine it at any time. The best time for a general potting is just when the plants have had a short rest after flowering. Those with seed left to ripen must be waited longer for. Those with valuable offsets, not yet begun to root, may be waited for a week or two. July may be considered a good medium time, if the plants are healthy and growing well. If potted much earlier there is a danger of the flower-stems showing early in winter; if much later, the roots will not have occupied the main soil sufficiently before winter. In turning the plants out of the pots, all the offsets, as already mentioned, should be removed. Most of the soil may be crumbled and shaken away. The main stem-root in old plants may be growing too long, or the base may be turning black and decayed. In either case shorten back to where it is sound, and daub the part cut with charcoal dust, and also any cuts of offsets from the stem. Shorten, but sparingly, the longest fibres if fresh. Remove all in the least sickly or decayed. In draining the pot, place the draining crock with its curved side over the hole. If there is from an inch to an inch and a half of drainage above, properly placed, the smallest uppermost, and covered with a sprinkling of moss, there will be no clogging of the drainage. Place some compost in the pot, hold the plant in it, regulate the roots all over the space nicely, and shake the soil among them, settling it by striking the pot on the bench, and then firm the soil a little with the fingers, and especially near the collar of the plant. Place the pots on a raised platform, on rough coal ashes, beneath the lights of the frame, which should be set with a north-east aspect, water with a fine rose, and keep them rather close, and shaded in the morning for a fortnight or three weeks.

Summer Treatment.—As soon as fresh growth is proceeding, the shading may be dispensed with. More air may be given at first, and then the sashes may be taken off completely; the frame being elevated on bricks, that the air may have free access all round the pots. Let waterings be duly given, the surface soil frequently stirred, decayed leaves removed, and slugs and worms hunted out. If the position is at all exposed to the mid-day or afternoon sun, shading will be required in the hottest hours. Mild, warm rains will be beneficial, but heavy rains must be guarded against, either by canvas or glass.

Winter Treatment.—From the first to the middle of October is a good time for removing the plants to their winter quarters. We suppose that the frame is again the Auricula house. The position on which it is to stand should be raised six or twelve inches above the ground level, and by grouting, or other means, the moisture should be prevented rising from below, as well as worms, &c. The ground should slope out from it all round, and the plants be set on rough coal ashes, the frame facing the south. The frame should be set on bricks, that air may pass below as well as above, the sashes being left off in all fine weather. Boards, or other means, must be ready to shut off the air at the bottom of the frames in frosty weather, and during severe frost the sashes must also be shut. No rain should fall on the plants in winter, and, if they become dry, the foliage should not be wetted, as, if long wet, mildew will be sure to seize them. Nothing in the shape of a yellow leaf should be twice seen. In dull, mild weather all the air possible should be given, back and front, without taking the glasses off, if the atmosphere is at all foggy. Dull foggy weather in December and January is a great enemy. Removing part of the ashes on a dry mild day, and replacing with dry and sweet materials of the same nature, will be an advantage. In severe weather the plants may be kept closed up and covered without injury. In very bright days, with cold frosty winds, it is better to shade instead of giving much air. When the weather is mild, in addition to giving air freely, the surface of the soil should be frequently stirred, and all green slime and moss removed. The pots should stand within six inches of the glass, and it is safest to plunge them in the rough ashes in winter. The roots are more easily injured by a severe frost than the leaves.

Spring Treatment.—In February, during a fine day, prick up the surface soil, throw off as much as you can without injuring the roots, and refill with rather dry, rich compost of equal parts of old, decayed dung, sweet loam, and silver sand, using it in a dry state, and pressing it firmly against the collar. Take this opportunity to add or replace fresh ashes, and thoroughly to clean and whitewash the frame inside with fresh lime. A watering will, before long, be wanted. The plants will require to be covered up at night when at all cold, and to be kept closer during the day in March, that the flower-stems may have no check, and that the pips may not be deformed or discoloured. What water is given after the end of February must be put carefully on the soil, without touching either the leaves, or, especially, the heart of the plant. As the flowering period approaches, remove the plants individually to a north aspect, under handlights propped up on bricks; or use a frame, and give air, shelter, and shading, in April, according to the weather. A little manure water will now be of great advantage in giving size to the flower and strength to the stem. Sudden changes of the weather to cold must be guarded against by mats, or other protection.

CALCEOLARIA.

This family is naturally divided into two groups, the *herbaceous* and the *shrubby;* the former having large flowers on long flower-stalks, the latter having small flowers on shorter flower-stalks, and coming from all parts of the plant continuously during the summer. The herbaceous ones, where treated so as to bloom several times during the summer, do so in successional efforts, each period of a mass of bloom being followed by one in which there are few or no flowers. On this account the herbaceous ones have come to be treated more particularly as florists' flowers and for pot culture; and the shrubby ones for pot culture and the flower beds in summer.

Characteristics of a good Flower.—If the flowers are equally good, the more shrubby the plants are the better, as the foliage makes a fine background for the flowers. The larger the flower, the better it will be, provided it is circular in outline, without crumples or serratures, and convex or globular in shape, instead of flat; the mouth of the purse cannot be too small; the colour should be bright, if a self; and if spotted, or blotched, the ground colour should be clear and distinct, and the spots, &c., well marked, not running or fouling into each other, or feathering into the ground colour.

Propagation by Seed.—*Time of Sowing.*—The second week in August is quite early enough. Sown in the second week in September, large flowering plants have been had in twelve-inch pots in May. They grow very fast at the end of autumn, and after the turn of the day in spring. The second and third week in August may be considered good medium times. Select a piece of ground in a shady corner, and there place a handlight or more. Strew the ground on which the handlight is to rest, and a space round it with salt. On this place a couple of inches of rough coal ashes, and when the glass is put down place two or three more inches of the ashes inside. These are precautions against worms and slugs. Then take one or several six-inch pots; fill them half full with drainage, then an inch of somewhat rough soil, filling up to within half an inch of the rim with fine, light, sandy loam, containing a little fine-sifted leaf mould. Press the surface, afterwards water the pots well, and allow them to drain for a day; then place a very little fine tolerably dry soil on the surface, press gently down to make smooth, and sow the seeds; then scatter over them the smallest quantity of fine sand. Press level again, place a square of glass over the pot, and set it underneath the handlight. If this is kept close, and the ashes inside moist, the seedlings will seldom want watering until they are fairly up—a matter of considerable importance. When fairly up, lift the top of the handlight a little; as they grow a little larger, edge up the square of glass over the pot, first at night, and then during the day. When a little larger, move the square of glass altogether, and give more air by the top of the handlight. By this time the tiny plants will have a few leaves, though it would be difficult, as yet, to handle them singly. To prevent them damping at the surface, lift little patches of several plants together, and prick out these patches an inch or so apart, in pots prepared as if for cuttings, or in shallow pans. If before this, notwithstanding the dampness of the ashes, the surface of the soil should be dry, soak it well, not by a rose overhead, but by flooding the surface, by pouring the water on a piece of tile close to the edge of the pot. Many young seedlings, if small, are destroyed by watering overhead; they rot off just at the surface of the soil. When thus pricked out, and thus watered, place under handlights again, and keep close for a few days. In two or three weeks it will be necessary to prick out the plants in the little patches separately, leaving about one inch or so between each two. As the autumn advances, the strongest, to bloom in April and May, may have each a four-inch pot, and be shifted to a larger one before the end of October; but the chief supply may be pricked out into shallow pans a couple of inches apart, or four may be placed round the sides of a five-inch pot. If there are more than are wanted, rather prefer the smallest and weakest-growing plants. They will soon acquire strength. Moisture, if not stagnant, will do little injury to them in winter. They may be grown with the protection of a cold frame in winter, paying great attention to air, and just securing them from frost. They are easily kept from frost in a greenhouse heated by a flue or hot water-pipes; but a close, warm, dry atmosphere is their bane. They will do well in a temperature ranging from 35° to 45°, with air and moisture in proportion. In greenhouses they will be much benefited if set or partly plunged in damp moss. They will grow rapidly, even in winter, at 45° to 55°, standing in damp ashes or moss, and having plenty of air. Whenever the pots are full of roots the plants will be inclined to throw up their flower-stems, and therefore they must be potted on, to prevent the roots matting, when large specimens are required. May and June are the best months for the herbaceous kinds. Seedlings will bloom well in six-inch pots. Plants sown in August would fill that size, and bloom in May. To bloom in June and July, they must be shifted at the end of April and the end of May. When a small plant proves good, and it is desirable to make a fine specimen, it is best to sacrifice all flower-stems, and give it a large pot, and in about six weeks it will bloom again. Seeds sown in March, April, or May, will produce plants to bloom in summer and autumn; they should be kept under glass at first, but after June will do best in a shady place out of doors.

Cuttings.—The best time for making cuttings is as soon as the young shoots can be had after flowering—generally the end of August, though cuttings will root at any time. They also strike freely in the spring with a mild bottom heat. Those truly herbaceous may likewise be divided. The pots should be prepared as for seeds, only having very sandy soil, or half an inch of sand on the surface. A north border, under handlights, is the best place for cuttings in summer and autumn; they should have no heat then. They will strike very fast in mild bottom heat in spring. Shrubby varieties, for flower-beds, strike best in a shady place, under glass, after the middle of September. They will strike in a quarter of the time, in spring, in a mild heat.

Soil.—Rich, light, sandy loam grows them to perfection. Four parts of sweet, fibry loam, one of sand, and one of flaky, dry cowdung, or leaf mould, will grow them admirably.

General Treatment.—From the time the seedlings are up, or the cuttings inserted, they should never be dry. If well drained, and in open material, there is less danger from damp than dryness. In all shiftings see that the ball is wet before giving it another pot, and use the soil in a condition neither hot nor dry. In winter they should be as near the glass as possible. In frosty weather, when much artificial heat is used, the plants should stand on a moist bottom, and frequent gentle syringing over the foliage in sunny days will help them to a moist atmosphere. The moisture should be in proportion to the artificial heat. In pits and frames where little or no artificial heat is given, the plants will be moist enough; and if young plants, and well drained, and not over-potted, they will seldom suffer from damp. Small sticks, as inconspicuous as possible, should be used for supporting the bloom. When in bloom they will be the better of a little shade. When saving seed is an object, the plants should have a drier atmosphere. When done flowering, those intended for propagating from should be placed on the north side of a fence, and the old flowers, &c., removed. When handlights are not to be had, many of the semi-herbaceous kinds will root freely if a little very sandy soil is heaped up to the base of the young shoots. Every one of these would make a better plant next year, wintered in a four-inch pot, than if you took the greatest pains with a plant in a 12-inch or 16-inch pot.

CARNATION AND PICOTEE.

The *Carnation* has the marks on its petals from the centre to the edge, and through the edge in flakes, or stripes of colour.

The *Picotee* has its coloured mark only on the outer edge of its petals.

Properties of a good Carnation.—Carnations are divided into five classes, namely:—1. Scarlet Bizarres. 2. Pink or Crimson Bizarres. 3. Scarlet Flakes. 4. Rose Flakes. 5. Purple Flakes.

Bizarre is a French word, meaning odd or irregular; the flowers in these classes have three colours, which are irregularly placed on each petal. *Scarlet Bizarres* have that colour predominating over the purple or crimson, but the *Pink* or *Crimson Bizarres* have more of these colours than the scarlet. *Scarlet Flakes* are simple white grounds, with distinct stripes or ribbons of scarlet. *Rose* and *Purple Flakes* have these two colours upon a white ground. The properties in other respects are—

1. The flower should be not less than two and a half inches across. 2. The guard or lower petals, not less than six in number, must be broad, thick, and smooth on the outside, free from notch or serrature on the edge, and lapping over each other sufficiently to form a circular rose-like flower; the more perfectly round the outline the better. 3. Each layer of petals should be smaller than the layer immediately under it; there should not be less than five or six layers of petals laid regularly, and the flower should so rise in the centre as to form half a ball. 4. The petals should be stiff, free from notches, and slightly cupped. 5. The ground should be pure white, without specks of colour. 6. The stripes of colour should be clear and distinct, not running into one another, nor confused, but dense, smooth at the edges of the stripes, and well defined. 7. The colours must be bright and clear, whatever they may be; if there be two colours, the darker one cannot be too dark, or form too strong a contrast with the

lighter. With scarlet, the perfection would be black; with pink there cannot be too deep a crimson; with lilac, or light purple, the second colour cannot be too dark a purple. 8. If the colours run into the white and tinge it, or the white is not pure, the fault is very great, and pouncy spots or specks are highly objectionable. 9. The pod of the bloom should be long and large, to enable the flower to bloom without bursting it; but this is rare; they generally require to be tied about half way, and the upper part of the calyx opened down to the tie of each division; yet there are some which scarcely require any assistance, and this is a very estimable quality. 10. Decided superiority of perfume should obtain the prize when competing flowers are in other respects of balanced merit.

Properties of a good Picotee.—Picotees are divided into seven classes. 1. Red, heavy-edged. 2. Red, light-edged. 3. Rose, heavy-edged. 4. Rose, light-edged. 5. Purple, heavy-edged. 6. Purple, light-edged. 7. Yellow grounds, without any distinction as to the breadth of the edge colour.

The characteristics of good *form* are the same as for the Carnation, but with regard to *colour*—1. It should be clear, distinct, confined exclusively to the edge of the petals, of equal breadth and uniform colour on each, and not running down (called sometimes *feathering* or *barring*), neither should the white ground run through the coloured border to the edge of any one of the petals. 2. The ground must be pure white, without the slightest spot.*

Disqualifications of a Carnation or Picotee.—1. If there be any petal dead or mutilated. 2. If there be any one petal in which there is no colour. 3. If there be any one petal in which there is no white. 4. If a pod be split down to the sub-calyx. 5. If a guard petal be badly split. 6. Notched edges are glaring faults, for which no excellence in other respects compensates.

Soil.—Fresh loam is absolutely necessary. It must be looked for in upland pastures, and prepared as directed for the ANTIRRHINUM. Add to this about one-fourth of two-year-old well decomposed cowdung, and the same quantity of leaf mould. A small quantity of finely-sifted old lime rubbish will be found useful to mix with it. The compost should be put into a place where it will gradually become moderately dry.

Potting.—The proper sized pots for blooming are from ten to eleven inches in diameter. If not new, they should be well washed and dried. Let the drainage be at least an inch thick, and cover it with another inch of the roughest part of the compost; turn the plants, in pairs, carefully out of the store pots; fill in sufficient compost to raise the ball nearly level with the rim of the blooming pot; then gently loosen some of the outer roots, and

* This rule renders the name, still retained by florists, inappropriate, for *Picoté* is the French for spotted.

rub off the old surface mould; place the plants in the pot, and fill round the ball till it is covered; press the soil down gently, and give a smart stroke or two upon the bench. This potting should be done before the middle or end of April. The plants should be protected by an awning from heavy rains and late spring frosts, but in fine weather should be fully exposed to its influences. Gentle showers will do them good.

Each plant only sends up one flower-stem, and where only a pair in each pot is exhibited, the blaze of flowers is too weak to be effective. Four strong plants would make a far better and more effective display.

For growing blooms to exhibit as cut flowers, one, or, as is generally practised, a pair of plants in a pot is not only sufficient, but desirable, in order to produce larger blooms.

After the potting is finished, and the plants so placed as to be protected from heavy rains, worms, and other insects, the only care they require is the supplying them duly with soft rain water, and sometimes with weak liquid manure as they require it, and placing stakes to them in time to support the rising flower-stems to keep them in an upright position. Tie loosely, so that the stems can lengthen without forming knees or bended joints. If tied very tightly this will certainly happen, and the stem will in time break off at the bended joint.

When the flower-buds are advanced to a considerable size they must have a ligature placed round them to prevent their bursting on one side. The best are made of india-rubber bands, which may be obtained at most stationers' shops. These are superior to a shred of the common garden mat, because they are elastic, and, consequently, allow the bud to swell.

When the flowers begin to expand it will be necessary to shelter them from the sun. The most effectual method is a stage with a covering of canvas on rollers that can be rolled up and let down at pleasure. This should be elevated on a frame high enough to walk under. Such cultivators as have not the convenience of a stage must have shelters formed like a small parasol, having a socket in the middle to slide down the support sticks just far enough to shade and protect the flowers. These may be made of tin, painted green, or of zinc, or a frame made of stout wire, of the same form, and covered with oiled canvas. This sort of shelter, however, can only be considered as a make-shift.

Thinning the Buds.—Select three or four of the most promising on each stem, and nip off the remainder. This rule applies to such as are intended for exhibiting as cut blooms; rather more should be left for those to be shown in pots. Six or seven would not be too many, if the plants are strong, in this case.

Propagation: by Seed.—A perfectly double flower cannot produce seed; to do so it must be only partially double, and the seed-pods will be shorter, and the seeds fewer in such flowers than in single flowers. Save seed from flowers as double as possible; gather it as soon as it is ripe, and keep it dry and cool through the winter. Sow in boxes in March, placed under glass or on a warm border. In April transplant the seedlings on a bed enriched with leaf mould, or very decayed hotbed manure as soon as they are large enough. Plant them nine inches apart, and let them remain on that bed through the succeeding summer and winter. They will all flower the season following. Mark such as are good, name them, and layer them in the way to be described presently. Afterwards treat them exactly like your old varieties.

By Layers.—A layer is a branch or shoot brought down to the ground, and when rooted, separated from its parent. The materials wanted for layering are a sharp, small knife, a quantity of hooked pegs (the fronds of the common brake or fern are the best, though the pegs may be made of birch or hazel), and some finely-sifted soil. When the shoots round each plant have made five or six joints, or pairs of leaves, choose a dull, cloudy day on which to perform the work, or if the plants are in pots, under an elevated awning, they may be layered in any weather. Commence by trimming off the leaves from the bottom of a shoot, leaving the two uppermost on and entire. Trim off the lower leaves on every shoot before layering one, because when a layer is tongued it is easily broken off. When this is done, take hold of the shoot, turn it up, and pass the knife blade through the third joint upwards, commencing the cut just below it; then reach a hooked peg, thrust it into the soil, catching hold by its hook of the layer as it descends, and press it gently down to the soil. Do the next in the same manner, and so on till every shoot is layered; then cover them all with the sifted mould about three quarters of an inch deep, and that pot or plant is completed. Then give a slight watering, and the layers want no further care till they are rooted, which will be in about a month or six weeks. Examine them occasionally, and, as soon as roots are emitted, pot them off into five-inch pots, a pair in each; or if your space is limited. and the layers small, three may be put into each pot. After they are potted they should be placed under glass, in a cold frame or pit, plenty of air being given in mild weather, and shelter from severe frost when it occurs. Very little water is required through the winter months, and the air in the frame should be kept as dry as possible. Should damp prevail, the plants, some fine day, should be taken out, and a coat of fine, dry coal ashes spread over the surface. The plants should then be replaced in the pit.

By Pipings.—Carnations may be propagated by this mode where there is the convenience of a gentle hotbed. It is, however, not so safe as layering, but where there are more shoots than can be layered, and it is desirable to propagate largely, the superfluous shoots may be piped. Cut off the lower part of the shoot up to the third joint, trim off the lowest pair of leaves, and pass the knife just through the joint. Prepare a pot by draining it, and filling it with the compost up to within an inch of the top; fill that inch with silver sand, water it gently to make it firm, and then insert the pipings all round it close to the pot sides; place them in a gentle hotbed, shading from the sun. Watch them daily, and supply water when the sand becomes dry. When they are rooted, which they will show by sending up fresh leaves, pot them in pairs, as directed for the layers, and treat them in the same way.

CHRYSANTHEMUM.

The characteristics of a good Chrysanthemum are as follows:— 1. The plant should be dwarf, shrubby, well covered with green foliage to the bottom of the stems; the leaves broad and bright; the flowers well displayed, abundant, and well supported by the stems. If the stems are more than eighteen inches high they are gawky, and show too much green in comparison with the bloom. 2. The flower should be round, double, high in the crown, perfect in the centre, without disc or confusion, and of the form of a segment of a ball. 3. The petals should be thick, smooth, broad, circular at the ends, and the point where they meet hardly perceptible. They must not show their undersides by quilling, and should be of such firm texture as to retain themselves well in their places. 4. The flowers to be large in proportion to the foliage, but the size only to be considered when plants are in all other respects equal. 5. The colour, if a self, is superior in proportion to its purity and brightness; if the colours are more than one they should be well defined and distinct. The worst of all colours are those which are mixed or clouded together; and we are inclined to place more than usual emphasis upon colour in the case of the Chrysanthemum, because many flowers now admitted even into exhibition stands are odious in this respect. We have given no rules for judging either *the quilled* or *the tasselled* varieties, because these should never be admitted to be shown, except in a separate class, as " Fancy Chrysanthemums;" and in that class we can only say, that those least offensive to the eye should receive the prize.

Soil.—The ordinary soil is formed of good loam and well-decomposed dung, in the proportion of two parts of the former and one of the latter. We have, when we desired to obtain extraordinary specimens, procured from a rich pasture some green turf about two or three inches thick; this was chopped up pretty small, and about one-third of two-year-old cowdung and a small quantity of sand added. The plants were bushy and strong; they were turned out of their pots, and put into 11-inch pots, in this rich soil. Growth was kept up by liberal supplies of water, both at the root and overhead. They were never allowed to flag, but at the same time care was taken that there was no stagnant water in the pots. In potting attention must be given that there is proper drainage. When the plants have nearly filled their pots with roots, give them a further stimulant by watering with weak liquid manure. Water twice with clear soft water, and once with liquid-manure water. The plants should be placed in such a position as to allow to each a due share of light. To keep them steady, it is advisable to plunge the pots about half their depth in coal ashes, or even soil or gravel. The best position to arrange them in is a single row, with a foot of space between the pots.

Chrysanthemums require training to form handsome bushes. Short sticks must be thrust into the pots, and a certain number of branches selected to tie to them; these should neither be too many nor too few. It is difficult to give precise instructions on this point; let it suffice to state that each shoot, and all its leaves, should stand clear of its neighbours, so as to let every leaf have light. Let the shoots be judiciously thinned out, and those that are left be trained outwards in part, so as to allow of a due admission of light and air to the centre leaves and shoots.

Propagation: by Cuttings.—The best are made of the young tops an inch long; and the best time is in March. They may be managed in two ways—either put them singly into two-inch pots, or place a number round the inside of a five-inch pot. Use sandy loam to strike them in. Place them in a frame heated slightly, and shade from the sun for a few days. They will quickly root, and should be then potted off, and replaced in the frame, if in five-inch pots; but if singly in small pots, they may be placed in a cool frame as soon as they are rooted, and repotted when the pots are filled with roots.

By Layers.—This is a good method to obtain very dwarf plants. Plant a few old plants out of doors in a row; let them grow as wild as they choose till the month of July; then take as many pots as plants are required, and plunge them, filled with some rich soil, into the ground, at such a distance from the plants growing in the ground as will allow the tops only, when bent down, to reach the pots; bring them carefully down, and lay a small stone upon each branch to keep it steady in its position in the pot. Leave about two inches of the top out of the soil. If the shoot is branched it is well, but if not it must not be topped, because there is some danger that the layer may continue to grow and not flower if topped so late in the season. The aim of this mode of propagation is to make them flower when very dwarf; and, therefore, the layer should have buds upon it just visible at the time when the layering is performed. Keep the soil in the pots moderately moist till roots are formed, and after that water more freely. When it is certain that the layers have made plenty of roots, cut them off from the parent plant, and remove them into a frame or pit deep enough to receive them. Should they flag during the day, give a sprinkling of water, and shade for a day or two till they recover; then give air and water freely. They will then be nice plants, about a foot high, with, perhaps, six or ten flowers on each.

By Seed.—It would be folly to expect good flowers from seed saved from a flat-petalled variety, or *vice versâ*; if an improved cup-shaped or flat-petalled variety is desired to be improved, the seed must be saved from a flower possessing these properties in the highest and best degree, and not from a quilled or tasselled variety. The flowers determined upon to save seed from should be protected from wind, rain, and insects; their own pollen should be dusted upon the stigma; and the seeds gathered as soon as they are ripe, and sown in the February following in a gentle hotbed, in shallow pots, and light, sandy loam. When the seedlings are high enough to be handled, transplant them into the smallest pots, and repot as soon as the pots are moderately filled with roots. They will make great progress during the summer if treated exactly in the same manner as described for the cuttings, and many of them will flower the same year.

In the northern counties Chrysanthemums will not bloom quite satisfactorily in the open air. It is necessary to give them greenhouse shelter early in October. In the greenhouse they should have plenty of moisture, both at the root and over the branches, especially when first placed there after having been exposed to the cool, moist evenings of autumn. Abundance of air must also be given every day, and at night, too, when sufficiently mild.

CINERARIA.

In cultivating the Cineraria there are two principal points to be aimed at. First, never allow the slightest frost to touch them; but, secondly, avoid the opposite extreme; for they should be kept as cool as they can be conveniently without the temperature falling to 32°.

Characteristics of a good Cineraria.—1. The petals should be thick, broad, blunt, and smooth at the ends, closely set, and form a circle without much indentation. 2. The centre or disc should rise boldly, and almost equal to half-globularly, above the petals, and be not much more than one-fifth of the diameter of the whole flower. In other words, the coloured circle formed by the petals should be about twice as wide all round as the disc measures across. 3. The colour of the petals should be brilliant, whether shaded or self; or if it be a white, it should be very pure. That of the disc should harmonise with that of the petals. 4. The trusses of flowers should be large, close, and even on the surface, —the individual flowers standing together with their edges touching each other, however numerous they may be. 5. The stems should be strong, and not longer than the width across the foliage. In other words, from the upper surface of the truss of flower to the leaves where the stem starts from should not be a greater distance than from one side of the foliage to the other. 6. The leaves should be broad and healthy. No worse symptoms of bad cultivation can be apparent than the leaves being stunted, discoloured, and showing other symptoms of having suffered from insects.

Propagation: by Offsets.—When a Cineraria has done blooming, remove it from the greenhouse, cut down the old flower-stems, excepting such as it is intended to save seed from, and place the pots out of doors upon a bed of coal ashes in an open situation. Give water moderately in dry weather, and as soon as the offsets appear, and have attained a leaf or two, take them off with a sharp knife, with the roots uninjured; plant them in small pots, and place them in a cold frame, shading them from the light for a fortnight, and from bright sunshine for another week. They will then be well rooted, and will require a pot a size larger.

By Seed.—Sow the seed as soon as it is ripe in shallow, wide pots, in light, fine soil, and slighty covered. As soon as the seedlings have formed two or three leaves, prick them out into the same kind of pots in a somewhat richer soil. They may remain in these pots till they have made some more leaves and fresh roots, then pot them off singly into small pots, shading for a few days. Afterwards, and at the proper time, repot them in the same manner as the offsets.

Soil.—The offsets and seedlings having attained the proper size for potting into larger pots, prepare the following compost:— Turfy loam from an upland pasture, two parts; fibrous peat, one part; decayed leaves two years old, one part; very rotten cow-dung, half a part; and a small addition of river sand Prepare, also, a sufficient quantity of broken potsherds of two sizes, one as large as walnuts, and the other about the size of peas. Have also a sufficient number of either new or clean-washed pots, two sizes larger than the plants are in.

Winter Culture.—By the time the plants, whether offsets or seedlings, are ready for repotting out of their first-size pots, cold nights will have begun to occur, which brings the time of culture under this head. Bring the plants on to the potting bench; prepare a pot by placing a large piece of potsherd over the hole at the bottom of the pot, then a layer of the larger size, and a second layer of the smaller size; place a thin layer of the rougher parts of the compost upon them, and as much soil as will be required to keep the plant just level with the rim of the pot; set the plant in the pot, and fill round it with the compost, pressing it gently down. Be careful not to break the leaves, as they are very brittle and tender. When the pot is quite full, give it a gentle knock upon the bench, to finally settle the soil. When all are finished, give a gentle watering, and place them in a cold frame; shade them if they flag from the sun, and water when necessary. They will soon require another shift. To know when they require it, turn a plant carefully out of its pot, and if the roots have reached the sides of the pot, and through the drainage, repot again immediately; for, if the roots once become closely matted, the plants will be crippled in their growth. The grand object is to keep them growing freely till they make large, broadleaved plants, in eight-inch pots, before they begin to show their flower-stems. Keep them in the cold frame or pit through the winter; only take care to cover them up securely every night, and day also, if the frost is severe. It will be necessary to pack round the sides and ends of the frame or pit with either short litter or dry fern, of sufficient thickness to keep out the severest frost. During severe weather it will sometimes be necessary to keep the covering on the glass all the day; but on all fine days take off the coverings, and give abundance of air; pick off all decaying leaves, should any appear, and only water when absolutely necessary. They grow and keep healthy much better in such a situation than in a greenhouse.

Summer Culture.—As soon as the warm, mild days of spring arrive, give the plants their last shift, and, if desirable, remove them into the greenhouse at once, placing them as near the glass as possible. The flower-stems will now be advancing rapidly; and, for some kinds, it will be necessary to use sticks to open out the heads of bloom, and show them to the best advantage, especially for those intended for exhibition; but all sticks should be removed a day or two before the show, as they are no addition to the beauty of the plants.

DAHLIA.

Characteristics of a good Flower.—1. *Form.*—Viewed in front, the flower should be a perfect circle; the petals broad at the ends, smooth at the edges, thick and stiff in substance, perfectly free from indenture or point, and should cup a little, but not enough to show the under surface. They should be in regular rows, each row forming a perfect circle, without any vacancy between them; and all in the circle should be the same size, uniformly opened to the same shape, and not rubbed nor crumpled. 2. Looked at sideways, the flower should form two-thirds of a ball. The rows of petals should rise one above another in rows; every petal should cover the join of the two petals under it, which the florists call imbricating; by this means the circular appearance is perfected throughout. 3. The *centre* should be perfect; the unbloomed petals lying with their points towards the centre should form a button, and should be the *highest* part of the flower, completing the ball. 4. The flower should be very double. The rows of petals lying one above another should cover one another very nearly; not more should be seen in depth than half the breadth; the more they are covered, so as to leave them distinct, the better in that respect; the petals, therefore, though cupped, must be shallow. 5. *Size.*— The size of the flower when well-grown should be not less than four inches in diameter. 6. *Colour.*—The colour should be dense, whatever it may be,—not as if it were a white dipped in colour, but as if the whole flower were coloured throughout. Whether tipped or edged, it must be free from splashes or blotches, or indefinite marks of any kind; and new flowers, unless they beat all old ones of the same colour, or are of a novel colour themselves, with a majority of the points of excellence, should be rejected.

Defects.—If the petals show the under side too much, even when looked at sideways,—if they do not cover each other well, —if the centre is composed of petals pointing upwards, or if those which are round the centre are confused,—if the petals are too narrow, or exhibit too much of their length,—or if they show any of the green scale at the bottom of the petals,—if *the eye* is sunk,—if the shoulder is too high, the face flat, or the sides too upright,—if the petals show an indenture as if heart-shaped,— if the petals are too large and coarse, or are flimsy, or do not hold their form,—in any or all these cases the flowers are objectionable; and if there be one or two of these faults conspicuous, the flower is second or third-rate.

If flowers are exhibited which show the disc, or a green scale, or have been eaten by vermin, or damaged by carriage, or are evidently decayed, the censors should reject them at once.

Characteristics of the Plant.—Although the form of the plant is of secondary consideration, yet it is a matter worthy of some notice. The general figure should be uniform and compact, that is, it should gradually enlarge from the lowest lateral shoots to the extremity of those highest, and it should be devoid of a straggling or rambling habit. Secondly, the plant should be disposed to bloom freely and numerously. Thirdly, its blossoms should stand out clearly from the foliage, on short, strong flower-stalks, so as to be presented boldly and advantageously.

Propagation: by Cuttings.—The time for striking these extends from February to August. The young shoots that spring from the tubers make the best cuttings, and are the most sure to grow; but the young tops taken off at a joint will strike root and form small tubers even so late as August, and often are more sure to grow in the spring following, if kept in small pots, than roots that have been planted out late. If the shoots on the old tubers are numerous, or there appear many buds ready to start, the shoots that have grown three inches long may be slipped off with the finger close to the tuber; but if the shoots are few, or only one, they must be cut off so as to leave two buds at the base of the shoot to grow again. The cuttings, or slips, must be put in pots filled with light earth, with a layer of pure white sand on the surface, and placed in a gentle hotbed. If the pot of cuttings can be plunged in coal ashes, or other material, the cuttings will strike the sooner; water very moderately and carefully, and shade from bright sun. They will strike root in a fortnight or three weeks, and should be immediately potted in 3½-inch pots, and kept close for a few days, till they make a few more roots. They may then be placed in a cold frame, shaded from the sun, und protected from frost and wet. Pot them again into 4½-inch pots before the roots become matted, and then begin to give air daily, and keep them well watered.

By Division.—The roots may be divided from the crown downwards, taking care to have a bud or two to each division. Pot them, if too early to plant out, or plant the divisions out at once in their places, but not earlier than the middle of April.

By Seed.—Save the seed from such double flowers as are partially fertile, having bright, distinct colours and good form. Gather it as soon as ripe, and hang the pods up in a dry place. When the scales of the pod turn brown, separate the seeds, dry them in the sun in the morning only, and when dry store them in a dry room. Sow them in March in shallow pans, and transplant the seedlings singly into small pots. As soon as the frosts are passed, plant them out a foot apart every way, and allow them to flower. All badly shaped or dull coloured flowers throw away; there is no hope of their improving by culture. Such as have good-formed petals and bright colours, though not perfectly double, may be kept another year for a further trial.

Soil.—The Dahlia requires a rich, deep, friable soil; and, as the branches are heavy and brittle, a sheltered situation should be chosen, neither too low nor too high. The ground should be trenched, if it will allow it, eighteen inches or two feet deep, and a good coating of well-decomposed dung spread on the surface after the trenching is completed, and immediately dug in one spit deep. Lay up the soil so mixed in slight ridges, to be levelled down just before planting.

Summer Culture.—Prepare the plants for planting out by constant and full exposure when the weather is mild. The season for planting is as soon as there is no fear of any more frost. Five feet apart every way for the dwarf-growing kinds, and six feet for the tall ones, will not be too much. It is a good method to have the places for each marked out, by driving in the stakes in the exact places first, and then there is no danger of the stakes injuring the roots. As late frosts might possibly occur, it is safer to cover the plants at night with clean empty garden-pots, of a sufficient size to cover them without touching the leaves, until all fear of frost has subsided. When the plants have obtained a considerable growth, cover the surface round each plant with some half-rotten, littery stable dung; this will preserve them from drought, and afford nutriment when the plants are watered.

Tying—As soon as the plants are high enough, they should be tied to the stakes with some rather broad shreds of soft bass matting; and the side-shoots must also be secured by longer pieces of matting, to prevent the winds and heavy rains from breaking them off. It may sometimes be necessary to place three or four additional stakes at a certain distance from the central one, to tie the side-branches to. The best kind of stakes are the thinnings of larch plantations. They should be stout, and six or seven feet long, at least. As the plants grow, if the weather is hot and dry, abundance of water should be supplied.

Protecting the Flowers.—Caps of oiled canvas stretched upon a wire frame are very good for the purpose; even a common garden-pot turned upside down is no bad shelter. They may easily be suspended over each flower by being fastened to a stake, and the flower gently brought down and tied to the stake under them. The best shade, however, is a square box with a glass front, and a slit at the bottom to allow the stem of the flower to slide into it, and thus bring the flower within the box. The flower has then the advantage of light and air, and is still protected from the sun, wind, and rain.

Winter Culture.—As soon as the autumn frosts have destroyed the tops of the plants, cut down the stems, and take up the roots immediately. If the roots come up clean out of the ground, they will only require gently drying, and may be stored at once in some place where they will be safe from frost. If the soil clings much to the tubers, these should be washed and dried, and then stowed away. The place should not only be free from frost, but from damp also, yet not so dry as to cause them to shrivel up too much. It is a good plan to have two or three of each kind struck late and kept in pots through the winter; but the soil must be perfectly dry before they are put to rest, and no wet or frost allowed to reach them. A good place for them is under the stage of a greenhouse where the pots may be laid on one side. In these winter quarters they must be frequently examined, and all decaying roots or stems removed.

FUCHSIA.

Characteristics of a good Fuchsia.—Commencing with the tube a first-rate Fuchsia should be well-proportioned, neither too thick, nor too short, nor too long; one inch and a half is a fair length, but if it is stout in proportion two inches might be allowed; the sepals or flower cups should stand at equal distances, and should be broad at the base, gradually tapering to the end; they should be refixed a little above the horizontal line, but not turned up so high as nearly to meet the tube; the corolla should be large and well rounded at the end, so that when the flower is turned up it may have the appearance of a little cup; the stamens and anthers at the top of them should project well out of the corolla; and the filament bearing the stigma must project considerably beyond the anthers; the stigma itself should be larger than the anthers, and should be of a clear white, so as to contrast well with the purple or crimson corolla. The colours should be clear and bright; the tube would be improved if of a waxy appearance, bright, and shining. If white, that white should be pure, not a pinkish white, but clear as the driven snow. The corolla should be of a clear colour, untinged by any other. The flower-stalk should be long enough to allow each flower to be seen distinctly from amongst the leaves. The habit should be rather dwarf than tall, and the plant should produce bloom when a foot high.

Soil.—Mellow, strong, yellow loam, one-half; well-decomposed hotbed manure, one-quarter; and one-year-old, decayed, tree leaves, one-quarter; all thoroughly mixed, will form a suitable compost.

Propagation: by Seed.—The seed should be carefully gathered when ripe. As the seeds are enveloped in a pulp, it is necessary, in order to preserve them, to cleanse them effectually. This is done by washing; bruise the berries with the hand, and mix them with water; as soon as the pulp is all washed off, pass the liquor through a hair-sieve fine enough to catch the seed, wash it repeatedly till it is quite clean, then dry it gradually; put it up in brown paper, and keep it in a dry room till spring. Sow it early in March in a mixture of light sandy loam and peat, cover slightly, and place the pots in a gentle hotbed. When the seedlings are half an inch high, transplant them in rows across pots five inches wide—these will hold about twenty or thirty plants each,— and then replace them in the hotbed. In these pots they may remain for a month or six weeks, and then they will require potting off singly into three-inch pots. Place them for a few days in a cold frame, and keep pretty close and shaded till fresh roots are formed, and they are then able to bear the full light, and a moderate admission of air. Give plenty of the latter as they acquire strength, and when the pots are full of roots give another shift into four-inch pots, and let them remain in these last till they flower. Many of them will flower the first year, and then is the time to make a selection. The selected one should be repotted, and grown on to the end of the season to prove them. Cuttings of the best may be taken off and propagated, and the whole kept in the coolest part of the greenhouse during the winter.

By Cuttings.—The best time to do this is in the early spring months; the first week in March, for instance. Place the plants intended to be increased by this mode in a gentle heat, to cause them to push forth young shoots. When these have attained two or three leaves, slip them off, and lay them to dry for a short time. The pots should be what are called 48's, measuring about four inches and a half in diameter. Let them either be quite new, or, if old, thoroughly washed clean. Drain them effectually, and place either some moss or rough siftings upon the drainage; then fill the pots with light, rich compost to within an inch of the top; fill the remainder with pure silver sand; give a little gentle watering to make it firm; let it stand a few minutes to dry, and then put in the cuttings, first smoothing the bottom of each with a sharp knife. Plant them round the edge of the pot, putting them so as to let the leaves point inwards. Remember, the cuttings cannot be too short. If the stems are just inserted within the sand, and the leaf or leaves are left out of it, they will strike root all the sooner. When the pot is planted with cuttings, fill up the holes the planting stick has made with some dry, fine sand; then give a gentle watering with the finest rose watering pot, and let them stand till the leaves and the surface of the sand have become moderately dry; then place them either in a gentle hotbed or under hand-glasses in heat; give them a change of air by tilting the lights of the frame upon the hotbed every morning, or by lifting off the handlights every morning early for an hour; and shade them well from the bright sunshine during the middle of the day until roots are formed. As soon as that takes place pot them off into $2\frac{1}{2}$-inch pots. Roots will be formed in fifteen or sixteen days from the time of putting in the cutting. After the plants are potted off, replace them where they came from for a week or ten days, keeping them pretty close, and shaded from the sun; give only just sufficient waterings to keep them fresh and growing. When more roots begin to show themselves, give more air and less shade till they are enabled to bear the full light of the sun. They may then be treated as established plants.

Summer Culture.—The plants struck in the spring make the finest specimens for exhibition in July. When the young plants have filled their pots with roots, shift them immediately into five-inch pots, in a compost of light loam and leaf mould, in equal parts, adding a due portion of sand to keep it open; this will be rich enough for the first two shifts. Place them in a house heated to 55° by day and 50° by night. Let them stand pretty close to the glass to cause a stout growth. Now is the time to determine upon the form the plants are to take when fully grown.

Pyramidal Form.—To furnish side-shoots nip off the tops when the plants are six inches high. Side-shoots will then be produced, and these should be tied out horizontally. The uppermost shoot should be tied upright, to be stopped again when eight or nine inches have been added to its stature. By the time this has taken place a fresh shift will be necessary. The diameter of the pot at this shifting should be seven inches. This shift should take place about the middle of April. Replace them in the house again, as near the glass as their shoots will allow. Give them every attention to cause strong, quick development, by watering freely at the roots, by syringing them overhead morning and evening, especially in sunny weather. and shutting up early in the afternoon, at the time the syringing is done. This will create a moist, stimulating atmosphere, and the plants will grow fast, and produce broad, healthy foliage. Stop them again, and tie the side shoots out in such a way as will furnish every side of the plant with horizontal branches equally distributed. If the house is a lean-to it will be necessary to turn the plant round every three or four days, to cause every side to be well proportioned and equally furnished. Continue this training till the plants have attained the requisite height, and begin to show bloom. The supports should then be removed. Repot twice more, first into nine-inch pots in May, and into eleven-inch pots in June. In this last size they may be allowed to flower. They should then be removed into the greenhouse, and have abundance of air night and day.

Winter Culture.—As soon as the bloom is over set the young plants out of doors in some open place in the garden. When the frost begins to appear take the plants under cover, either under the stage of the greenhouse, or in a back shed, or even a cellar, where the severe frost cannot reach them. Here they may remain without water till the potting time comes round again.

HYACINTH.

Characteristics of a good Hyacinth.—Size and Form of Spike.—To be a fine specimen the spike ought to be at least six inches long, and two inches in diameter at the lowest and broadest part, tapering gradually up to a single pip. But form, or proportion, is the greatest merit; and the handsomest proportions for the spikes are for its length to be twice the diameter of its lowest part, and for the whole spike to form a cone.

Size and Form of Pips.—The outline of each, looking at it in front, should be circular; and, looking at it in profile, it should be semi-circular. In other words, each pip should be half a globe. To effect this the petals (if the flower is single) require to be strongly bent back, or reflexed, so as to throw forward the centre. In double flowers it is not needed for the outer petals to be much bent back, as the semi-globular form in these is partly attained by the inner petals being imbricated, or lapped over each other in tiers, like the tiles on a roof. The lower pips should be large—an inch and a quarter in diameter is a superior size; and the pips of each circle should gradually diminish in diameter as they approach nearer to the summit. The petals should be thick, glossy surfaced, as if made of wax and rounded at the end. Sharp-pointed petals always injure the outline of the form of the spike.

The footstalk, or stem, of the spike should be straight, stout, and of a height sufficient to raise the lowest part of the spike just above the points of the leaves. The footstalk of each pip should be gradually shorter as it approaches nearer the top; and each should spring from the stem at an angle just a little less than a right angle, so as to aid the pips in adapting themselves to a conical form, and yet to keep their broad faces, or discs, full before the eye.

Colour.—What we say on this point is applicable to competing flowers of every species, for in all it should be esteemed as entirely subordinate to form and size. The reason for this is sound; for form and size, if no accident interferes, are superior just in proportion to the skilfulness of the cultivation. Colour, therefore, should have no further weight than to turn the scale in favour of the best coloured, provided that two specimens are equal in form and size. In the case of selfs—that is, flowers of one colour—the most uniform and brightest are best; but in flowers of more than one tint the colouring is best where the colours are distinct, and not clouded into one another.

Fragrance.—When flowers, such as the Hyacinth is, are of a kind yielding a perfume, if the rivals are equal in other qualities, we should award the prize to the most fragrant. It is even a criterion of good cultivation.

In Glasses.—The glasses ought to be at least nine inches long, with a cup at the top to contain the bulb. The bulbs should be put into the glasses at two or three times, if a lengthened season of bloom is desired; the glasses should be filled with soft clean water, just up to the neck, but not actually to touch the bulb. If wanted early, they should be put into the glasses as soon as the bulbs arrive from Holland. When they are so placed, and at whatever time, they should be put into a dark, cold room for a fortnight, to cause roots to be formed previously to the bloom-buds appearing. Examine them occasionally, and remove gently any scales that may be decayed, but be very careful not to injure the young roots. Should the water become foul, let it be changed, keeping each glass filled up to within a quarter of an inch of the bulbs, but do not let it actually touch them. When the buds and leaves have made a little growth they should be brought into the full light of the window, but even then, if possible, avoid a window facing the mid-day sun, or one in a room where there is a fire. These precautions induce a gradual growth, and, consequently, a much stronger foliage and finer bloom.

When the roots have nearly reached the bottom of each glass there will be seen, at the extremity of each, a pellicle or covering of mucous matter. This soon stops up the mouths of the roots by which the food of the plant is conveyed to the leaves. To prevent this the roots should be drawn carefully out of the glasses, and a wide vessel should be placed handy filled with clean water. In this immerse the roots of the bulb, and draw the mass carefully through the hand, pressing them gently. Do this two or three times until the roots appear quite clean, and perfectly white. Whilst one person is doing this, let another be washing out the glass, and wiping it quite clean and dry. Then gradually work the clean-washed roots into the glass before putting in any water. To get them in when numerous it will be found necessary to twist them round and round till they reach their old quarters, and the bulb rests upon the neck of the glass. Then fill the glass with clean water, and replace it in the window. It will generally be found that once washing will be sufficient. After this no more care will be necessary, excepting occasionally changing the water. Bulbs bloomed in glasses are afterwards only fit for the border. As soon as the bloom is over, the bulbs should be taken out of the glasses, preserving all the roots. Lay them in a border in the garden, and give a good watering. Here they will gradually ripen the bulbs, and the leaves will as gradually turn yellow and decay. Then take them up, and keep them dry and cool until October, and they may then be planted in the borders in the flower garden.

Culture in Pots.—Soil.—This should be rich and not over light, such as sound loam of rather a strong texture, mixed with about one-fourth of horse-droppings. Well-rotted cow-dung will be a good substitute for the horse manure, provided the compost has a liberal addition of sharp sand added to it.

Size of Pots.—The kind denominated "hyacinth pots," which are at least one-third deeper than the ordinary ones, are the best for these bulbs. When one bulb only is put in a pot, use the size called large 48's, which are nearly five inches in diameter at the top, and for two bulbs, use the small 32's, which are six inches in diameter. Three, or even five, bulbs might be planted in pots large enough to contain them, with a good effect, where they are to bloom in a greenhouse or a conservatory.

Potting.—Whatever kind of pots are used they must be well drained. Then upon the drainage place a thin covering of very fibrous turf, broken into pieces. This has been used with great success in a green state. Then put a layer of the compost, and press it down very firmly, only take care that it is in a proper state, neither too wet nor too dry. Keep adding more soil, and pressing it down till the pots are full enough to receive the bulbs. When the bulb is placed in the pot, upon this firm bed of soil, the top should be about a quarter of an inch below the level of the pot rim; then fill in more soil around it, pressing it also firm, and close to the bulb. If this is not properly done, when the roots begin to push they will lift the bulb out of its place, and these roots will be liable to be broken. When this rising of the bulb does happen it should be carefully lifted up, and a little soil taken out to make room for the roots, the bulb replaced gently, and the soil pressed again firmly around it. The season for potting is the last week in September, or the first week in October, for early blooms; but bulbs may be potted even to the end of November, if not forced too hard at first.

A bed, four feet wide, in an open place in the garden, will be suitable to plunge the pots in. If the situation is dry the soil may be excavated about four inches deep, and a layer of coal ashes spread over the bottom to keep worms out of the pots. Place the pots containing the bulbs on the bed, and cover them over with spent tanners' bark or coal ashes about two inches above the pots. Here they may remain till they are required, either for forcing into flower, or till the spring.

Take a portion of them into a warm pit, heated by some means, as hot water, dung, or tanners' bark, to bring them on into flower early, only let the forcing process be gentle, especially for the first three or four weeks, when the heat may be increased five or ten degrees. Begin with 50°, and then increase it to 55° or 60°, with sun heat.

To have them in flower at Christmas they should be placed in heat about the middle of October, so that the forcing may be gradual. If forced too quickly the flower-stems will be weak, and the colours anything but bright; whereas, if they are brought on gradually, the flower-stems will be strong, the flowers large, and the colour better. Some sorts of Hyacinths are better adapted than others for either growing in glasses or forcing in pots. For growing in pots, to flower late in the spring, almost any variety will answer.

When the bloom is in perfection the pots should be taken into a cool greenhouse or window, and plenty of air given. They will last much longer in bloom than if kept in heat. After the blooming is over the pots may be placed behind a wall, and duly watered to perfect the bulbs. They will not answer again for forcing, but may be planted in the borders the October following.

Culture in Beds.—Soil.—To grow Hyacinths well in beds the soil should be rich, light, and deep. If the soil of the garden is a sound loam, and well drained, then excavate the soil to the depth of fifteen inches. Level the bottom, and place a layer of small stones, or brick-ends broken small, two inches thick.

Cover this drainage with two inches of littery dung; then mix the soil that has been thrown out with some well-decomposed cowdung, some leaf mould, and plenty of river or sea sand, well screened. The proportions to be one part cowdung and one part leaf mould, to six parts of loam. Should the substratum be clayey or gravelly that part must be wheeled away, and as much good loam added as will replace it; then mix the compost well together, and fill the bed with it; let it be four or five inches above the former level, to allow for settling; lay it perfectly level, so that it may have the full benefit of the rain that falls upon it. If cowdung cannot be procured, hotbed dung, well rotted, will do.

Planting.—The best time is the first week in October; though, if the weather is mild, they may be planted as late as the middle of November. The soil should be moderately dry, and, therefore, it is better to wait a week or two should the season of planting be wet. To prevent treading upon the bed lay upon it a narrow piece of board long enough to reach across it, or have the board strong enough to bear the planter's weight, and raise it up at each end high enough to clear the bed; plant them with a dibber thick enough to make a hole as wide as the largest Hyacinth is in diameter, and the end that is thrust into the soil should be cut across, and a mark made just as far from the bottom as the bulbs should be covered with soil; the proper depth is three inches from the top of the bulb. Each Hyacinth should have at least five inches square of surface to grow in, but six inches would not be too much space for the leaves to expand, especially if the same bulbs are to be planted again the following season. If the colours are to be mixed, place the bulbs so that the colours will succeed each other in rotation, as, for instance, 1, red; 2, blue; 3, white; 4, yellow; then 5, red, and so on, till the bed is full; or, if there are several beds, and it is desirable to keep the colours separate, so that one bed shall be red, another blue, another white, and another yellow, then plant accordingly. As the planting proceeds have some of the compost ready, sifted through a coarse sieve, and fill up the holes with it. When so covered they are sure to be at the right depth; then rake the bed very lightly.

Shelters.—The Hyacinth is hardy enough to bear a moderate degree of frost; but it is advisable to cover the bed with about two inches of spent tanners' bark, to be removed early in spring, before the shoots appear above ground. Half-decayed leaves would answer the same purpose, or a mat or two thrown over the bed. If an amateur or florist cultivates the Hyacinth in long, common beds, like Tulips, a permanent shelter should be put up in the form of the bed, or the beds might be sheltered with hoops and mats. If so protected when in flower the season of bloom will be considerably prolonged.

Water.—During dry, parching winds, which sometimes occur in March, a slight sprinkling over the beds will be acceptable to the rising buds. In frosty weather this should be applied in the mornings only; but if there is no appearance of frost, then water in the evenings also, previously to putting on the shutters for the night. This sprinkling may be continued with advantage till the blooms begin to expand. As soon as the bloom is over the old flower-stems, but not the leaves, should be cut off, but not quite down to the ground, the covers removed, and, as soon as the leaves turn yellow, the bulbs should be taken up and laid upon a mat to dry; they can then be lifted easily under shelter. When the leaves are all quite decayed dress them off carefully, without bruising the bulbs, and then put these away in a dry, cool room till the planting season comes round again.

PANSY.

There are three classes, 1, Selfs, all of one colour. 2. Having yellow, orange, sulphur, or straw-coloured ground, with margins of maroon, crimson, chocolate, bronze, puce, and their intermediate tints. 3. Having a white ground, with margins of purple, blue, mulberry, and their intermediate tints.

Characteristics of a good Pansy.—Many have written upon the characteristics which belong to it when really a superior flower, and their opinions are combined in the following:—1. Each bloom should be nearly perfectly circular, flat, and very smooth at the edge; every notch, or unevenness, being a blemish. 2. The petals should be thick, and of a rich velvety texture. 3. Whatever may be the colours, the principal, or ground colour of the three lower petals, should be alike; whether it be white, yellow, straw colour, plain, fringed, or blotched, there should not in these three petals be a shade difference in the principal colour; and the white, yellow, or straw colour should be pure. 4. Whatever may be the character of the marks or darker pencillings on the ground colour, they should be bright, dense, distinct, and retain their character, without running or flushing, that is, mixing with the ground colour. 5. The two upper petals should be perfectly uniform, whether dark or light, or fringed or blotched. The two petals immediately under them should be alike; and the lower petal, as before observed, must have the same ground colour and character as the two above it; and the pencilling or marking of the eye in the three lower petals must not break through to the edges. 6. If flowers are equal in other respects, the larger, if not the coarser, is the better; but no flower should be shown that is under one inch and a half across. 7. Ragged or notched edges, crumpled petals, indentures on the petal, indistinct markings or pencillings, and flushed or run colours, are great blemishes; but if a bloom has one ground colour to the

PELARGONIUM.

Propagation: by Seed.—When the seed is ripe gather it carefully, and divest it of its arils, or feather-like appendages, wrap it up in paper, and keep it in a dry drawer, in a cool room, till spring. Sow it early in March, and place it in a gentle heat; a hotbed that has been at work for a few weeks will answer admirably. Sow in wide, shallow pots, well drained, in a light, rich compost, press the seed down gently, and cover it about a quarter of an inch deep. If the seed is good it will quickly germinate, and should then be removed from the hotbed and be placed upon a shelf in the greenhouse near to the glass. Water very moderately, or the plants will be apt to damp off. As soon as the seedlings have made their second leaf, pot them off singly into two-inch pots, in a compost of loam and leaf mould in equal parts, with a liberal addition of river sand, finely sifted. Replace them on the shelf, and shade for a time from hot sunshine. The seedlings will soon fill these small pots with roots. They must then be repotted into pots a size larger, and may afterwards be treated in the same way as those which have been propagated by cuttings. Keep them close to the glass, and give abundance of air on all favourable occasions. As soon as the weather will permit, place them out of doors, upon a bed of ashes of sufficient thickness to prevent worms from entering the pots. The situation should be an open one, to ripen the wood, and induce a stocky or bushy habit, so as to insure their flowering the following season. The size of pots to flower them in need not be more than four inches and a half. When there is a fear of autumnal frosts, remove them into the greenhouse and place them on a shelf, at such a distance from the glass as will serve to keep them dwarf and bushy. There is no need to top them in the manner recommended hereafter for plants raised from cuttings, the object being not to make fine specimens, but to get them to flower as quickly as possible the spring following. This brings us to consider what are the *characteristics of a first-rate Pelargonium.*

Form is the first; the flowers should be nearly flat, neither too much cupped nor in the least reflexed. Each petal should be nearly equal in size, rounded at the end, and quite smooth at the edges. The whole flower should be as near a perfect circle as possible. It should be of such a *substance* as to keep its form when expanded. If thin and flabby, it will turn backwards and forwards as it advances in size, and the general effect will be marred. The *size* of each bloom should be at least one inch and a half in diameter. The *colours* should be clear, distinct, and bright; the edging of the upper petals should also be uniform; the dark blotch should never run into the edging. The *habit* should be rather dwarf than otherwise, and it should flower freely;

the *truss* should stand up well above the foliage, and the number of blooms forming the truss should never be less than five; each flower-stem should be long enough to bear the flower as high as to form an even truss.

By Cuttings.—Cuttings may be put in and struck from March to August; the general time, however, is when the plants have done flowering, and require cutting down to make bushy plants for the next season. This generally happens from the end of June to the beginning of August. The best place to strike the cuttings in is a well constructed propagating house; but they may be very successfully propagated in a frame set upon a spent hotbed, first removing the soil, and replacing it upon a thick coat of coal ashes to keep out the worms. Upon this coat place another of dry sawdust to plunge the cutting pots in. This dry sawdust will serve to absorb the moisture from the earth in the pots and the necessary waterings. The best soil is pure loam mixed with silver sand. Five inches wide at the top is the most proper size for the pots. The pots must be well drained. Fill them to the top with the prepared loam, which should be put through a rather coarse sieve to take out the stones, &c. It should not be pressed down too hard, but made firm enough to hold the cuttings fast. Use it in a state neither wet nor dry. The side-shoots which have not flowered, and are not more than two inches long, make the best cuttings. These should be cut off close to the stem. If taken off with a sharp knife they will not require to be cut again at the bottom, unless the cutting is too long; then they should have a clean horizontal cut just under a joint, to make the cutting the right length. Cut off the bottom leaves close to the stem, leaving only two of the uppermost. Place the cuttings in a shady place, to dry up the wound. This will take an hour on a dry day, or two hours on a dull, cloudy one. Then put them in the prepared pots, round the edge, inclining the leaves inwards, so that they may not touch the leaves of those in the contiguous pots in the frames or in the propagating house. When a pot is filled, give it a gentle watering, and set it on one side to dry up the moisture on the leaves and surface of the soil. Then plunge the cuttings in the frame, and shade them from the sun, or even from the light, till they form a callosity (a swelling at their base). After that, reduce the shade gradually, using it only during bright sunshine. A little air may also be given every day by tilting up the lights behind, if in a frame. The propagating house will only require air when the heat is too great, to reduce the temperature to 55° or 60°. The cuttings must be frequently examined, to see if roots are formed; and as soon as they are an inch long, pot them off into the smallest 60-pots, which are generally about two inches in diameter. A small addition of well decomposed leaf mould may be mixed amongst the loam with advantage. When potted off give another gentle watering, and replace them in the frame or propagating house until fresh roots are formed; renew the shading, but disuse it as soon as it is safe to do so, and then give plenty of air to prevent them being drawn up and spindly. To cause them to become bushy plants, nip off the top bud; the lower side-buds will then break, and the shoots from them must be again stopped as soon as they have made three leaves. The plants will then be ready to receive a second potting, and should be removed into the open air. The above directions, as far as the cuttings are concerned, relate only to the *show* varieties, as they are called; but *fancy* varieties are more difficult to increase by cuttings. Insert the cuttings of these in shallow pans, one inch and a half deep, with a hole in the centre, in the usual loam and sand, placing them on a shelf in the propagating house, or in the frame, close to the glass, upon inverted pots. Make the cuttings very short, with a portion of the old wood at the bottom of each. Very little water is to be given till the callosities are formed; afterwards give it more freely, and when roots make their appearance, immediately pot off, and give the usual treatment.

By Buds.—Make a shallow pan ready for them, by putting in a portion of pure loam and sand, then a covering of pure sand alone, and give a gentle watering to settle it. Take a shoot of moderate strength, cut off the leaves, but not quite close to the stem, then cut off the two lowest buds, leaving about a quarter of an inch of wood below each bud. After that, split the shoot containing the two buds down the centre. If the two buds are not exactly opposite, but one a little below the other, the upper one must be shortened below the bud to the proper length. The upper cut should be nearly close to the bud. Make a sufficient number ready at once to fill the pan or pot. Plant them, using a short, blunt stick a little thicker than the bud-cutting. Insert them so as only to leave the bud just above the sand. Plant them close to and round the edge of the pan, placing the cut side against the pot. Fill up the holes with a little dry sand, and water gently again. Place them either in a propagating house, a shady part of a stove near the glass roof, or in a frame. Shade from bright sunshine, and water as required. The buds will soon break and show leaves.

By Roots.—Some kinds of *Fancy Pelargoniums*, and most of the *Cape original species*, are difficult to increase except by cuttings of the roots. Take an old plant, shake off all the soil, and cut the roots into short pieces, retaining as many fibres as possible to each. Put each root-cutting singly into as small pots as they can be got into, leaving the top just visible. Place them in the house or frame appropriated to propagation; give a gentle watering, and shade. New roots will soon push forth, and then shoots will appear. When that takes place, reduce the shade to give colour to the leaves and strength to the shoots. As these advance in growth, thin them gradually, by slipping one or two off at a time, till finally they are reduced to one which is to form the future plant. As soon as this shoot attains the height of two or three inches, nip off the top to form a neat bushy plant.

House.—Pelargoniums require a house to themselves. The span-roofed form is the best; because the plants in such a house grow on all sides alike. The sides should be of glass, the side windows should move up and down, to allow a large circulation of air, and the top lights should also be moveable, to let out the heated air. The plants should be placed upon stages near to the glass. These stages ought to be broad enough to allow large specimens to stand clear of each other upon them. To exhibit collections of ten or twelve in number, three or four times during the season, the house should be at least fifty feet long and twenty feet wide.

The heat wanted is just enough to keep out the frost, and the best mode of obtaining that heat is by hot water circulating in cast-iron pipes. They should be placed near, but not close, to the walls, and about a foot from the floor. For a house of the size we have described, two four-and-a-half-inch pipes running round it will keep out any frost we are likely to have in this country.

Compost.—Procure from an old pasture where the grass is fine as much turf three or four inches thick as will serve to pot the collection for one year; have it chopped up into small pieces, and lay it up in a long ridge. The ridge or bank should not exceed two feet high, on a base of three feet wide. The grassy surface and green roots will soon begin to ferment. Let it be turned over every three months for a year, and then it will be fit for use. Unless it be very heavy, or of a close texture, it will not require any addition. The grand object is to have a soil just rich enough to grow a plant to a certain size, without too much luxuriance of growth, but still of such a stimulating power as to enable a plant to grow to three feet high, and as much through, and to produce so many flowers as to completely cover a plant. If, however, the soil should be so poor as to need a supply of manure, then use leaf mould a year old, and mix the necessary quantity, one-fourth in most cases being amply sufficient.

Winter Management.—Strict attention to giving air on all favourable occasions; keeping the house as dry as possible; giving a due supply of water, but no more; pulling off every decaying leaf, and keeping the surface of the soil frequently stirred, are the main points to attend to during winter. The temperature of the greenhouse during winter should never exceed 45°, nor fall lower than 34° or 36°. If kept too warm, the plants will draw up weak and spindling; if too cold, the leaves will turn yellow, or spot, or damp off.

Spring.—In potting them care should be taken that it is not overdone. Buds should be visible first, or the plants will continue to grow, and will not flower until late in the season. Again, the size of the pots should be taken into consideration. For a plant two feet and a half high, and three feet through, a pot only eight inches in diameter is needed. The nourishment is supplied by means of liquid manure, given at intervals only, and in a diluted state.

Training.—During spring attention must be given to tying out the plants. Use but few sticks, and those keep out of sight as much as possible. A good plan is to tie round each pot a broad piece of strong bass mat, and when the shoots are long, to bring them down with short pieces of bass tied to the piece which goes round each pot. This does away with the sticks in a great measure, gives a direction to the branches, and opens out the centre.

Summer.—The plants will now require shading to prolong the season of bloom. Too much air cannot be given, and to prevent the approach of bees and other insects the apertures where air is admitted should be covered with netting. A much larger amount of water is now required; it will frequently be necessary twice a day. If a dash or two of water is thrown upon the floor occasionally during hot sunshine, it creates a moist and cooler atmosphere. Smoke frequently with tobacco, to destroy the green fly. As the plants go out of bloom, cut them down, and set them out of doors to be repotted, as directed in the autumn treatment.

PETUNIA.

Characteristics of a good Petunia.— 1. *Form.*—The flower should be round, without notches on the edge, and it should be rather inclined to cup, that is, the outer edges should not bend back. 2. *Substance.*—The petals should be stout, and able to keep the form nearly as long as the colour lasts perfect. 3. *Colour.*—When a self, it should be clear without fading at the edges; when striped, each stripe should be well defined, and each colour distinct. 4. *Size.*—Each flower should be at least one and a half to two inches across; if large they are liable to bend back. 5. *Habit.*—The plant should be rather dwarf, and produce flowers abundantly; the foliage should be rather small, in order that every flower may be seen distinctly.

Propagation : by Cuttings.—Petunias are easily propagated by cuttings from February to October. The best cuttings are the young tops of rather weakly-growing plants. In spring the cuttings require a gentle hotbed; but in summer and autumn they strike root readily enough in a cold pit or frame. The cutting pots should be drained in the usual way; then place a layer of rich, light, very sandy compost nearly up to the rim of the pot; and lastly, fill up the pot with fine silver sand; then give a gentle watering to make it firm. For the cuttings, choose young weak shoots, and cut them off close to a joint, dress off the lower leaves so as to allow about an inch to be planted in the sand, and not more than three or four leaves at the top. Plant them with a short stick, pressing the sand closely to each. The pot may be filled with cuttings in rows across it, or, if space is plentiful, place them out round the edge. Observe that the holes made by the planting stick are filled up with dry sand; it runs more readily into the holes than moist sand would do.; then give a gentle watering again, which firmly fastens the sand round each cutting; leave them on the bench for an hour to dry off the surface moisture. After that, place them, if in spring, in a gentle hotbed, or, if in summer or autumn, in a pit or frame; shade from bright sunshine, and water when the surface becomes quite dry. Mind the watering-pot, and do not use it too freely upon cuttings until they are fairly rooted, and show evident signs of having made roots and growth. Then give plenty of air, and expose them fully. The spring and summer cuttings should be potted off immediately when rooted; but those struck late in the year may remain in the cutting pots through the winter. When they are potted, whatever may be the period, they should be placed in a frame or pit where they can be shaded and kept close for a few days until fresh roots are produced; let them then be gradually inured to bear the full light and air.

By Seed.—The seed should be gathered as soon as it is ripe, carefully cleaned from the seed vessels, and kept dry and cool through the winter. Sow it in the spring in shallow pans, placed in a gentle hotbed, or on a shelf close to the glass, in a warm greenhouse or propagating house. When the seedlings come up, prick them out in similar pans rather thinly. This can scarcely be done too early, for if allowed to remain too long in the seed-pan there is great danger of their damping off. When they have made three or four leaves pot them singly into thumb-pots; and, as soon as there is no fear of frosts injuring them, plant them out in a nursery-bed till they flower.

Soil.—Loam procured from the surface of a pasture, and prepared as directed for the ANTIRRHINUM. Of this loam take one-half, add to it one-quarter leaf mould, one-eighth well-decomposed hotbed dung, one-eighth sandy peat, and as much sand (river would do) as would give the compost a sandy character.

Summer Treatment.—Supposing a plant to be in a 60-pot, and to have passed through the winter unscathed, it should be a low, bushy plant, well furnished with branches and healthy leaves. The soil for repotting being moderately dry, let the plants be brought out of the greenhouse to the bench, and prepare the pots to receive them. If old and dirty, let them be clean-washed, and do not use them till they are perfectly dry; put in drainage i he usual way; place some rough siftings over the drainage, an upon them place as much soil as will raise the ball of earth the plants are growing in to the level of the rim of the new pots; then turn the plants in succession out of the pots; remove carefully the drainage that may be attached to each ball; place the plant in the fresh pot, and fill round the ball the new compost till the pot is full; then give a gentle stroke upon the bench, and fill up the deficiency; the old ball should then be covered about half an inch, and a small space left below the level of the rim; then give a gentle watering, and return them to the greenhouse, placing them close to the glass. As they grow, take care to stop each shoot, thereby inducing a bushy habit. The tops, if required, may be made use of as cuttings. In this stage the plants will require constant attention to keep them duly supplied with water, and plenty of air whenever the weather is mild.

About the middle of April they will require a second shift into larger pots, into the same compost, using the same precautions as to drying the soil, draining the pots, and so forth. Most probably the green fly will now make its appearance, and it must be instantly destroyed by frequent fumigations of tobacco. When the weather becomes warmer they will grow much stronger and more bushy in a cold frame or pit, upon a layer of coal ashes, than on the greenhouse stage.

A third and last shift will be necessary in June; the plants should then be put into pots nine inches in diameter, and in these they are to flower. As soon as the usual inhabitants of the greenhouse are removed into their summer quarters the Petunias will be in a fit state to take their place. Plenty of air must be given, and the roof should be shaded whenever the sun shines brightly.

Winter Treatment. — Old plants that have flowered freely through the summer will be so exhausted as to be hardly worth keeping through the winter; but for scarce kinds or seedlings a winter treatment is requisite. Let such be cut down early in August, leaving all the young shoots that are near the soil; turn them out of their blooming pots, reduce the ball pretty freely so as to repot them in five-inch pots, give no water, and place them either in a close pit or in a shady part of the greenhouse, where no air can blow upon them. Shade closely for a week or two till fresh growth is induced, then inure them gradually to light; stop the top shoots, and give a small watering. Keep them through the winter as close to the glass as possible, and rather dry than otherwise. If these plants can be preserved they will make fine, strong, early-blooming plants the season following.

Growing for Exhibition.—The time to exhibit them to perfection is about the last week in June, which is early, to the last week in July, which may be considered, in the generality of seasons, to be late.

Plants for this purpose should be well established the preceding autumn, and should not be allowed to flower till within a month of the time of exhibition. They may be kept in pots from three to four inches in diameter through the winter. From the first potting, up to the month of May, they should be frequently topped; that is, the two upper leaves, with the buds attached, should be carefully and neatly cut off with a sharp knife.

They must be repotted as soon as the roots reach the sides of the pots. The roots should never be allowed to become matted till the plants are placed in their blooming pots. In March provide a number of short sticks, painted a light green. At one of the spring pottings, before the roots have pushed into the new earth, thrust a circle of these sticks round the pot at some distance from the shoots; tie a short piece of small bass mat to one of these sticks, so that the two ends of the mat are equal in length, then bring each end round a branch nearest to the stick, and, with the mat, draw it gently down to the stick, and tie it to it rather loosely. This requires a steady hand. Proceed round the plant till every side-shoot is brought down, and the centre left thinly furnished. Cut off the ends of all the strong shoots, and the plants will soon form bushy, round-headed specimens. As the shoots advance in number and length this must be repeated, and longer sticks made use of. If the shoots are too numerous let them be thinned, so as not to crowd each other. The short sticks may be removed when the shoots do not require their directing support. In May the plants ought to be strong and bushy, eighteen inches high and twelve inches through, and be showing plenty of flowers, which may then, if the show is in June, be allowed to come into bloom; but if in July, the buds must be taken off, and none allowed to remain till the middle of June.

PINK.

Characteristics of a good Pink.—The flower must be fully double; so much so, that it should form the half of a ball, rising up to the centre, and should be perfectly circular in outline. Each *petal* should be stout, broad, and smooth at the edges. This smoothness is called *rose-edged;* that is, without any notches or teeth. The lowest tier of petals should be the widest, reaching in diameter at least from two to two and a half inches. The next row should be shorter, so much so as to show the lacing fully on the lower petals; and the next shorter again, and so on up to the centre, which should be well filled up without confusion. The *ground colour* should be pure white. The *lacing*, or circular stripe, should leave an edge of white outside of it, and another inside; this lacing of colour should be of the same width as the outside edging of white, and should be smooth and even at the edges; in fact, laid on as if it had been traced by a skilful hand with a fine camel-hair pencil. Then, at the bottom of the petals, there should be another body of colour, the same as the lacing, to form a bold, rich eye.

Soil and Situation of the Bed.—The best situation is the slope of a bank, or even the top of a middling-sized hill, where the bottom is dry. If moderately elevated it may, if on a wet bottom, be more easily drained. If the soil is naturally of a good quallity, and not more than three years under culture, it is well. The Pink requires a generous soil, moderately manured with thoroughly-decayed stable litter. This, if the soil is good, may be laid upon the bed intended for Pinks, two inches thick, about October, and it should be immediately dug in deep, and the soil well mixed with it. To accomplish this well it is of advantage to dig the bed or piece of ground two or three times over. If the soil is heavy, and the situation low, the soil had better be entirely removed, and the bottom of the bed well drained; then bring in some good light loam, the top spit of an old pasture that has been laid up, and turned over, and mixed with dung twelve months previously. Raise the bed from four to six inches above the natural level of the garden, keeping up the edges either with long slates or boards.

Propagation: by Seed.—As soon as the seed is judged to be ripe, let it be gathered and separated from the pod, dried moderately, packed in brown paper, and placed in a dry drawer in a dry room till the sowing season.

Sowing.—Sow in March, in shallow pans, or boxes, placed under a frame without heat. Set the pans upon coal ashes, and carefully close every crevice, to prevent slugs from entering. Cover this frame up every night to keep out the frost, give abundance of air during warm, sunny days, and water very gently whenever the surface appears dry. The seeds, if good, will quickly germinate, and the seedlings will require particular attention to prevent them from damping off. Give air every day, and on very warm, sunny days, pull off the light entirely. The watering, also, must be very judiciously performed, giving it in the mornings only of such days as are likely to be sunny. When the plants have attained a sufficient size to be handled, let them be carefully pricked out into similar pans or boxes, replaced in the frame, and kept there till they have six or eight leaves each. They may then be fully exposed to the weather for a week or two, and after that be planted out, four inches apart, into a bed prepared according to the preceding directions. By the autumn they will be strong plants, and will all flower the following season. If you have not a frame you may choose a warm border, sow your choice Pink seed upon it in April, transplant your seedlings in June, and have them tolerably strong before the autumn. Protect them through the winter with hoops and mats, or some other cheap covering, and you will succeed in blooming some the first year, and all the second.

By Cuttings, or, as they are called, *Pipings*.—The time for this work depends upon the growth of the plant. As soon as the side-shoots are long enough, they may be taken off and planted. This generally happens about the end of May, or beginning of June. The earlier it can be done, the better plants the pipings will make, and the finer they will flower the following season.

The pipings may be planted either in pots, under a frame, or under handlights. For an amateur the pot method will be the most certain. The materials necessary for this purpose are a good sharp knife, a few bell-glasses, and pots of a size to match them. The soil most suitable is good, light, sandy loam, without any admixture, and a portion of pure white sand to place on the surface. When the pipings are two or three inches long, proceed to cut, not pull, them off. Cut them close to the old plant, but do not injure its stem. When as many pipings as one variety will afford, or as many as may be required of it, are cut off, put a number or name to them, and then dress off close the lower leaves, plant the pipings, and place the tally to them at once. Do not cut off the ends of the leaves that are left. Give a gentle watering to settle the sand close to each piping; and plant them so far within the rim of each pot as to leave room for the bell-glasses to rest upon the sand within the pot. Place them with the bell-glasses over them in a frame covered with glass, on a very gentle hotbed, either of stable litter or spent tanners' bark. Give shade, and water. Directly roots are formed give plenty of air, and leave the bell-glasses off every night, replacing them during the day for a short period. Leave the glasses off entirely as soon as the plants will bear the light, and then remove them out of the frame, and place them out of doors upon a bed of coal ashes or gravel for a week or two. By this time the planting-out season will have arrived. The beds to receive them should then be in a state of readiness, and they may be carefully taken out of the cutting pots, and planted where they are to bloom the following season. This propagating process must be performed every season. One-year-old plants only produce blooms fit for the exhibition table. Two-year-old plants will do to plant in the flower garden.

If the pipings are to be planted without pots in a bed prepared in a frame heated underneath with any lasting fermenting material, the mode of preparing the piping is exactly the same. The soil on the surface is also the same, only let it be of sufficient depth to prevent the heat being too great. Level the surface, and plant the pipings in rows. When they are put in shade, water duly, and give air as soon as roots are formed. Then take the plants up carefully with a trowel, and put them in the blooming bed. Pipings of Pinks will root under hand-glasses also, if planted in a bed of the same soil, with a coating of sand, in a shady part of the garden. The cuttings, however, are much longer in forming roots, and are, therefore, liable to damp off by being so long confined under the glass.

Pinks may be propagated by layers, exactly in the same way as directed for the CARNATION, and when the layers are rooted, take them up and plant out at once in the blooming bed.

General Management: Planting.—The bed to receive the plants being duly prepared, and the pipings rooted, they may be planted out. The best time to do this is in the early part of September. If planting is delayed a considerable time after the pipings are rooted, they become weak and long-legged, and are so tender that they suffer from the autumnal winds, and many perish if the winter sets in severely. By being planted in the blooming bed as early as September, the plants become well established, firmly rooted, and even make some growth before winter sets in. By being well rooted, the frost will have less power to throw them out of the ground. Plant across the bed in rows six inches apart, and six inches from plant to plant in the row. When planting take the pot of pipings to the bed, turn them out, and carefully divide them, retaining every root, and even a small portion of soil to each. Commence with No. 1; plant it with a trowel, taking out a small quantity of earth; then put in the plant, and press the earth firmly to it. The first row may be planted from the walk at the end of the bed. The first row being finished, procure a board nearly as long as the bed is broad, lay this across it, and when planting the second row place the foot upon the board. After the second row is finished planting, and the tally or tallies correctly placed, remove the board backwards, stir up the soil where it has been laid, and proceed to plant the third row; and so on till all are finished. The only point to attend to is not to have too many plants out of the soil at once, as, if that were the case, the young roots being tender would perish at the ends.

Mulching.—A little protection from very severe frost will be useful. That protection consists in laying upon the bed, between the rows, a thin covering of either very short, littery dung, or one-year-old leaf mould. If neither of these is at hand, a covering of decayed tanners' bark will answer the purpose.

Spring and Summer Culture.—When the severe weather of winter is over, see if any of the plants have been disturbed by the frost; press them down gently into the earth, and close it to them with the hand. The heavy spring rains will soon make the soil hard, and when such is the case, stir the surface of the soil with a very short three-pronged fork, being careful not to disturb the roots of the plants. The mulching, if very long, may be partially removed, and the rest mixed with the soil in the operation. This forking may be repeated as the plants advance in growth, and will be useful to keep down the weeds, as well as keeping the surface of the soil loose and open. As the season advances, and the heat of the sun becomes powerful, a second mulching will be desirable. The former mulching was used to protect the roots from the frost; this second one is to shelter the roots from the heat and drought.

The Blooming Season.—By the time the flower-stems begin to spring forth, the plants will be in good health, and strong in grass—*grass* is the term for the leaves and shoots before the flower-stems appear. This period will be fast approaching about the end of May or beginning of June. As the flower-stems advance in height, sticks will be required. Place them to the plants for that purpose before the flowers open, because, if delayed till that takes place, a heavy fall of rain might break them off. The best kind of sticks are made from double laths, split into the required thickness, made round and smooth. From fifteen to eighteen inches will be a proper length. Give them a coat of lead-coloured paint, and when that is dry, a second coating of light green, approaching as nearly as possible to the colour of the stems of the plants. These sticks should be prepared some time beforehand. When the flower-stems have advanced to six or nine inches in length, place the sticks and tie the stems to them. Be careful in thrusting in the sticks not to injure the roots. If any of the stems are uncommonly vigorous, let them have the longest sticks. The best article to tie them with is shreds of soft new bass mats. In tying the stems great care must be exercised; if tied tight the stem is prevented elongating, and it then bends outwards, and forms what are called "knees," which, if not immediately relieved by loosening the string, will snap off at the joint. To prevent this it is prudent to tie loosely at first. The string should be tied tightly round the stick, and then brought round the flower-stem, and tied so as to leave room for it to expand. This tying will require to be often repeated to keep the stems perfectly straight and upright. When they have attained their full growth, which happens when the flower-buds have become large and full, the ties may be tightened, and there is then no danger of breaking.

Thinning the Buds.—If the stem is weak, one flower will be as many as it will bring to perfection; but if strong, two or sometimes three, may be allowed to bloom. In taking off the extra buds, be careful not to crack or injure the stem. The next point to attend to is to place something round each bud, to prevent it from bursting on one side, or irregularly. Very small india-rubber rings are the best for this purpose; they readily expand as the bud swells, and yet are tight enough to answer the purpose of preventing the buds from bursting. If, notwithstanding, the buds still show an inclination to open on one side, then take a pair of sharp-pointed scissors, and cut open the calyx or flower-cup on the opposite side to where the bursting is likely to take place. Tying should be done in an early stage of the bloom, and the ring or tie should be fixed nearly in the middle of the bud. If it be lower, it will not prevent the bursting, and if above, the bud will swell out below it, and then form a monstrous, mis-shapen flower. Protection will be needed from sunshine, stormy winds, and beating rain. The most effectual protectors are oiled canvas covers stretched over the whole bed, upon a frame of hoops and rods. Caps of the same material, nine inches in diameter, kept expanded by a frame of wire, will answer almost equally as well. Thrust in near to the flowers a strong stick, just low enough to be above the flower. These shelters may be fastened to the stake by a socket on one side of the cap, wedged firmly to keep it fast in its place.

POLYANTHUS.

Characteristics of a good Polyanthus.—The *plant* should be healthy; the *foliage* large and abundant; the *stem* stout enough to bear the truss well up above the leaves, which should cover the pot, and rise up in the centre; from the centre of the leaves the stem should rise; the *truss* should consist of at least five flowers, and the footstalks of each flower be able to support each bloom level with the rest. Each flower, or *pip*, should be round and flat, neither inclined to cup nor reflex. The pips should be divided, near the outermost edge, into segments; each division, or *segment*, should be slightly indented or scolloped in the centre. Each flower should have a yellow centre, or *eye*; in the centre of that there should appear a *tube* containing the anthers, but the pistil should not be seen. This yellow centre, including the tube, should be of the same width as the *ground* or *body colour*, which colour should either be a rich dark crimson or a bright red. Round this body colour the *margin*, or *lacing*, should appear of a uniform width surrounding each petal, and continuing down the centre of each to the yellow eye. The colour of this lacing, or margin, should be uniform, whether it is sulphur, lemon colour, or clear yellow.

Propagation: by Seed.—This should be saved only from flowers of good form and clear bright colours. As soon as the seed is ripe, gather it before the pods burst. The seed is generally ripe when the pods turn brown; cleanse the seed, and keep it dry till March. Then sow it in the soil hereafter described, and place it in a gentle heated frame, or pit, close to the glass. As soon as the seedlings are large enough to take hold of, transplant them, six inches apart, into a prepared border, rather shaded from the mid-day sun. Keep them watered in dry weather, and let them remain there through the winter. They ought to flower the following season. All the care they require is to keep them clear from weeds and slugs. As soon as they have done flowering, those worth keeping should be taken up with a trowel and potted, and afterwards treated as proved and established varieties.

By Division.—The Polyanthus generally sends out plenty of offsets. When these have made roots they may be taken off the parent plant, potted, and treated the same as the seedlings, only they should be taken up out of the border early in August, potted, and placed amongst the old plants. Care must be taken in dividing them that the stem or root-stock of the old plant is not injured.

Soil.—They do well in the following mixture, formed of the top spit of an old pasture kept for twelve months, two-year-old cowdung, and one-year-old decayed leaves, in the proportion of two parts loam, half a part cowdung, and half a part leaf mould, with less sand than that recommended for Auriculas.

Spring Treatment.—Top dress the plants, and keep them well supplied with water. A gentle syringing over the leaves will be found beneficial, done early in the mornings of fine spring days, and withheld when the weather is dull, cold, and gloomy. When the blooms appear they should be slightly shaded from bright sunshine; but they will bear more sun than Auriculas, especially the dark-ground varieties. The shades should be put on about ten and removed by three o'clock; in almost all cases, plenty of light greatly brightens the colours, so that no more shade should be used than is absolutely necessary. When the blooms are fully expanded, they will last much longer if the plants are placed under handlights where the sun cannot reach them during the middle of the day.

Summer Treatment.—After the bloom is over they should be placed in their summer quarters. The north side of a low wall is the best situation for them; and in order to prevent the attacks of the red spider, the grand enemy to these plants, place the pots in saucers or garden pans. When watered, that portion that runs through the pots remains in the pans, and by keeping the air round them moist, prevents the red spider from attacking them. In this situation they remain till August. In the early part of that month they should be repotted, and that is a proper time to take off the offsets; strong plants should be potted into pots from six to seven inches diameter. These should be moderately drained. If the plants are already in the full-sized pot, the balls should be reduced, and the roots partially pruned, so as to allow of a large quantity of fresh soil being added. Give a gentle watering to settle the soil, and keep them a fortnight longer under the shade of the wall.

Autumn Treatment.—This commences in the last week in

August. The plants should then be removed into a more open place. The west border will answer admirably; if the weather is then moist, the pans should be dispensed with, and the pots set upon a bed of coal ashes, thick enough to keep worms from working in at the holes at the bottom of the pots.

Winter Treatment.—This commences about the end of October. The Polyanthus is more hardy than the Auricula, and will do better if kept in a separate frame, where it can have more air, and rather less protection from frost. We have known the pots so hard frozen that they could scarcely be lifted up, and yet the plants flowered well the spring following. The care necessary is, to place them upon a bed of coal ashes, sufficiently thick to prevent worms entering the pots. At the time they are placed under the frame let each pot and plant be examined. If the pots are green and dirty they should be washed clean, the hole at the bottom of the pot should be examined to see that it is quite open, to allow the superfluous water to run off freely; the soil on the surface should be stirred, all weeds and moss cleared away, a thin top-dressing of fresh soil put on, and every decayed or decaying leaf removed. If the leaves project over the edge of the pots, let the latter stand in the frame so that the leaves of one plant do not touch the leaves of the others. In the winter months they require only just enough water to prevent them flagging. During hard frost, protect them every night with a covering of double mats, or with good water-tight wooden covers.

RANUNCULUS.

This requires especial attention to the following requirements:—

Situation.—It is only a waste of time and money to attempt to grow it within the influence of a smoky atmosphere near large towns, or upon a high hill in a dry soil, or in a swamp. The florist must choose a place for the Ranunculus-bed neither too high nor too low; let it be a level surface, and if it be sheltered from the northern blasts so much the better.

Soil.—The soil should be retentive of moisture. The best kind is the virgin mould of some alluvial soil on the banks of a river, or some lowland pasture. It should be of a rather close texture, without any small stones or sand amongst it. Lay it up for a year, turn it over until it is well incorporated, wheel out the old soil to the depth of a foot or more, place a thin layer of very rotten cowdung at the bottom, and upon that the fresh soil. If the situation is low, with a wet subsoil, it must be well drained; but if the subsoil is dry there is no necessity for drainage. If the soil should be thought too poor, a small addition of decayed cowdung will be advisable; but it must be so decomposed as to appear like a black powder. Let it be thoroughly mixed with the soil whilst making the bed, in dry weather, about the month of September.

Planting.—The season for planting is in the early spring, as soon as the most severe frosts have passed and the ground has become tolerably dry. Some time about the end of February or the first week in March, rake the surface of the bed in the morning of the day previous to that fixed upon for planting. Some recommend steeping the roots for twelve hours in water before planting, but we think this not necessary, except the planting season has been from some cause or other put off till the middle of April; then it may be useful. Supposing, then, that the weather is propitious, and all things prepared, commence by drawing with a hoe a drill across the end of the bed, one inch and a half deep; if deeper the roots will be weakened the succeeding year, by forming a kind of stem nearer the surface; and if shallower, the plants are more liable to be struck with drought. The drill being drawn the right depth, plant the whole of No. 1, and press each bulb, or tuber, slightly down into the ground; plant them, if large, four inches apart in the row; if small, three inches and a half will be a sufficient distance. If one row across the bed will not contain the whole of the first variety, draw a second drill five inches from the first, and place the tally at the end of the variety. As soon as the first kind are all planted, cover the crown of each tuber with fine sand. This will cause the tubers, when they are taken up in July, to come out of the ground quite clean for keeping. Then, with a short-toothed rake, draw the soil over the bulbs, and when it is level, with the head of the rake gently press the soil pretty closely upon them. Draw another drill for No. 2; proceed in the same way in planting and covering up, and so on till the whole are planted. Then fix over the bed, or beds, some hoops three or four feet apart, with rods running lengthways, and tied to each hoop with either wire or tar-twine. This is to form, with mats thrown over it, a shelter from severe frosts, and also from heavy snow showers, which sometimes visit us late in the spring. This shelter will also serve to protect the blooms from sunny days. We, however, earnestly warn against too much shelter in early spring. Too much covering up is quite as injurious as none. Even heavy showers of rain will be advantageous. All the shelter required in early spring is, protection from very severe late frosts, heavy showers of snow, or from heavy storms of hail, after the plants have made their appearance above ground.

Watering.—In order to do this effectually, have the beds perfectly level; and each bed should have an edging either of narrow boards or long narrow slates, projecting an inch, at least, above the level of the bed. This edging will check the water running off the bed into the walks. Previously to the first watering, immediately after the plants have broken through the soil, and when the surface is moderately dry, tread down the soil between the rows pretty firmly with the feet. After the bed is regularly pressed down, then press the soil close to the neck of each plant, and between them, with the hand. Then proceed to water the bed with a rather coarse-rosed watering pot; give it freely and liberally; and to do this well, go over the whole bed with a heavy shower, and as soon as that has sunk in and disappeared, commence again, and repeat the shower. In most cases this will be amply sufficient for a week's consumption. If the weather still continues dry, at the end of the week repeat the watering, and do so until heavy showers take place. It is probable that the soil will, with such heavy waterings, become baked on the surface, and will crack. Whenever that is observed, let the surface be broken fine with a small three-pronged fork; but the roots must not be disturbed nor the foliage injured by this operation. A gentle watering should be given immediately after the forking. Continue this abundant supply of water, whenever the weather is dry, up to the bloom beginning to open, and then discontinue it, and more especially if the plants are shaded during the time the sun has its greatest power.

Shading.—This shade should be applied at the time the flowers begin to expand, and not before. A shelter formed like the one we shall describe for the Tulip would be the best, as it would allow the blooms to be constantly seen, and would protect them from heavy rains and dews, which very soon tarnish the bright colours almost as much as the scorching rays of a June sun. Those who may not choose to erect such a summer shelter may form one of arched hoops and long rods, covered with sheets of canvas, to be taken off when the sun does not shine brightly, and in fair weather. The arches may be made of hazel rods, bent over a long stout rail, nailed to upright posts at each end of the bed, with a sufficient number of posts in the bed itself; or hoops of the right length may be procured from a cooper's yard. Whichever they are, they will require short stakes placed at the side of the bed, at such a distance from each other as will support two long rods, either of wood or iron, on each side. These rods must be fastened firmly to each hoop, and then they will support the canvas cover perfectly, so that it will not touch the flowers.

Taking Up and Storing.—The right time to take up the roots is as soon as the leaves are withered. When the bloom is quite over, cut down all the flower stems, and remove the shades entirely, day and night. If the weather be hot and dry, the leaves will soon decay after the flower-stems are removed. Some seasons, however, happen now and then to be very wet; in such it would be prudent to replace the canvas shades so as to protect the roots from too much wet and hasten their maturity. In either case taking up roots must not be delayed more than a week, or, at the farthest, a fortnight, after the foliage has become dry and withered. If delayed longer, and rain should fall, the warmth left in the soil and the rest they have had will cause them to make new roots, and that will weaken them much. Having got them into a fit state for taking up, fix upon a fine dry day. Commence with No. 1, and put all that variety into a garden saucer, or a sheet of paper of a size proportionate to the number of tubers; dress off the dead leaves, and shake off any soil that may adhere to the roots; place the number upon the lot, and remove them off the bed entirely before a single root of the No. 2 is disturbed. Proceed similarly with No. 2, and so on till the whole are taken up. Let them remain in the open air, if it is fair weather, the whole of the day, and at night remove them into some place where the rain or dew cannot reach them. Let them remain open to the air until they are thoroughly dried, then pack them up in paper, and keep them in a dry, airy room, not much exposed to the sun. Here they may remain till the season of planting returns, requiring only to be looked over occasionally, and all decaying roots or other injurious matter removed. Should mouldiness appear upon the tubers, you may be certain either that the room is too damp, or that they have been put away before they were properly dried.

Propagation by Divisions, or rather, *Offsets.*—The best time to separate the offsets from the old tubers is when they have been taken up a day or two, and have become soft and flabby, and before they have attained that firm, dry state, fit to be put away for the season of rest. It happens frequently, with some varieties, that the old tuber forms two, and sometimes four tubers, equal in size, and capable of flowering the next season; when that is the case, they may be placed among the flowering tubers. If they are too small to bloom, plant them in a bed by themselves, made of the same materials as the blooming one. This bed of small offsets will not require to be shaded so much as the bed of blooming tubers. Water must be applied liberally to enable the plants to grow freely. Take them up when the leaves are decayed, and manage them exactly like the blooming tubers above described. If any of them have attained to a size likely to bloom, promote them to that class at once.

Propagation: by Seed.—The seeds must be saved from flowers likely to improve the breed; they must be looked for in semi-double flowers. Form is the first property to attend to. When the seed is ripe gather it immediately, or the wind will soon disperse it. Keep gathering it as it ripens. Lay it upon a sheet of paper in a room where the sun will shine upon it for an hour or two in the forenoon. When it is perfectly dry, wrap it up in paper, and keep it in a dry, cool room till wanted.

Sowing.—Early in spring mix a compost of strong loam and leaf mould, and fill some boxes or seed-pans, well-drained, very nearly full; sift a portion of it, and place a thin layer over the rough compost, and press it very gently down. Mix the seed with some fine soil, rubbing the seed and the soil well together till the seeds are separated from each other. Sow this mixture upon the soil in the boxes or shallow pans; press it down level, and with a fine sieve sift some of the compost evenly over it, the thickness of a shilling; then, with a watering-pot, the nozzle of which has the finest holes, give a gentle watering. Place the seed-pans under glass in a cold frame or pit, or in front of a low wall facing the east, and contrive a covering or shelter of some kind to protect them from heavy showers. Whenever the soil appears dry, give water with the fine-rosed water-pot, and in strong sunshine place a shade over them till the seedlings appear above ground, and have attained a leaf or two to each plant. Search well about where the boxes or seed-pans stand, and even lift them up, and examine under them, to see if any slugs or wood-lice have crept there to hide themselves. Continue this attention till the leaves begin to decay, and then cease watering, but keep the plants clear of weeds. When the leaves are all decayed, and winter is approaching, place the pans of seedlings in some very cool place where no rain can fall upon them, and keep them there till spring. About the middle of April bring them out, and give them a good watering. Sift over the soil a thin layer of fresh compost, and repeat the care and attention with regard to watering, looking after insects, and keeping clear of weeds, as in the previous season. This second year, when the leaves fail, and the plants are at rest, the tubers will have attained some size. They should now be taken out of the soil, and the surest way to accomplish this without losing any roots is to sift the upper part of the soil through a fine sieve, fine enough to catch even the smallest roots. Store them away in a cool, dry room, and in the spring plant them out, and manage them like the named varieties.

ROSE.

We write expressly on the culture of the Rose as a florist's flower; or rather, for purposes of exhibition only.

ROSES IN POTS.—*House and Pit.*—To have fine specimens of Roses in pots, to flower in May or June, there should be a house properly constructed, and a pit to shelter the tenderer kinds in from severe frost and heavy rains, and to place the plants in after potting. The best kind of house is a span-roof, with aspects east and west, because then the plants have the benefit of the sun early in the morning and late in the afternoon. The house should be wide enough to allow room for a tolerable platform in the centre and a narrow one round the sides. The centre platform will serve exceedingly well to hold large plants, and those round the sides will do to place the smaller ones on. It should be high enough to bring the tops of the plants within at least two feet of the glass. Covering the platform with coal ashes or sand, for the pots to stand upon, is of great use. If it be thoroughly wetted now and then, it slowly gives out a moisture to the atmosphere of the house, which is very agreeable and healthful to the inmates. The house should be heated by a boiler and hot-water pipes. Air should be given so as not to come in direct contact with the young leaves of the Roses. Sliding doors in the walls will allow ingress of fresh air the best way of any, because then it becomes heated by passing over the pipes previously to reaching the plants; yet it is necessary not only to let in fresh air, but also to let out that which is heated. This can be done best by having a portion of the roof moveable.

Glazed Pit.—Though, if the cultivator has a house for cultivating his Roses for exhibition, he may dispense with a pit, yet, if he has a pit in addition, he will find it exceedingly useful. The best form for a cold pit is the common lean-to; that is, the walls should be highest at the back. If after potting, and a good watering to settle the earth of the roots, they are placed in a cold pit, syringed gently two or three times a week, and shaded from the sun, under such favourable treatment they will soon make fresh roots, and scarcely suffer from the removal. In such a case, the pit is invaluable as a shelter from drying. cold winds, and from heavy rains, frost, and snow. Again, this pit is of great use as a protection to the more tender kinds, not exactly from cold alone, but also from excessively heavy autumnal or winter rains. Another advantage of having such a pit at command is, to retard the plants from coming into bloom too early.

Soil for Roses in Pots.—For the strong-growing varieties, three parts strong turfy loam taken from some pasture not more than three inches deep, and one part good hotbed manure. Chop the loam well up, and mix the manure thoroughly into every part of it; a small quantity of quick-lime cast in amongst it at the time will be beneficial. For the slender-growing varieties. three parts of the same kind of loam, two parts leaf mould, and one part sharp river sand, with the lime added as before.

Potting.—The potting season for them all, at whatever time they are to bloom, is early in October. At the time of potting, the stems below ground should be diligently examined, and every bud likely to produce a sucker rubbed off close to the stem, as well as the suckers already produced. Drain the pots moderately well, and proportion their size to that of the plants. In potting, prune off any roots that may have been broken or bruised; then open the roots from each other, and spread them equally on every side amongst the soil, covering the highest layer about one inch, and leaving about half an inch below the rim of the pots. After the potting is finished, place the plants in the cold pit, syringe them frequently, and keep them close, shading from bright mid-day sun. As soon as new roots are formed, give them plenty of air, and draw off the lights every fine, dry day. The tender kinds would pass the winter more securely in the pit, but the hardy ones should be removed out of it, and plunged in a bed of coal ashes, there to remain till the time arrives to start them into growth.

Pruning.—Some varieties are strong growers, others are weak growers; some bear their flowers on short spurs, whilst the greater number bear them on terminal shoots; hence it is necessary to know all these peculiarities before the knife is applied at all.

1. *Roses requiring close pruning.* By this term is meant to cut in the wood made the previous year to within three or four buds of the base of each shoot. Under this head we class Provence and Moss Roses, excepting two or three very strong growers, which will be noticed presently; also the Damask, Alba, Gallica, Hybrid Provence, Damask Perpetual, the weak-growing Hybrid Perpetuals, the weak-growing Bourbons, the weak-growing Noisettes, the China, and the Tea-scented. All the Roses that are classed under these heads, with the exception of strong growers, require to be closely pruned. The best season for this operation is about the end of February or beginning of March. If pruned much earlier, the buds will break, and probably be caught and injured by late spring frosts. If the heads are crowded too much, thin out some of the weaker old branches, leaving the rest so as to form an open, compact bush.

2. *Such as require moderately shortening.*—These are strong, robust growers, and if cut in closely would generally produce few flowers, and abundance of coarse, strong shoots. They may be arranged under the following varieties:—All the strong-growing Moss Roses, especially such as Moss Baronne de Wassenaer, Du Luxembourg, and Lanei; also hybrids of Chinese, Bourbon, and Noisettes; all climbing Roses, except the Banksian varieties; also the strong-growing Hybrid Perpetuals, such, for instance, as Comte Bobrinsky, Gloire de Rosomènes, and such-like; the strong-growing Bourbons, and the strong-growing Noisettes. These require the shoots to be thinned out, and very little shortened; the season for the operation is in early spring.

3. *Such as require only to have their shoots thinned out*, leaving the moderately strong shoots with scarcely any pruning. Under this head we include the Scotch dwarf Roses, the Austrian Briar, Harrisonii and Persian Yellow, the Sweet Briars, the Banksian, the Rosa multiflora, the Macartney, and the Perpetual Scotch.

These require only their strong, over-robust shoots to be pruned clean away, and the best time for the operation is about Midsummer. The moderately-growing shoots should be kept growing until they reach the height of the wall or paling, excepting the Scotch varieties (*Rosa spinosissima*), which are dwarfs, and should be grown on their own roots as compact bushes. When the shoots of these become long, weak, and straggling, cut them in pretty severely, sacrificing one year's bloom for the sake of throwing fresh vigour into the plants. This may require to be done once in five or six years. If the others become naked towards the bottom, train in a fresh strong shoot or two from the bottom of the trees, thinning out some of the weakest branches to make room for the young strong shoots; and as these advance from year to year, clear away the exhausted old shoots to make room for them. Do this gradually, or there will be few flowers, till they become furnished with weak flower-bearing branches.

A considerable amount of pruning at the proper season would be avoided if the Roses in pots, and, indeed, in the open ground, were thinned during the season of growth. At that time cut away, close to the old wood, all the very strong shoots, and all the weak, straggling ones.

Thinning the Blooms.—Take away all small, deformed, or imperfect buds, leaving the largest and most healthy to expand and come to perfection. Such buds should be left as are likely to bloom at the same time. This rule, of course, applies only to plants intended to be exhibited.

Summer Treatment.—Such plants as have finished blooming in May should at once be placed in the pit, where they should have abundance of air night and day, unless frost intervene, when they should be protected. If there are no pits or frames to spare, they must be set out of doors, and protected by hoops and mats. The mats should be placed over them at night for three or four weeks, and also during the day, in bright, sunny weather, but on cloudy, showery days expose them fully. If the wood become ripe, and the leaves fall, they should then be placed where the sun will not reach them, behind a wall or a low hedge, and plunged in a bed of coal ashes. Care should be taken that they are not deluged with water, especially the China and Tea-scented varieties. By thus having them at rest early they will, when set to work again, after being duly pruned, start into growth, and bloom again much more freely than newly-potted plants.

Such Roses as are grown in pots for exhibition as late as September should, during the early part of summer, be placed in such a situation as is most likely to retard them from blooming early. The large class of autumnal-blooming Roses are the best adapted for such seasons of exhibition; yet numbers of China and Tea-scented, with their hybrids, will bloom in great perfection during the latter part of the summer and commencement of the autumn. The early shoots of blossoms are pruned off.

Plants that have been exhibited in June or July should be,

as soon as their bloom is over, plunged in a bed of ashes, fully exposed, excepting for a week or two at first, when they should be shaded from the burning summer's sun.

Watering.—In the house or pit they must be liberally watered, not on the drip-by-drip system, but by a thorough wetting of the entire quantity of the soil in each pot. The China and Tea-scented varieties must be watered cautiously even in the house or pit; for they are more impatient of wet at the root than the rest. In the open air the plants should be plunged in coal ashes, and, consequently, do not require so often watering as when the pots are exposed; still less water would be required if a mulching of short manure were spread over the surface of the mould in the plunged pots. This mulching is highly beneficial; the most successful growers of Roses in pots make use of it.

During the early part of summer the plants will be greatly benefited now and then by liquid manure. Roses thrive well with guano water, but it must be a very weak solution; a quarter of a pound of genuine guano will make three gallons.

Winter Treatment.— At the beginning of this season the pruning should be all done. Afterwards, the more tender of the China and Tea-scented varieties should be placed under some kind of shelter not so much from cold as from wet. If the Roses are in pits set the pots upon a stratum of clean pebbles or broken bricks; then, if the drainage in the pots is open, any excess of water accidentally given will easily escape. It will be necessary to repot most of those that have been grown one year or more in pots. If any are weak discard them at once, and procure fresh plants; they need not be thrown away, but may be planted in the open ground, where, if well treated, they will recover health and vigour, and may be grown in pots again. In shifting those that are in good health into larger pots let the roots be carefully untwisted, and take away part of the old soil; let the stems be cleaned thoroughly from moss or loose bark, and all 'the old drainage picked out from amongst the soil and roots; then drain the new pots well, and cover the drainage with some pieces of turf; upon that lay a thin layer of fresh soil, and then place the plant in the pot, spreading out the loosened roots, mixing the soil well amongst them; fill in the soil round the ball, and gradually bring it up to the top of the ball, and cover that about half an inch. This repotting should be done early in October.

Seasons of Starting.—The Rose, more than most other plants, *will not bear either sudden or violent changes of temperature.* The sap must be slowly set into movement; therefore, to cause them to bloom in May, which is the month in which Roses are generally exhibited the first time in the year, the batch intended for that time should be set to work about the second week in

January by bringing them into the Rose-house. A low temperature is proper for the first month or five weeks, the maximum being 45° by day and 35° by night. A slight increase of water will be necessary during that time. Plenty of air should be given whenever the state of the external atmosphere will allow it. They should also be syringed overhead twice or three times a week. After the first month is over a small increase of heat may be given. Allow the thermometer to rise to 50° by day and 40° by night. Water may now be given more liberally, with a dose now and then of weak liquid manure; this treatment should continue for another month or five weeks; this will bring them towards the end of March. The buds should then be just visible, and then a farther advance in heat will be desirable; let the maximum be 55° by day and 45° by night. As the foliage will now be pretty fully developed, the plants will require a proportionate increase of food in the shape of water and liquid manure. Use the water twice, and the liquid manure once, never giving either till the plants require it, but never let them flag for the want of water. Use the syringe, too, freely at least once a day, remembering that when once the blooms begin to expand it cannot then be used. If the blooms appear to advance too rapidly for the time of exhibition means must be used to retard them; the temperature should be gradually lowered, and, during bright sun, they should be shaded.

For June exhibitions, the first week in March will be time enough to bring the Roses in pots into the house. If there is only one house, these new comers should be placed in the coolest parts of the house, and brought on as slowly as possible.

Roses in pots to bloom in the autumn should be moderate-sized in February, and should then be repotted and kept as backward as possible, by placing them either behind a north wall, or by shading during the day with hoops and mats. Prune them late, and as soon as the first flower-buds appear nip them off. When they do begin to grow, keep them growing as slowly as possible and do not allow them to produce any flower-buds till the middle of July for August, and till the middle of August for September. Put in practice the precepts already laid down with regard to training, watering, &c. When the Roses begin to open, remove them into a more light and airy situation. A greenhouse would be a good situation for them, if well aired and properly shaded, and if plentiful supplies of water be given to them.

TULIP.

Florists call Tulips *seedlings* until they have bloomed; after this those preserved on account of their good form and habit, as well as the offsets they produce, are called *breeders*. After some years the petals of these become striped, and they are then said to be *broken*. If the striping is good, they are said to have a *good strain*; if it be inferior, they are described as having a *bad strain*. A *rectified* Tulip is synonymous with a Tulip having a good strain. A *feathered* Tulip has a dark-coloured edge round its petals, gradually becoming lighter on the margin next the centre of the petal; the feathering is said to be *light*, if narrow; *heavy*, if broad; and *irregular*, if its inner edge has a broken outline. A *flamed* Tulip is one that has a dark-pointed spot, somewhat in shape like the flame of a candle, in the centre of each petal. Sometimes a Tulip is both *feathered* and *flamed*. A *Bizarre* Tulip has a yellow ground, and coloured marks on its petals. A *Byblæmen* is white, marked with black, lilac, or purple. A *Rose* is white with marks of crimson, pink, or scarlet.

Characteristics of a good Tulip.—1. The cup when fully expanded should form, as nearly as possible, half of a hollow ball. The petals, six in number, must be broad at the ends, smooth at the edges, and the divisions where the petals meet scarcely showing an indentation. 2. The three inner petals should set close to the three outer ones, and the whole should be broad enough to allow of the fullest expansion without *quartering* (as it is called), that is, exhibiting any vacancy between the petals. 3. The petals should be thick, smooth, and stiff, and keep their form well. 4. The ground colour* should be clear and distinct, whether white or yellow. The least stain, even at the lower end of the petal, would render a Tulip comparatively valueless. 5. Whatever the colours or marks upon a Tulip, all the petals should be marked alike, and be perfectly uniform. 6. The *feathered* flowers should have an even, close feathering all round, and whether the feathering be narrow or wide, light or heavy, it should reach far enough round the petals to form, when they are expanded, an unbroken edging all round. 7. If the flower have any marking besides the feathering at the edge, it should be a beam, or bold mark down the centre, but not to reach the bottom, or near the bottom of the cup; the mark or beam must be similar in all the six petals. 8. Flowers not feathered, and with *a flame* only, must have no marks on the edges of the flower. None of the colour must break through to the edge. The colour may be in any form not in blotches, so that it be perfectly uniform in all the petals, and does not go too near the bottom. 9. The colour, whatever it be, must be dense and decided. Whether it be delicate and light, or bright, or dark, it must be distinct in its outline, and not shaded or flushed, or broken. 10. The height of a Tulip should be from eighteen to thirty-six inches: the shortest is proper for the outside row in a bed, and the tallest for the highest row. 11. The purity of the white, and the bright-

* *Ground colour* is that upon which the other colours are laid.

ness of the yellow ground colours, should be permanent, that is to say, should continue until the petals actually fall.

Early in September is a good time for preparing the Tulip bed.

Situation.—The aspect should be open to the south and south-east, but well sheltered from the north, north-east, and north-west winds. We prefer a perfectly level surface. The elevation of the site is also a consideration worth serious attention. Wherever, then, it is in the power of the cultivator of Tulips intended for exhibition to choose the site, let him select the happy medium, neither too high nor too low. If there are no shelters already on the spot to protect the flowers from the northern blasts, there ought to be some prepared. A close wooden paling is the one most ready and effectual, and if made of deal or oak, and well painted, will last several years. Beech, Hornbeam, Yew, or Arbor Vitæ hedges are very excellent, but they require several years' growth before they are high enough to screen the flowers effectually. Whatever shelter is made use of, it should be placed at a sufficient distance from the beds not to draw up the flowers, or prevent a full exposure to light; therefore the wind shelters should never exceed six or eight feet high.

Draining.—The Tulip loves a deep soil, and a dry subsoil. Where there is a good depth of good loam, with a dry, gravelly, or sandy bottom, no more draining is required than one or two formed with drain-pipes and tiles, to carry off the water that may fall in wet seasons on the surface. When the natural soil is shallow and the subsoil clay, set out the bed the desired length and breadth; then cast out on one side all the good soil, shovelling out the small crumbs; then dig out the subsoil, till the bed is eighteen inches deep. After that is finished dig a drain in the centre of the bed six inches deep, and wide enough to allow the operator to lay down, first the flat tiles, and then the circular pipes, with holes in the latter to admit of the water escaping into them, and then being carried clear away. When the pipes, &c., are laid down, cover them with rubble, and then lay all over the bottom of the bed three or four inches of either small stones, broken clinkers, or brick ends. Upon this drainage lay a stratum of short straw or small brushwood; make this smooth, and you may consider the drainage complete.

Manure and Soil.—A rich soil is necessary, yet it must not be over rich. Procure some one-year-old cowdung; spread over and upon the drains a stratum of this cowdung two inches thick; then mix about one-sixth of very well-decomposed hot-bed dung with the loam thrown out and laid on one side on commencing the operation of draining. If there is not enough soil to make the bed up level as before, procure some good loam for the purpose, mixing it with the same proportion of well-decomposed dung. If the situation is low and damp, it will be advisable to place an edging round the bed, six or eight inches deep, of sufficient strength to bear up the soil when it is raised to that height. The best material for an edging of this kind is blue slate, and the next, slabs of wood nailed to strong uprights driven into the ground at proper intervals. Mix the top surface with a considerable quantity of river sand; this will cause the bulbs to come out of the soil at taking-up time, clean, and of a bright brown colour. Should the collection be large, there should be two parallel beds, with a walk between them.

Shelter for the Flower before and when in Bloom.—Where the collection is small, hoops, either of wood or iron, with canvas covers or mats to be thrown over the hoops, which ought to be high enough to keep the covering clear of the flowers, will do. This covering should be applied, not only when the plants are in bloom, but also to shelter them from the late frosts after the plants make their appearance, as well as the cutting winds during the early months of the year. Too much shelter only coddles the plants, and makes them tender. On all favourable occasions remove the coverings entirely, and let the Tulips have the benefit of fine weather and gentle rains. If the spring is unusually forward and warm, so as to bring the flowers on too early, retard them by putting on the covers only on the side exposed to the heat of the sun. For a large collection, a regular tent, formed of a frame of wood and covered with canvas, is required.

The best planting season is about the beginning of the second week in November, as near the 10th of that month as the weather and the state of the ground will permit. This rule applies to all the country north of London; perhaps, in the milder climate of the southern counties, a week later would be better. Offsets may be planted a little sooner or later, as may be covenient.

Planting.—The tallest should be in the centre of the bed. This renders it necessary to plant them in rows lengthways of the bed, and not across it. This being determined upon, let the soil be levelled; then with a hoe draw a drill the length of the bed, as nearly two inches deep as possible. As soon as the drill is drawn, bring out all the tall growers, and plant them, five inches apart, at the bottom of the drill, giving each a gentle pressure. When the row is finished, thrust in at each end a strong stick, to mark where the row of bulbs is when covered up. Cover up the bulbs by the aid of a short-toothed rake. After that let the soil on each side of the planted row be stirred up with a three-pronged fork. Then set the line at the right distance from the centre (we mentioned that the beds should be four feet wide, which would allow nine inches between each of the five rows, and six inches next the edging); the line then must be set at such a distance from the centre that the next row of bulbs will be exactly nine inches apart from the centre one.

Draw the drill the same depth as the first, and plant the next tallest flowers in it. Then mark the row with a stick at each end, and so proceed till the whole is finished; the lowest growers will then be next the paths all round the bed. Each variety must be numbered.

Taking Up and Storing.—As soon as a Tulip has done blooming cut down the flower-stem, but do not injure the leaves. Expose these fully to the light and air. As soon as the leaves are turned yellow take up the bulbs. If delayed some time, and the weather should be wet, there is danger of their starting fresh roots, which would injure the bloom next year. When taken up, expose them to the sun a few hours every morning until they turn brown; and when perfectly dry, divide from the flowering bulbs all the offsets. They should be kept in a cool, dry room till the planting season arrives again.

VERBENA.

Characteristics of a good Flower.—1st. The flower should be round, with scarcely any indenture, and no notch or serrature. 2nd. The petals should be thick and flat, and bright. 3rd. The plant should be compact, the joints short and strong, and distinctly of a shrubby habit, or a close ground creeper, or a climber; those which partake of all are bad. 4th. The trusses of bloom should be compact, and stand out from the foliage, the flowers touching each other, but not crowding. 5th. The foliage should be short, broad, and bright, and enough of it to hide the stalks.

The colours should be perfectly clear and distinct in selfs, no shade should prevail, and in stripes the line where the colours separate should be well defined. The form of the truss should be as nearly flat as possible, so as to show off every individual flower to advantage.

Soil.—The best is a mixture of old turfy loam, leaf mould, and peat, in equal parts. If vegetable mould cannot be had, use the loam and sand, and about a sixth part of very rotten dung, or good old hotbed manure.

Situation.—Beds are best in an open exposure, sheltered by hedges or walls from the north-west, north, and north-east winds. The bed or beds should be long, and not more than four feet wide; and then would contain two rows, allowing them space to spread out a little every way.

Plants in Pots.—The plants intended for exhibition in pots should be in a pit or frame deep enough to keep them at least nine inches from the glass when in bloom. The best plan would be, first, to cover the bottom of the pit or frame with a layer of dry coal ashes two or three inches thick; then to turn upside down a sufficient number of empty pots to set those containing the plants upon. When they are first placed in the pit they should be within six inches of the glass. As they advance in growth they may be lowered accordingly by using lesser pots or bricks for them to stand upon, or place them upon the bed of ashes itself.

Potting.—The plants must be healthy, clear from insects, well furnished with leaves, low, bushy, and with numerous branches close to the soil; and the kinds such as produce good trusses of well-shaped, bright-coloured flowers. The best season for this operation is March. Place some of the compost where it may become moderately dry; have ready a sufficient number of either new or well-washed old pots. If the plants have been kept through the winter in pots about three inches in diameter, a shift into five and a half or six-inch pots will be sufficient at this early season. Provide also a good quantity of materials for drainage; also a few hooked pegs to pin the plants down with. Any time from the 1st of March to the middle of the month will be suitable. Drain the pots well; and, in potting, loosen the roots a little, and spread them out amongst the fresh soil. Fill the pots nearly to the top, but be careful not to bury the neck of the plant deep in the soil. As soon as the potting is finished give a gentle watering, and place them in the frame. Peg down such shoots as are long enough for the purpose, spread them out equally over the surface of the pot, and nip off the ends of every long shoot, which will cause them to break out more shoots, and the pinning down will also induce shoots to spring from the centre of the plant. The plants should be in the pots at least two months before the exhibition.

The newly-potted plants must be placed upon the pots in the frame or pit, and be carefully attended to, with due supplies of soft water, but in this early stage the watering must not be excessive. Water early in the day, and give plenty of air to dry up the damp.

The plants will grow rapidly, and will soon require a second shift. At this shift they will require at least an inch of drainage. There should be about an inch of space between the ball and the sides of the pots. Turn the plants carefully out of the pots, pick out the greater part of the old drainage, place as much soil upon the new drainage as will raise the ball nearly level with the rim of the pot, avoid deep potting, press the earth down round the ball firmly, but gently, and give a smart stroke upon a firm part of the bench to settle the whole. This will leave sufficient space within the rim of the pot to hold a good watering. As potting is finished, return the plants to the pit, and water them moderately overhead. During the operation peg down the shoots when long enough, trim off decayed leaves, stop the shoots, apply sticks, and clear off insects if any appear.

Training.—The flat mode of training is to a circular, table-like, wire trellis about fifteen inches in diameter, with three strong feet to thrust into the soil, and of sufficient length to elevate the trellis above the soil—about six inches for weak growers, and eight inches above the soil for stronger ones. It should be formed in circles, less and less towards the centre, with diverging rods to the outermost circles, to keep each circle in its place at equal distances from each other: three inches will be ample space between each circle. As soon as the plants are shifted for the last time into their blooming pots is the time to fix the trellises to each plant. The trellises should have first a coat of lead colour, and afterwards two coats of light green paint, to prevent them from rusting, and to give them a neat appearance. When the plants are ready, or large enough for training, apply the trellises by thrusting the three feet into the earth a sufficient depth to keep them firm in their places. Then, as the plants advance in growth, train the shoots equally over the trellis, stopping them to cause a sufficient number of branches to cover the whole trellis, nipping off all the flower trusses till within six or seven weeks of the day of exhibition, if that happens in May; but if in June or July, or still later, *the flowers will expand sufficiently in five weeks* (this rule applies to every mode of training). The aim must be to let every part of the trellis, bush, or pyramid be fully furnished with bloom.

Planting.—The bed or beds to receive the plants should be in good order about the last week in May or the first week in June; the plants should, by a little extra pains in potting and stopping, be nice little bushes at the time. Choose a warm, cloudy day for the operation. The beds should be four feet wide; then stretch a line fifteen inches from the edging, and plant the first row of Verbenas close to it at eighteen inches apart; when that row is complete shift the line to fifteen inches from the other side of the bed, and put in the first plant so as to form a triangle with the two plants in the first planted row, and so proceed till the whole are planted; then give a gentle watering to settle the earth to the plants.

The best tool to use in planting is a garden trowel. Set the plants in their places, turn the first plant out of the pot, pick out the crocks from the bottom of the ball, loosen the roots a little from amongst the soil, make the hole with the trowel just so deep as to allow the ball to be a quarter of an inch below the level of the bed, level the earth about the plants, pressing it firmly close to them. Proceed thus till all are finished, then rake the bed smooth; give each plant a good watering, cover them with pots every night, till all danger of late frosts is over; stir up the surface of the bed with a short three-pronged fork, leaving the soil rather rough. As the plants advance in growth, peg the shoots down to the earth; they will soon root into it and obtain fresh support. Let the shoots be equally spread out all over the bed; but should the centre of each plant become naked, it may be filled up with shoots brought back again from the extremities. Blooming shoots must be allowed to rise up pretty equally distanced from each other, and will soon require a stick to each to support them and keep them in proper order.

To prevent the plants being exhausted, nip off the greater part, if not the whole of the buds, till within six or seven weeks of the day when they are wanted for the show. Should the weather in the meantime prove dry, it will be of advantage to give them occasionally such a watering as will descend to the lowest roots. A mulching of short litter would prevent a too great evaporation, if laid on immediately after this liberal watering.

Protecting Bloom.—As soon as the flowers begin to expand they require to be sheltered from the bright rays of the sun, and the rough ungenial storms. Those in pots, in frames, are very easily protected from too bright sun by a covering of thin canvas.

Shelter for Beds.—The kind of shelter we recommend is that formed with hoops, long rods, and lengths of oiled canvas; garden mats might be used, but the shade they give is too much. In frosty weather, which sometimes occurs even so late as April, the mats might be used during the night with good effect.

Watering.—In the early part of the season, whilst there is the least appearance of cold nights, the water should be given in the morning, but when the days lengthen, and the power of the sun increases, and the growth of the plants is progressing rapidly, it is advisable to give water in the afternoon. When the plant is healthy, and shows the least inclination to droop its foliage, then it requires water.

Giving Air.—On mild, cloudy days it will be advisable to draw off the lights of the frame or the pit entirely, and let the plants revel in the mild atmosphere.

Propagation: by Cuttings.—There are two seasons for this operation, the spring and the latter end of summer. The cuttings made in spring are for planting out the same season; and those made at the end of the summer for keeping a store of young plants through the winter. The best place for striking Verbena cuttings is a pit, consisting of a platform supported upon walls, with a frame set upon it, heated with stable litter under the platform, and by linings of the same material. In this frame almost every cutting will take root in ten or twelve days. The season for making the first crop of cuttings is about the middle of February. They may be put in till April, so that with diligence and care thousands of young plants may be raised for planting out in May. It will be desirable to place the plants to produce cuttings in a gentle heat, to cause them to make young shoots. When they have grown a sufficient length, drain the pots for the cuttings effectually; then place some rough parts of the compost upon the drainage; fill the pots with the compost (consisting of light loam, peat, and leaf mould, with a free mixture of sand), to within an inch of the rim of the pot, and this inch should be filled up with pure white sand. Cut off the tops of the plants; trim off the lower leaves, and plant them round the edge of the pots pretty thickly; then give a little water to settle the sand, and place them in the frame. Make the cuttings small. They should not be more than two inches long, even rather less would strike sooner.

When they are in the frame, great attention must be paid to shading them from the sun, and to giving air every morning, to let out the moisture. Should the weather be cold, the frame should have a covering of double mats. As soon as roots are formed, let them be potted off into what are called small 60-pots. These are about two inches and a half across; replace them in the frame for a very few days till they have made fresh roots, then put them either in a greenhouse or a cold frame, well covered up at night as long as cold weather lasts.

The tops of these first-struck plants may be taken off and made use of as cuttings. This will cause the plants to break side-shoots and become bushy. When the plants are fairly established abundance of air must be given. In mild weather draw off the lights of the frame; and, in rainy weather, give air by tilting the lights.

The method of putting in cuttings for winter stores is somewhat similar. The only point to mind is to have them well-rooted before the cold weather sets in.

The winter storing consists in placing the plants in a cold frame, covering them up securely in frosty weather, giving air on all favourable occasions, and just water enough to keep them alive. Every decayed leaf must be removed, and should any mildew appear, the plants should be dusted with sulphur to keep it down. If the cultivator possesses a greenhouse, a few bushy plants may with advantage be placed on a shelf near the glass.

INDEX.

Alpine plants, 172
American Cress, 11; Blight, 80
Anemone, 191
Annual flowers, 152
Antirrhinum, 194
Apple, 78; varieties, 81
Apricot, 82; varieties, 84
Aquarium, 175; plants for, 176
Arrangement of Garden, 6
Artichoke, 12
Asparagus, 13
Aspects for fruit-trees, 70
Auricula, 108
Bean, Broad, 14; Kidney, 35
Beet, 15
Biennials, 159
Blossoms, protecting, 77
Borders, crops for, 9; formation of for fruit-trees, 67
Borecole, 16
Broccoli, 17
Brussels Sprouts, 16
Budding fruit-trees, 75
Bulbs, flowering, hardy, 163, 167; in beds, 166
Burns' Onion, 52
Cabbage, 18
Calceolaria, 201
Capsicum, 20
Carnation, 204
Carrot, 21
Cauliflower, 22
Celery, 24
Cherry, 84; aphis, 86; Morello, 85; varieties, 87
Chrysanthemum, 208
Ciboul, 26
Cineraria, 210
Composts for flowers, 136
Couve Tronchuda, 26
Cress, 26
Crown Imperials, 165
Cucumber, 27
Currant, 87; varieties, 91
Dahlia, 212
Digging flower-beds, 134
Edgings, 9
Enclosures, 5
Endive, 31

Eschallot, 32
Fennel, 33
Ferns, list of, 171
Fernery, 170
Fig, 91; varieties, 94
Filberts, 98
Flower-beds, 133; plans of, 183—188
Flower Garden, arrangement, 131 ornaments, 138
Form of Garden, 5
Fruit Garden, situation for, 67
Fruit-trees, sites for, 6
Fuchsia, 215
Garlic, 33
Gladioli, 165
Gooseberry, 94; varieties, 98
Gourd, 33
Grafting, 74
Grafting clay, 74; wax, 75
Hamburgh Parsley, 34
Hedges, 6
Horse-Radish, 34
Hotbed, to make, 27
Hyacinth, 218
Iris, Persian, 165
Jerusalem Artichoke, 35
Kale, 16
Kidney Bean, 35
Kohl Rabi, 64
Lawns, 137; to renovate, 138
Leek, 37
Lettuce, 38
Love-Apple, 40
Manures for flowers, 136
Marjoram, 41
Melon, 41
Mint, 43
Mulching, 73
Mushroom, 44
Mustard, 46
Narcissus, 164
Nectarine, 101; varieties, 107
New Zealand Spinach, 46
Nuts, 98; varieties, 98
Onion, 48
—— Burns', 52
—— Canada, 62
—— Potato, 52
—— Tree, 62

Onion, Underground, 52
—— Welsh, 26
Paling, 6
Pansy, 228
Parsley, 48
Parsnip, 48
Pea, 49
Peach, 101; varieties, 107
Pear, 107; varieties, 112
Pelargonium, 226
Perennials, 159; lists of spring, summer, and autumn-blooming, 161—163
Petunia, 230
Picotee, 204
Pillars, rustic, for flowers, 146
Pink, 233
Planting fruit-trees, 72
Plum, 113; varieties, 115
Polyanthus, 238
Potato, 50
Potato-Onion, 52
Protecting fruit blossoms, 77
Pumpkin, 33
Radish, 53
Rampion, 53
Ranunculus, 240
Raspberries, 115; varieties, 117
Rhubarb, 54
Rockwork, 172
Root pruning, 75
Roses, various kinds and uses, 145—152; insects on, 149; culture in pots, 244
Rotation of crops, 10
Rustic baskets, &c., 138; plants for, 140
Sage, 56

Savory, 56
Savoy, 57
Scallions, 26
Sea-kale, 57
Shallot, 32
Shrubs, list of flowering, 142; for a wall, 143
Shelter, 67
Situation of garden, 5
Size of garden, 5
Soil of garden, 5; preparation for fruit-trees, 70
Spinach, 61
Squash, 33
Stations for fruit-trees, 70
Strawberry, 118; varieties, 120
Tansy, 61
Tetragonian Spinach, 45
Thyme, 62
Tomato, 40
Top-dressings, 73
Tree-Onion, 62
Trees, ornamental, 141
Trellises for fruit-trees, 69
Trenching, 134
Tulips, 165; early, 163; for exhibition, 249
Turnip, 63; stemmed cabbage, 64; rooted cabbage, 64
Underground Onion, 52
Unfruitfulness, its causes, 75
Vegetable Marrow, 33
Verbena, 253
Vine, 121; varieties, 126
Walks, 67, 131
Walls, 5
Welsh Onion, 26

First-class Weekly Illustrated Gardening Publication,
Price Threepence; Stamped Fourpence.

THE

JOURNAL OF HORTICULTURE,

Cottage Gardener,

AND

COUNTRY GENTLEMAN,

EDITED BY GEORGE W. JOHNSON, F.R.H.S.,

AND

ROBERT HOGG, LL.D., F.L.S.,

Assisted by a Staff of the best Writers on Practical Gardening, and numerous Correspondents engaged in the pursuit of Horticulture and Rural Affairs.

THIS Publication some time since commenced a New Series of that old-established and popular Periodical "THE COTTAGE GARDENER," permanently increased to Thirty-Two Pages, and richly Illustrated with Wood Engravings in the highest style of the Art.

The subjects treated on embrace every department of Gardening, and Rural and Domestic Economy; from the small plot and allotment of the Cottager to the Villa Garden of the Country Gentleman and Merchant, the grounds of the Parsonage-house, and the more extensive establishments of the Nobility and Gentry.

The Horticultural Department consists of all Out-door and In-door operations of the Fruit, Flower, and Kitchen Garden; Notices of all the New Fruits, Flowers, and Vegetables; Arboriculture, and more particularly Fruit Tree Culture, and Pomology; Landscape Gardening, and Garden Architecture; descriptions of all the newest Inventions in Garden Structures, Tools and Implements; and a detail of work to be done in each department during every week in the year.

In Rural and Domestic Economy, it treats of the Farm and Poultry-yard; Allotment Farming; the Dairy; the Pigeon-house; and Rabbit and Bee-keeping. The Treatment of Soils, Manures, Cropping and Rotation of crops. Brewing; Wine Making; Vegetable Cookery, and the Preserving of Fruits and Vegetables.

Natural History and Botany, so far as they relate to Gardening and Husbandry, are amply treated on, and embrace Zoology, Geology, Mineralogy, Meteorology, and Physiological, Structural, Systematic, and Popular Botany.

Biographies and Portraits of the most celebrated Horticulturists.

Reviews of New Books relating to the above subjects; Reports of Horticultural and Poultry Societies' Meetings throughout the country; and Scientific Notices.

To ADVERTISERS, the JOURNAL OF HORTICULTURE will be found a valuable and effective medium, from the extent of its circulation among the middle and higher classes.

A SPECIMEN NUMBER FREE BY POST FOR FOUR STAMPS.

Journal of Horticulture and Cottage Gardener Office,
162, FLEET STREET, LONDON, E.C.;
And to be had of all Booksellers, and at the Railway Stalls.

WORKS PUBLISHED
AT THE
JOURNAL OF HORTICULTURE OFFICE.

THE FRUIT MANUAL, containing Descriptions and Synonymes of the Fruit and Fruit Trees commonly met with in the Gardens and Orchards of Great Britain, with Selected Lists of the Varieties most worthy of Cultivation By ROBERT HOGG, LL.D., F.L.S., Secretary to the Fruit Committee of the Royal Horticultural Society of London. Price 3s. 6d.; post free, 3s. 10d.

SCIENCE AND PRACTICE OF GARDENING, in which are Explained and Illustrated the Principles that Regulate all the Operations of Horticulture, including Demonstrations of the Phenomena of the Germination, Growth, Diseases, and Death of Plants. With numerous Wood Engravings. By GEORGE W. JOHNSON, Esq., F.R.H.S., Co-Editor of THE JOURNAL OF HORTICULTURE, &c. 400 pages, with 50 Illustrations, price 3s.

THE CHEMISTRY OF THE WORLD, being a Popular Explanation of the Phenomena daily occurring in and around our Persons, Houses, Gardens, and Fields. By G. W. JOHNSON, F.R.H.S. 6s., bound in cloth. Free by post, 6s. 6d.

THE AILANTHUS SILKWORM AND THE AILANTHUS TREE. Abridged and Translated from the French, by LADY DOROTHY NEVILL. Price 1s.

THE BRITISH FERNS, popularly Described, and Illustrated by Engravings of every Species. By G. W. JOHNSON, F.R.H.S. Fourth Edition, with an Appendix, 3s. 6d., bound in cloth, gilt edges. Post free, 3s. 10d.

A PRACTICAL TREATISE ON THE CULTURE OF THE VINE, as well under Glass as in the Open Air. By JOHN SANDERS. Third Edition, price 5s.

RAMBLES IN SEARCH OF WILD FLOWERS, and how to Distinguish them. By MARGARET PLUES, Author of "Rambles in Search of Ferns;" "Rambles in Search of Mosses." Post 8vo., with Eighteen Coloured Illustrations, price 6s.

ORCHARD-HOUSES, HINTS ON THE CONSTRUCTION AND MANAGEMENT OF. By J. R. PEARSON, the Nurseries, Chilwell, near Nottingham. Second Edition, in limp cloth, price 1s. 6d.

THE ORCHID MANUAL, for the Cultivation of Stove, Greenhouse, and Hardy Orchids. By THOMAS APPLEBY. Price 2s. 6d. Free by post for 32 postage stamps.

HOW TO FARM TWO ACRES PROFITABLY; including the Management of the Cow and the Pig. By JOHN ROBSON. 1s. Post free, 1s. 1d.

OUR VILLAGERS. By the Authoress of "My Flowers," &c. 1s., bound in cloth. Free by post, 1s. 2d.

THE GARDEN MANUAL. Seventh Edition. 1s. 6d., bound in cloth. Post free, 1s. 8d.

OUT-DOOR GARDENING. Second Edition. 1s. 6d., bound in cloth. Post-free, 1s. 8d.

IN-DOOR GARDENING. Second Edition. 1s. 6d., bound in cloth. Post-free, 1s. 8d.

THE PIGEON BOOK. 1s. 6d., bound in cloth. Free by Post, 1s. 8d.

PRIZE ESSAY ON THE CULTIVATION OF EARLY POTATOES. By the Rev. E. F. MANBY. 2d. Post-free, 3d.

THE AGRICULTURAL AND HORTICULTURAL USES OF the Ammoniacal Liquors produced during the manufacture of Gas. 4d., or 8s. per 100.

OFFICE: 162, FLEET STREET, LONDON, E.C.
And to be had of all Booksellers, and at the Railway Stalls.

Monthly, Price 1s., with Four Coloured Illustrations.

THE WILD FLOWERS
OF
GREAT BRITAIN,

ILLUSTRATED BY COLOURED DRAWINGS OF ALL THE SPECIES,

BY CHARLOTTE GOWER,

And Botanically and Popularly Described, with Copious Notices of their History and Uses,

BY ROBERT HOGG, LL.D., F.L.S.,
And GEORGE W. JOHNSON, F.R.H.S.,

Editors of "The Journal of Horticulture and Cottage Gardener."

Vol. I., with 80 Coloured Plates, is now ready, elegantly bound in cloth, gilt extra, price 21s.

JOURNAL OF HORTICULTURE OFFICE, 162, FLEET STREET.

Beautiful Coloured Engravings of the New Flowers and Fruits, appear in the

FLORIST AND POMOLOGIST;

A PICTORIAL MONTHLY MAGAZINE OF

FLOWERS, FRUITS, & GENERAL HORTICULTURE,

CONDUCTED BY

ROBERT HOGG, LL.D., F.L.S., AND JOHN SPENCER, F.G.S.,

ASSISTED BY

MR. THOMAS MOORE, F.L.S.,

AND NUMEROUS ABLE CONTRIBUTORS.

ONE SHILLING MONTHLY.

The Volume for 1862, with Twenty-three highly Coloured Illustrations, price 14s., bound in cloth, gilt extra, is now ready.

LONDON: JOURNAL OF HORTICULTURE OFFICE, 162, FLEET STREET,
And Sold by all Booksellers and Newsmen.

MANUALS FOR THE MANY.

GARDENING FOR THE MANY. Threepence.
ALLOTMENT FARMING FOR THE MANY. Threepence.
BEE-KEEPING FOR THE MANY. Fourpence.
GREENHOUSES FOR THE MANY. Sixpence.
KITCHEN GARDENING FOR THE MANY. Fourpence.
FLOWER GARDENING FOR THE MANY. Fourpence.
FRUIT GARDENING FOR THE MANY. Fourpence.
FLORISTS' FLOWERS FOR THE MANY. Fourpence.
POULTRY BOOK FOR THE MANY. Sixpence.
WINDOW GARDENING FOR THE MANY. Ninepence.
MUCK FOR THE MANY. Threepence.

* Any of the above can be had post free for an additional postage-stamp.

LONDON: "JOURNAL OF HORTICULTURE AND COTTAGE GARDENER" OFFICE, 162, FLEET STREET, E.C
And to be had of all Booksellers, and at the Railway Stalls.